Best Interests of the Student

Applying Ethical Constructs to Legal Cases
in Education

Best Interests of the Student

Applying Ethical Constructs to Legal Cases in Education

Jacqueline A. Stefkovich
The Pennsylvania State University

Routledge
Taylor & Francis Group
New York   London

First published by Lawrence Erlbaum Associates
10 Industrial Avenue
Mahwah, New Jersey 07430

Reprinted 2009 by Routledge

Routledge
Taylor & Francis Group
270 Madison Avenue
New York, NY 10016

Routledge
Taylor & Francis Group
2 Park Square
Milton Park, Abingdon
Oxon OX14 4RN

Cover design by Tomai Maridou

Illustration by Hector L. Sambolin, Jr.

Library of Congress Cataloging-in-Publication Data

Stefkovich, Jacqueline Anne, 1947-
Best interests of the student : applying ethical constructs to legal cases in
    education / Jacqueline A. Stefkovich.
        p. cm.
    Includes bibliographical references and index.
ISBN 0-8058-5183-6 (pbk : alk. paper)
1. Educational law and legislation—United States. 2. Students—Legal
    status, laws, etc.—United States. 3. School management and orga-
    nization—United states—Decision making. 4. Education—Moral
    and ethical aspects—United States. I. Title.

KF4150.S72 2006
344.73'079—dc22   2005035476
                                                                CIP

Printed in the United States of America
10 9 8 7 6 5 4 3 2

To Beth Stefkovich
Once a student, always an inspiration

Contents

Preface

As the title suggests, this book is aimed at applying ethical decision making to school-based legal cases with a primary focus on the best of interests of the student. Questioning the implications of court decisions for educational policy and practice is not new. However, courts are often hesitant to tie school officials' hands when it comes to making decisions related to practice. Likewise, at times there have been actions on the part of school personnel that courts have ruled as legal, which other educators have criticized as bad law or bad practice. These types of cases have long served as grist for vigorous debate in education law classes. If one agrees with Foster (1986), "administration at its heart is the resolution of moral dilemmas" (p. 33), then most if not all of these education-related legal opinions carry with them ethical consequences.

Focus on the "best interests of students" emerged from earlier work on the Shapiro and Stefkovich (2001, 2005) book, where Joan Shapiro and I described ethical paradigms based on models of justice, caring, and critique and proposed a fourth paradigm, that of the profession. This fourth paradigm considered the other three as well as issues such as (a) what does the profession expect, (b) what happens when personal and professional ethics clash, and (c) how community influences educators' ethical decision making. At the center of this model lies the *best interests of the student*. Educators have often used this concept to justify important moral and ethical decisions; therefore it seemed apt that this concept would lie at the heart of a professional paradigm.

When Joan and I presented our model at the annual conference of the American Educational Research Association (AERA), Dr. Paul Begley, Director of the University Council for Educational Administration's (UCEA) Center for the Study of Leadership and Ethics, raised this question: "What is in the best interests of students? How do we define it?" Although our ethics book provided some direction in this regard, it never fully explored this question. With two advanced doctoral students at Penn State, Michaele O'Brien and Josie Moore, I subsequently conducted research on this topic, finding the absence of a definition or a trend in how decisions were made. This book includes a discussion of those findings, examines the concept of best interests of the student, and presents a model to guide educators as they confront legal and ethical dilemmas.

FILLING THE KNOWLEDGE GAP

This book fills a unique gap in the knowledge base, that is the juncture between educational law, ethics, and the best interests of the student. To my knowledge, there is no text using a case study approach that analyzes legal decisions from the perspective of multiple ethical decision-making paradigms. The case study method has been effective in teaching school leaders in finance, organizational theory, decision making, and ethics itself (Ashbaugh & Kasten, 1995; Cooper, 1995; Goodlad, Soder, & Sirotnik, 1990; Greenwood & Fillmer, 1997; Kirschmann, 1996; Merseth, 1997; Strike & Soltis, 1992; Zubay & Soltis, 2005). In addition, numerous scholars have written law-related texts that include legal cases. Although some of these texts stress the importance of policy issues related to the law (e.g., Rossow & Stefkovich, 2005), the primary emphasis still focuses on legal analysis.

There are also a number of fine books that discuss ethics for school leaders from multiple paradigms but do not address legal responsibilities in any detail and do not employ a case study approach (Beck & Murphy, 1994; Noddings, 1992, 2003; Starratt, 1994, 2004). Shapiro and Stefkovich (2005) combine cases with multiple paradigm analyses, but the cases do not, for the most part, focus on legal issues.

Strike et al. (1998) come closest to combining legal dilemmas with ethical analyses, but their book only analyzes dilemmas from a justice and sometimes legal perspective and their dilemmas are fictitious rather than based on real court cases. None of these books, except Shapiro and Stefkovich (2005) even begin to address the question of what is in the best interests of the student. Thus, I believe this book fills an important gap in the knowledge base and instruction of educational leaders.

TEACHING NOTES TO THE INSTRUCTOR

This text is designed primarily for use in university courses related to the preparation of educational leaders including administrators (e.g., principals, superintendents, curriculum coordinators, personnel directors, school business officials) and teachers. It could also be an integral part of an education law or ethics course, used as either a basic or supplementary text. It could be used at either the introductory or advanced levels of educational administration, school leadership, and supervision programs. The information in this text could be infused into the core curriculum of a doctoral, masters, or certification program.

Aspects of law and ethics can easily be integrated into foundations courses that emphasize the social sciences and education such as history, philosophy, sociology, and psychology of education. This book may also benefit school counselors, social workers, psychologists and others who deal with students and their rights in the schools. Others interested in educational policy and the law, including central office personnel, educational policymakers, state department personnel, regional educational centers, federal level education staff, school board members and professional organizations might find this book helpful as a reference on law and ethics.

No one book can adequately cover all of the ethics literature and still provide an in-depth view of the law. The purpose of this book is neither. Instead, it is designed more to provide a broad-based view of that intersection where educational law and ethics meet. Those teaching education law and wanting more in-depth coverage in that area may want to assign students the entire case rather than the annotated versions provided in this book. Those instructors preferring to focus on ethics and philosophy may want to assign readings from these areas of scholarship. This book provides a fairly comprehensive reference section that should be of assistance.

ACKNOWLEDGMENTS

It is difficult to adequately express my appreciation to the many individuals who have assisted me with this book throughout the years. First go my deepest thanks to Naomi Silverman of Lawrence Erlbaum Associates, Publishers, who has always given me support and from the very beginning believed in my vision for this book. I would also like to acknowledge those persons who reviewed the manuscripts and provided extraordinarily helpful suggestions. They include: Patricia First, University of Arizona; Jamie B. Lewis, University of Georgia; Martha McCarthy, University of Indiana at Bloomington; Nelda Cambron-McCabe, Miami University; and Paul Begley, The Pennsylvania State University.

A special note of thanks goes to these advanced doctoral students at Penn State: G. Michaele O'Brien, who worked with me to conceptualize earlier outlines for the book, select initial cases, and write early case summaries; Marilyn Begley, who summarized a number of the later cases and provided invaluable editorial assistance and suggestions, including the graphic for Figure 5.1; and Lance Potter, attorney and graduate assistant extraordinaire, who came to the rescue with his outstanding research skills in my last few months of polishing and adding cases.

I also appreciate the efforts of other students: Caroline Watral, whose research and background in philosophy immensely informed my thinking in Part I; Karen Morris, whose research supplemented my understanding of the justice and caring frameworks; Josh Fischel, who explained the intricacies of critical theory to me and my class; William Frick, who questioned my representation of respect and helped me to rethink its meaning; Fabian Roche, who reviewed Part I providing feedback from an Australian perspective; and Hector Sambolin, who was able to present a visual model for the best interests conceptual framework, which appears on the book cover and in chapter 3.

In addition, there are a number of graduate students who assisted me in various capacities along the way, including: Josie Moore, Todd Hosterman, David Hermann, and Robert Griggs. This book was piloted at different stages in three of my summer school courses in The Law and Ethical Decision Making and in two of my Ethics in Educational Leadership classes. I thank the students in these courses who generously commented on the coherence of the best interests theory and the appropriateness of the legal cases; and many colleagues along the way, including: Joe McKinney, Ball State University; Preston Green, Penn State University; and Joan Shapiro, Temple University, who suggested cases to be included, commented on the best interests model, and encouraged me to write this book.

Finally, I extend my gratitude to Judy Leonard, Staff Assistant for Penn State's Department of Education Policy Studies, who provided detailed and meticulous assistance in the final editing and formatting stages of this document, and to my mother, Betty Stefkovich, who steadfastly encouraged me in this endeavor even when the work took me away from family and friends, which was often the case.

Part I

A CONCEPTUAL FRAMEWORK

Before applying ethical concepts to legal cases, it is important to have some understanding of the underlying conceptual framework of this analysis as well as its various components. This section includes five background chapters. The first provides an introduction to the topic. The second describes various educational paradigms that may be used to analyze ethical dilemmas. The third focuses on the literature surrounding the "best interests of the student" and presents a conceptual model for determining best interests. The fourth discusses the role of the courts and legal opinions as related to administrative discretion and ethical decision making. The last chapter discusses how to apply the best interests model to court cases.

1

Introduction

Confronted with difficult situations, school leaders frequently rely on the rule of law to guide their work. On the other hand, many, if not most, of the situations that these educators face on a day-to-day basis require ethical rather than, or in addition to, legal decision making. This chapter focuses on school leaders' recognition of ethical dilemmas and application of ethics in their professional decision making.

LAW, ETHICS, MORALS, AND VALUES

Educators, and many others for that matter, often confuse and intersperse terms such as *law, ethics, morals, values,* and *personal preferences*. Therefore, it is important to begin with some working definitions that should be helpful in sorting out these various concepts. Black, in his comprehensive legal dictionary (Garner, 2004), defines law as: "The regime that orders human activities and relations through systematic application of the force of politically organized society, or through social pressure, backed by force, in such a society; the legal system [as in] respect and obey the law" (p. 900). Thus, citizens are bound to obey laws or else face legal sanctions.

Both ethics and morals are defined as "custom or usage" and, in this respect, they are synonymous. Some philosophers, however, have drawn a distinction between the two. For example, Grenz and Smith (2003) conceptualize ethics as moral philosophy or "the division of philosophy that involves how humans ought to live" (p. 77). Ethics focuses on questions of right and wrong, what is humanly good, and why practices are moral or immoral. On the other hand, morality involves the actual process of living out these beliefs.

Perhaps more relevant to this discussion is the distinction between morals, values, and personal preferences. As Grenz and Smith (2003) point out:

Despite the affinity between the terms *morals* and *ethics* in philosophical treatments of the topic, in the media or in casual conversation, people today often distinguish between the two, so that morality comes to be linked to sentiments, personal preferences, or scruples. As a consequence, *moralize* is often used in a pejorative sense to refer to the attempt to inculcate one's own moral conclusions on others. (p. 77)

For purposes of this book, the terms *ethics* and *morals* will be used in their true philosophical sense as distinguished from personal preferences or values. In no manner does this discussion support the imposition of any person's individual value system on others. Rather, the aim here is to understand the inherent limitations of the law in solving everyday problems, the broad discretion provided to school authorities by the judiciary, and the importance of self-reflection and inquiry in making ethical decisions that may, and often do, have a profound influence on students.

Unlike scholars (Begley, 2004) who see ethics as only a small part of a larger valuation process, something used mostly in times of high-stakes urgency, the premises here are that ethics should guide school leaders' decision making, that there can be common ground even in a multicultural, pluralistic society, and that, rather than impose their own values on students and teachers, school leaders should strive to reach a higher moral ground in making decisions. This is not easy. As Shapiro and Stefkovich (2005) point out, ethical decision making involves reflection, an acknowledgment of various approaches to ethics, and constant self-assessment and reassessment. As Begley (2004) notes:

The study of ethics should be as much about the life-long personal struggle to be ethical, about failures to be ethical, the inconsistencies of ethical postures, the masquerading of self-interest and personal preference as ethical action, and the dilemmas which occur in everyday and professional life…(p. 5)

ETHICS AND EDUCATIONAL LEADERS

In the past decade, there has been recognition of the need, as well as increased demand, for courses in ethics for school professionals. A number of educators have recognized the importance of training educational leaders in ethical decision making (Beck & Murphy, 1994; Shapiro & Stefkovich, 2005; Walker, 1998). Campbell (1999) observed: "central to much of this literature is the argument that educational leaders must develop and articulate a much greater awareness of the ethical significance of their actions and decisions" (p. 152). Beck et al. (1997) refer to an "unprecedented amount of interest in *explicit* consideration of ethical issues by educators and students" (p. vii).

There has been a renewed interest in including ethics as part of educators' preservice training. Impetus for this movement came about after leaders in the field produced a number of books on this topic (Beck & Murphy, 1994; Noddings, 1992, 2003; Starratt, 1994, 2004). Interest increased exponentially after the Interstate

School Leaders Licensure Consortium (ISLLC; 1996) released standards for the licensing of school administrators. Standard 5 requires that school leaders promote the success of all students by "acting with integrity, fairness, and in an ethical manner" (p. 18).

To meet this standard, school leaders are required to possess knowledge of various ethical frameworks and perspectives on ethics, to be committed to bringing ethical principles to the decision-making process, and to developing a caring school community (ISSLLC, 1996). These standards are reflected in a licensing exam for school leaders developed by the Educational Testing Service (ETS) and in college and university-based school leader training program requirements as set forth by agencies such as the National Council for the Accreditation of Teacher Education (NCATE; Murphy, 2005).

THE LAW AND EDUCATIONAL LEADERS

School law courses remain a staple of many educational leadership programs. Treated in isolation, this training can create a tension for practitioners between the legal and moral aspects of school leadership. For example, there have always been actions on the part of school personnel that courts have ruled as legal, which other educators have criticized as unethical or simply bad practice.

These types of cases have long served as grist for vigorous debate, particularly in education law and policy classrooms. Part of this tension lies in the fact that courts have been hesitant to tie school officials' hands when it comes to making decisions related to practice and thus have given practitioners considerable discretion in day-to-day decision making. These conflicts highlight the importance of legal and ethical decision-making models that allow educators to make informed choices about resolving problems in practice.

ETHICAL/LEGAL/EDUCATIONAL THEMES

In discussing case law related to what is legal and what is ethical, a number of important themes emerge. These themes are also apparent in educational literature that focuses on what constitutes good administrative practice. They include issues related to (a) the importance of access to education for all students; (b) the tension between equality (treating all students the same) and equity (recognizing that students do not all start out as equal and some need more or different attention than others in acquiring an education); (c) the extent that schools inculcate values; (d) cultural differences in our ever-changing society; and (e) the rights of parents in relation to the school's responsibility to act *in loco parentis* (in the place of the parent). Table 1.1 presents these themes and their prevalence in the various cases.

TABLE 1.1
Ethical, Legal, and Educational Themes

Case Name	Access to Education	Equity	Values Inculcation	Cultural Differences	Parents' Rights
Cornfield v. SD 230 (1993)		X			X
Beussink v. Woodland (1998)	X		X		X
Boroff v. Van Wert (2000)			X		X
LaVine v. Blaine (2001)	X		X		X
Settlegoode v. Portland (2004)	X	X			X
Mozert v. Hawkins (1987)	X	X	X	X	X
Lassonde v. Pleasanton (2003)			X	X	X
U.S. v. Bd. of Ed. of Philadelphia (1990)		X	X	X	X
C.H. v. Olivia (2000)	X	X	X	X	X
Fleming v. Jefferson County (2002)		X	X	X	X
Gay Straight Alliance v. Boyd (2003)	X	X	X		
Boring v. Buncombe (1998)		X	X		X
Gruenke v. Seip (2000)	X	X	X		X
Doe v. Pulaski (2002)		X	X		X
Davenport v. YMCA (1999)	X	X	X	X	X
Joye v. Hunterdon (2003)	X		X		X
Ratner v. Loudoun (2001)			X		X
Seal v. Morgan (2000)			X		X
S.G. v. Sayreville (2003)			X		X

Case Name	Access to Education	Equity	Values Inculcation	Cultural Differences	Parents' Rights
Hearn v. Bd. of P. Ed. (1999)			X		X
People Who Care v. Rockford (1997)	X	X			
Hoffman v. Bd of Ed. (1978)	X	X		X	X
Pro. Standards v. Smith (2002)	X		X		
Immediato v. Rye Neck (1996)			X		X
Nabozny v. Podlesny (1996)	X	X	X		X
Billings v. Madison (2001)		X	X	X	X
Selman v. Cobb County (2005)	X		X	X	X
Thomas v. Roberts (2003)			X		X
Hasenfus v. LaJeunesse (1999)			X		X
Garcia v. Miera (1987)			X	X	X
Doe v. Hawaii (2003)			X	X	X
Timothy W. v. Rochester (1989)	X	X	X		X
Kadrmas v. Dickinson (1988)	X	X		X	X
Garrett v. Detroit (1991)	X	X	X	X	
Taxman v. Piscataway (1996)		X	X	X	

2

Conceptualizing an Ethical Framework for Educational Leaders

This chapter presents an explanation of four paradigms aimed at understanding how to approach ethical decision making in schools. They include the ethics of justice, care, critique, and the profession. Close attention is also given to the community, which is not viewed as a separate ethic in this discussion, but rather as an integral part of the ethic of the profession.

In grappling with day-to-day ethical dilemmas in schools, it is important that educators understand the various frameworks that philosophers and educational scholars have developed over the years. Some of these approaches date back centuries; others are relatively new. Some build on the writings of earlier philosophers; others borrow from social science inquiry in fields such as law, psychology, sociology, political science, language literacy, and education.

Each of these approaches to ethics is important to educational leaders who are asked to make ethical decisions. By considering these frameworks or paradigms as complementary parts of a whole, educators have access to a more advanced set of tools for decision making. A caution is in order here. It is clearly impossible, in one short chapter, to adequately cover any of the theories presented or to include all of those many scholars who have contributed to these fields.

Instead, the aim of this chapter is to provide a structure for understanding various approaches to making ethical decisions and highlight some of those theories and theorists most relevant to education. Thus, readers are strongly encouraged to take

advantage of the ample reference section provided at the end of this book and to explore topics of interest or fill gaps in their knowledge (or in this chapter) on their own.

THE ETHIC OF JUSTICE

Until fairly recently, most scholars and practitioners equated ethics with a more traditional approach to philosophy, a view of ethics as justice. Indeed, this paradigm was apparent as early as writings by Aristotle and Plato. The ethic of justice provides the basis for legal principles and ideals. Here, one may ask questions related to the rule of law and more abstract concepts of *fairness, equity* and *justice.*

Starratt (1994) characterizes this ethic as originating in two schools of thought, one stressing society as its key component and the other focusing on the individual as central. The former conceptualizes justice as emerging from "communal understandings" (p. 50). The latter includes the concept of *social contract,* where the individual gives up certain rights for the good of society. Strike, Haller, and Soltis (1998) draw similar comparisons as they emphasize differences between the principles of benefit maximization and equal respect. The principle of benefit maximization or utilitarianism determines morality in relation to consequences. Here, "the best and most just decision is the one that results in the most good or the greatest benefit for the most people" (p. 17). *Utilitarianism* is a type of ethics where the fundamental purpose is to promote certain ends.

Bentham and Mill are well-known defenders of this concept. However, there are various versions and differences within utilitarianism. For example, Bentham (1948) argued for the Principle of Utility, that is, an action should be judged according to the results it achieved, whereas Mill (1978) was concerned with the social contract and the minority being oppressed by the majority. One of the additions that Mill made to the notion of social contract was that the majority (or the state) should only interfere with the minority if the minority is doing something that is directly harmful to the state.

On the other hand, the principle of equal respect assumes that persons are free and rational moral agents and are of equal value. Exemplified by the Golden Rule and later influenced by the work of Kant (1966), this principle requires that persons be treated as ends rather than means. In Kant's approach to ethics, *moral principles* are laws that issue from reason and derive their authority from the sovereignty of reason.

Kant's ethics form the basis for the social contract theories of Locke and Rousseau (Audi, 1995). Of particular relevance is Rousseau's (1967) *Social Contract,* where he reflects on the nature of responsibility (contract) and rights such as liberty:

What man loses by the social contract is his natural liberty and an unlimited right to anything which tempts him, and which he is able to attain; what he gains is civil liberty and property in all that he possess.... Besides the preceding, we might add to the acquisitions of the civil state moral freedom, which alone renders man truly master of himself; for the impulse of mere appetite is slavery, while obedience to a self-prescribed law is liberty. (p. 23)

A number of contemporary philosophers have also grappled with issues of liberty and responsibility. Rawls' (1999) *Theory of Justice,* based on the social contract theories of Locke, Rousseau, and Kant, envisions justice as fairness. Rawls' theory rests on two principles. First, each person has an equal right to basic liberties. These liberties include freedom of speech, assembly, conscience and thought, property rights, and freedom from arbitrary arrest and seizure. Second, social and economic inequalities must provide the greatest benefit to the least advantaged as well as conditions of fair equality of opportunity.

Thus, Rawls' general conception is that all primary goods, which include liberty and opportunity, income and wealth, and the bases of self-respect, should be distributed equally unless an unequal distribution of any or all these goods advantages those who are least favored. Rawls suggests that a moral decision is one that one would make, not knowing his or her role in the situation. In this way, the person in the least advantaged position would always be given fair treatment.

Stressing reasoning and rationality in his six-stage approach to moral development, Kohlberg (1981) based his work on that of Kant and Rawls and also relied heavily on the theory of psychologist Jean Piaget. Kohlberg characterizes his first two stages as reasoning at a preconventional level. In Stage one, persons base their moral actions on obedience, that is, adhering to literal interpretations of laws and rules, and avoidance of punishment. Stage two reasoning, sometimes referred to in early writings as "tit for tat," involves instrumental purpose and exchange, that is, deal cutting based on fairness. In other words, "I will do this for you if you do this for me."

Stages three and four operate at the conventional level. Stage three considers the role of the individual in relation to others and takes into account factors such as mutual expectations, concern for others, loyalty, and trust. Stage four involves making decisions from a democratic or societal point of view. Here, the welfare of society is key. Kohlberg classifies Stages five and six as postconventional, or principled, ways of making moral decisions. His Stage five focuses on rights, social contract, and utility. Finally, those making moral decisions at stage six would do so based on universal principles. Here, Kohlberg stresses, among other things, Kant's respect for other persons as ends, not means.

THE ETHIC OF CARE

Out of the ethic of justice, the ethic of care shifts the emphasis on rights and laws to compassion and empathy. When the ethic of care is valued, school leaders emphasize

relationships and connections in the decision-making process, rather than strategies and rules associated with a hierarchical approach (Shapiro & Stefkovich, 2005).

Coming from a justice perspective, Kohlberg identified elements of caring as an approach to ethical decision making but categorized it as *stage three reasoning* in his six-stage approach. He attributed this style of thinking mostly to women. Gilligan, a professor at Harvard University and former student of Kohlberg, challenged this model of ethical decision making. According to Gilligan, Kohlberg characterized women as "stuck" at Stage three. In her seminal book, *In a Different Voice,* Gilligan (1982) observed a paradox in Kohlberg's depiction of women at Stage three, pointing out: "The very traits that traditionally have defined the 'goodness' of women, their care for and sensitivity to the needs of others, are those that mark them deficient in moral development" (p. 18).

Gilligan (1982) pointed out that Kohlberg's longitudinal study, which served as a basis for his moral development scale, included only adolescent boys. She urged researchers to reconsider Kohlberg's research as applied to women, concluding that women's moral reasoning was different from, not inferior to, that of men. Gilligan's groundbreaking research paved the way for other scholars to consider women's voices.

Two years after Gilligan's book was published, Noddings firmly established an ethic of care in the scholarly literature with her publication of *Caring: A Feminine Approach to Ethics and Moral Education* (Noddings, 1984, 2003). Her view centers on mutuality, emphasizing connections, and interdependence. She recognizes commitment in the form of devotion and loyalty but also stresses the importance of a relationship between the person who gives the care and the person who receives the care. Building on the research of Noddings and others, Beck (1994) conceptualizes caring as a foundational ethic that "transcends ideological boundaries" (p. 3). For her, an ethic of care assumes that human beings have intrinsic worth and emphasizes unconditional commitment to others. Caring, concern, and community building go hand-in-hand with fraternity and "compassionate justice" (p. 2) as key values.

Combining the paradigms of justice and care, Sernak, in 1998, urged school leaders to balance their power with caring, noting that these two qualities are not necessarily at odds with one another. She advanced a theory of caring power in which a leader, regardless of gender, uses power to create a caring climate within the school. Three factors intrinsic to this concept include (a) understanding self both as separate from and in relation to community, (b) building a just and democratic pluralistic school community, and (c) experiencing personal freedom in order to fully function in a community.

THE ETHIC OF CRITIQUE

The *ethic of critique* seeks to challenge the status quo and give voice to the marginalized sectors of society. It is firmly routed in critical theory, which goes

beyond just maintaining a criticism of a system or situation. Audi (1995) defines this approach as one that integrates philosophical reflection and social sciences' explanatory achievements with the ultimate goal of "linking theory and practice, providing insight, and empowering human beings to change their oppressive circumstances and achieve emancipation" (p. 279). Developed by Max Horkheimer, the term *critical theory* was first used as a self-description of the Frankfurt School and its revision of Marxism (Audi, 1995). Other prominent critical theorists of that time include Theodor Adorno, Herbert Marcuse, and Hannah Arendt.

Critical theory is "any theory that is at the same time explanatory, normative, practical and self-reflexive" (Audi, 1995, p. 170). These theories are normative and critical in that they bring to light negative practices in our society. They are practical because they focus on self-understanding and improvement of social conditions. The latter includes empowerment and emancipation from oppression. Critical theories are self-reflexive in that "they must account for their own conditions of possibility and for their potentially transformative effects" (p. 170). Another way to consider the self-reflexive aspect of critical theory is that the critic cannot be separate or outside of the condition of the critique. This approach varies greatly from, and contradicts, traditional positivistic approaches to scientific theory that require separation of fact and value.

Although newer approaches to critique have diverted somewhat from the original intent of the Frankfurt School, nonetheless they all tend to challenge educators to rethink traditional ideas of law and justice to consider who has the power. Concepts supporting the notion that some groups in our society have historically had more say when it comes to determining what is legal, just, and, consequently, ethical are central issues here. Within this paradigm, one might question who makes the laws and how they apply to a different people. Other key concepts include issues of *power, privilege, culture,* and *language.* A number of feminist scholars have been at the forefront of this movement asking these questions in relation to gender (e.g., Capper, 1993). In a similar vein, contemporary scholars including Apple (2001, 2003), Freire (1970, 1985, 1993, 1998), Giroux (1994, 2000, 2001, 2003a, 2003b), and Purpel (1989, 2003) have focused on racial and social-class inequities as well as gender. Some have criticized this country's system of public schooling, which "celebrates meritocracy, privilege, competition, and hierarchy" (Purpel, 2003, p. 95).

One way to approach these issues is through the curriculum. In his classic work, *Pedagogy of the Oppressed,* Freire (1970) contends that students have often been treated as objects, depositories such as in a bank with teachers as the depositors. For Freire, students are not depositories, nor are they empty vessels. The ability of educators to communicate with their students is central to Freire's approach to pedagogy. For him, human life holds meaning through communication. Authentic thinking must involve communication. Teachers can neither think for their

students nor impose their thinking on students. Indeed, student thinking authenticates teacher thinking (Freire, 1970).

Influenced by Freire's work, Purpel (1989) proposes a curriculum that emphasizes justice and compassion, which educates and empowers. Purpel believes our culture and, thus, our schools stress individual competition rather than community building. Similarly, Apple (2001, 2003) points out the danger of emphasizing business approaches and markets in education at the expense of addressing serious social problems, and Giroux (2003b) asserts that corporate culture eliminates or, at the very least, devalues injustices rooted in racial and class differences. Applying this culture to schools as we do now creates serious detrimental effects. Educators, Giroux (2001) maintains, have a key role to play in linking economic democracy and social justice to equality of rights.

> Under these circumstances, many students increasingly find themselves in schools that lack any language for relating the self to public life, social responsibility, or the imperatives of democratic life. In this instance, democratic education, with its emphasis on respect for others, critical inquiry, civic courage and concern for collective good, is suppressed and replaced by an excessive emphasis on the language of privatization, self-interest and brutal competitiveness. (pp. 83–84)

In the past few years, other scholars have joined the ranks of those urging educators to consider issues of social justice in their ethical decision making. Shields (2004) encourages educational leaders to address social justice issues by engaging in moral dialogue that would develop strong relationships, engage the voices of those involved in the education of children, and question existing practices and beliefs.

Marshall (2004) squarely puts the onus on educational leaders and those who train them, observing that educational leadership programs reflect a culture that has marginalized social justice issues. This marginalizing not only affects those with unequal status "but also limits the voices of allies within educational administration that would confront issues of injustice and inequity in our field" (p. 6). Marshall's comments extend widely to include race, class, ethnicity, language, gender, poverty, and differences in sexual orientation, religion, and ability.

THE ETHIC OF THE PROFESSION

Starratt's (1994) articulation of a multidimensional ethical framework paved the way for subsequent scholars to think of the paradigms of justice, care, and critique not as totally distinct entities but as complementary, as a "tapestry of ethical perspectives," the blending of which "encourages a rich human response to the many uncertain ethical situations the school community face every day...." (p. 57).

In *Ethical Leadership and Decision Making in Education,* Shapiro and Stefkovich (2005) discuss these paradigms and argue for a fourth that includes

these three and then moves beyond this multiparadigmatic approach to consider "moral aspects unique to the profession and the questions that arise as educational leaders become more aware of their own personal and professional codes of ethics" (p. 18).

Shapiro and Stefkovich (2005) note that although standardized codes are meant to inform, rather than prescribe practice, a disparity often exists between professional codes and policies and the personal judgment or moral values of administrators. Thus, a key component of the ethic of the profession is "an integration of personal and professional codes" (p. 60). Educational leaders must develop an awareness of their own personal codes of ethics. Professional codes consist of standards set forth by groups, organizations, and sometimes even lawmakers to serve as a guide for practice. In contrast, personal codes are unique to the individual. Such codes, which consist of ideals and principles for the educational leader based on life experiences, cannot be divorced from educational decision making.

In this paradigm, educators must acknowledge that their personal values are likely to influence their actions (Begley & Johansson, 1998, 2003; Willower & Lacata, 1997). Duke and Grogan (1997) identified greater clarity concerning personal values as an important step in making moral decisions. Czaja and Lowe's (2000) survey of ethical responses to problematic school situations indicated, "the importance of self-assessment for identifying personal values ran parallel with the importance of writing a personal … code of ethics" (p. 10).

On the other hand, this integration of professional and personal codes of ethics can lead to a type of inconsonance or a "clashing of codes." Shapiro and Stefkovich (2005) respond to these inevitable clashes by grounding the professional paradigm in the needs of the student. This focus is in concert with Walker's (1998) observation: "The well-considered shibboleth that the best interests of children will be taken to override conflicting interests may be considered both a safe and essential ground for educational decision making" (p. 300).

Therefore, the ethic of the profession considers the ethics of justice, care, and critique as well as what the profession expects, what happens when personal and professional ethics clash, and how the community influences educators' ethical decision making. This ethic calls for school leaders to consider professional and personal ethical principles and codes, standards of the profession, and individual professional codes to create a dynamic model that places the "best interests of the student" as central. This ethic is illustrated in Fig. 2.1.

THE IMPORTANCE OF COMMUNITY

Furman (2003, 2004) proposes a fifth ethic for educational leaders, that of community. For Furman, *community* is the context within which the other ethical postures are applied as school leaders make decisions in an ever-changing environment. She defines the ethic of community as "the moral responsibility to

FIG. 2.1.   Ethic of the profession.

engage in communal processes as educators pursue the moral purposes of their work and address the ongoing challenges of daily life and work in schools" (2004, p. 215). Here, the community, rather than the individual, is the major focus of schools' moral agency. Thus, communal processes, rather than people, are emphasized.

Furman's approach is very different from scholars who view community as an entity and/or see it in relation to the individual (Beck, 1999; Purpel, 1989; Sergiovanni, 1994; Shapiro & Stefkovich, 2005). Many of these scholars do not discuss community as a separate ethic, but instead, join it with another paradigm. For instance, Shapiro and Stefkovich (2005) portray community as an integral part of their model for the ethic of the profession. Community plays a critical role in both Noddings' (1992) and Beck's (1999) conceptualizations of caring. Influenced by critical theorists such as Giroux and Freire, Purpel's curriculum for justice and compassion encompasses community. For purposes of the analyses in this book, community will be viewed in a way similar to that proposed by Shapiro and Stefkovich (2005), that is, as a vital part of the ethic of the profession but not as a separate paradigm.

Some of these authors also see a negative side to community as well as a beneficial one. Noddings (1992) cautions us when she observes: "… communities often act like bloated individuals. Just as an individual may have a personal rival or enemy, so may a community or group" (p. 118). For Noddings, this situation is problematic and potentially more dangerous than with individuals because one feels safer acting in a group. Noddings' vision of community as positive entails the ability to remain in the community accepting its "binding myths, ideas, and commitments" (p. 118) while resisting community pressures for conformity or orthodoxy. To accomplish this vision, one must have self-knowledge but also a knowledge of others that is gained through ongoing communication.

Beck (1999) captures this complexity of community and pulls it into the other paradigms when she writes that:

> Even though many of us acknowledge that communities can be forces for evil, oppression, and corruption, our language about them suggests that we typically think of them as social systems in which people engage in honest reflection and critique, pursue justice, and care for and respect one another. (p. 36)

However community is viewed, as a separate paradigm or part of a larger schema, as positive or negative, its influence on ethical decision making in schools may be profound and should never be underestimated.

3

A Model for Promoting
the Student's Best Interests

Not all those who write about the importance of the study of ethics in educational administration discuss the needs of children; however, this focus on students is clearly consistent with the backbone of our profession. Other professions often have one basic principle driving the profession. In medicine, it is "First, do not harm." In law, it is the assertion that all clients deserve "zealous representation." In educational administration, we believe that if there is a moral imperative for the profession, it is to serve the "best interests of the student." Consequently, this ideal must lie at the heart of any professional paradigm for educational leaders.

—Shapiro & Stefkovich, 2005, pp. 24–25

Even though the term *best interests* is used frequently, there is a lack of clarity as to what constitutes a student's best interests. School leaders tend to interpret this phrase in a variety of ways, oftentimes disagreeing on the best course of action or what is truly in the best interests of the student. Thus, the time has come for developing a more robust model to determine the best interests of the student when making ethical decisions. Based on a new conceptualization of the three Rs with the correlates as rights, responsibilities, and respect, this model presents a guide for school leaders as they make ethical decisions.

THE STUDENT: AS AN INDIVIDUAL AND IN CONTEXT

This best interests model intentionally refers to the best interests of the student as an individual as opposed to students in a group. The underlying assumption here is that if the individual student is treated with fairness, justice, and caring, then a

17

strong message is sent to all students that they will also be afforded justice and caring and that they should treat others similarly. Thus, rights carry with them responsibilities, so much so that the rights of one individual should not bring harm to the group.

Beck (1994) eloquently lends support to the caring aspect of this concept of best interests in relation to the individual. Here, she focuses on the benefits of caring:

> For those who hold a caring ethic, the value of lives, their own and others', has a very different basis. They believe that persons possess inherent worth and dignity. A caring, community-oriented ethic frees persons from pressuring others and themselves to constantly strive to earn or maintain value [through achievement]. (p. 55)

If a clash between individual and group needs emerges, an ethic of justice requires that the educational leader must first decide if the individual is acting responsibly in asserting his or her rights. If not, then what better opportunity is there to take advantage of the situation as a teachable moment for the student? Take, for example, one case where a student took a weapon from another student who was about to commit suicide. Rather than expelling the student who took the weapon—as was done—would it not make more sense to praise the student for being a Good Samaritan and explain to him the importance of reporting such matters? Granted, this task of teaching responsibility is challenging and requires vigilance. However, in this way, there is great potential here for educators to grow both personally and professionally and for students to share responsibility for their own development.

In a similar vein, context is critical to this conceptualization of best interests in that it may influence actions. Take, for example, zero tolerance rules. No one would question that it is critical to enforce tough rules when weapons are brought into schools. On the other hand, it might not be in the best interests of the individual student or of the entire school community to expel a student who has a weapon in his car that he did not know about. Yet, as chapter 10 illustrates, this event occurred, as did the attempted suicide mentioned previously, and in each instance school officials expelled the student.

Therefore, just as judges render their opinions on a case-by-case basis, carefully weighing the facts of the case in the context of prevailing laws, so must educational leaders work within the confines of their school communities, calling upon their own discretion and professional judgment within the context of each particular situation to determine what is truly in the best interests of the student.

WHAT ARE BEST INTERESTS?

The best interests concept is rooted in legal jurisprudence. In such cases, usually involving custody, child labor, and compulsory education, the courts often refer to the "best interests of the child" (Goldstein, Freud, & Solnit, 1973, 1979; Goldstein, Solnit, Goldstein, & Freud, 1996). It is *the* legal standard used by courts in determining issues of child custody, child support, and visitation (or access, as it is called in some jurisdictions) in regard to the child or children's parents or legal guardians (Wikipedia Online Encyclopedia, 2004).

In determining the best interests of the child, courts often order various investigations to be undertaken by social workers, psychologists, and other experts to determine living conditions of the child and his or her custodial and noncustodial parents. Although parents may often request visitation or custody to fit their own interests, the overriding consideration is how the child will benefit from interacting with these parents. Historically, courts have allowed children some capability to make decisions in regard to their own welfare. However, in the absence of the maturity to make decisions, adults who care for these children have been ultimately responsible.

Stability of the child's life, links with the community, and a stable home environment by the proposed custodial parents are some of the issues courts consider in deciding the outcome of custody and visitation proceedings. More specifically, in determining best interests, courts often consider the age and gender of the child; the mental and physical health of the child; mental and physical health of the parents; lifestyle and other social factors of the parents; emotional ties between the parents and the child; ability of the parents to provide the child with food, shelter, clothing and medical care; established living pattern for the child concerning school, home, community and religious institutions; the quality of schooling; and the child's preference (Wikipedia Online Encyclopedia, 2004).

Walker (1998) cites Canadian Supreme Court cases that use "the best interests of children test" (p. 288) as applied to child custody cases where the child's safety and well-being is balanced with the value of the family unit. However, Walker found that even within the court system, "best interests" is determined by a variety of factors beyond age, physical and emotional constitution, and the relationship that the child has with parents, with little agreement as to what constitutes the best interests of children.

Stefkovich, O'Brien, and Moore (2002), in an analysis of court cases and articles in law reviews and education journals, revealed no specific definitions of best interests beyond those already mentioned. In addition, the context in which the term was used varied greatly. For example, *Nettleton School District v. Owens* (1997), a case involving interpretation of the Teacher Fair Dismissal Act as it applies to the influence of alcohol on a teacher's professional conduct, based its decision on the "best interests of students." In *Jergeson v. Board of Trustees* (1970), the President of the Board of Education based a teacher's dismissal on a "philosophy and practice of education" that "is detrimental to the best interests of the high school students" (p. 482). Other court decisions referred to the best interests of students, but did not define the term. Instead, it was generally used as part of a larger argument and was not the focus of the case itself.

A content analysis of over 60 law review articles using this term (best interests of the student) or a variation of it (e.g., best interests of students, best interests of children), revealed no common theme and no shared use. Instead, these articles focused on a wide variety of educational issues at both the primary and secondary levels including, among others, students with disabilities, bilingual education, students' constitutional rights, student athletes, school choice, children's rights, local control, and student services. In each of these articles, when "best interests" was used, no explanation of the term was provided (Stefkovich et al., 2002).

Oftentimes, the term "best interest" supported a point being made by the author with no clear definition of what specifically is in the best interests of the student and no specific guidance as to what action/decisions are consonant with a student's best interests. Use of the phrase, however, generally implied great discretion on the part of school officials. For example, Dupre (1996), in her comprehensive analysis of students' constitutional rights, writes: "… once a society that generally respected the authority of teachers, deferred to their judgment, and trusted them to act in the best interest of school children …" (p. 50).

Finally, the Stefkovich et al. (2002) research revealed that neither educators nor the popular press either defined or commonly used the term "best interests." In a review of 71 news articles, the term "best interest(s) of students" covered over 21 topic areas and was used to justify a wide variety of K–12 administrative decisions ranging from special education placement, to disciplinary sanctions, to school consolidation. Similar results were found in analyzing doctoral dissertations, trade journals, and professional academic journals in education and related social sciences.

Walker, a Canadian scholar, seems to offer the best advice on this topic (Walker, 1998). His research, which involved extensive interviews with school principals and superintendents, revealed a widespread but varied commitment to what he termed "kids' best interests" (p. 4). In other words, school leaders see children as primary stakeholders in schools but use the term "best interests" in a variety of ways. Indeed, these leaders' ethical decision making was based on a variety of factors in addition to students' best interests, including the overall well-being of stakeholders, "the preeminence of educational goals," and the "maximization of long-term benefits" (p. 4). More recently, Begley (2004) found similar results in his study of U.S. and Canadian principals.

WHOSE BEST INTERESTS?

Although Walker (1995) observes that the best interests maxim carries with it "enormous potential to direct and to measure goodness, rightness, and appropriateness of policy and practice," he also notes it has "the same potent ability to cover non-action or detrimental choices with respect to the long term quality of children's lives" (p. 4). Even when well-meaning, there is a danger here. "Sadly, adult-centricity may be one of the largest obstacles to securing the best interests of children" (Walker, 1998, p. 291). Accordingly, scholars have commented that the interests, needs, rights, and perspectives of adults often determine the best interests of minors (Goldstein et al., 1973, 1979) and call for a consideration of students' voices in determining best interests (Ehrensal, 2002, 2003; Levesque, 1997; Mitra, 2001, 2003, 2005).

An editorial by a 16-year-old honors student, published in *The San Francisco Daily Journal,* makes the point most profoundly (Ducote, 2002). Addressing guardians *ad litem* in private custody cases, she observed: "Instead of being actually represented, children get their 'best interests' represented by adults. We children have no choice and no recourse when those adults have their own agendas" (p. 106). She was referring to the abuse she claims she underwent for years while living with her father. Adults who were supposed to protect her, instead, tried to convince her that living with the abuser was in her best interest. She concluded: "The practice of trying to ascertain what is in a child's best interest exists because minors supposedly cannot speak for themselves. Yet, at 11, I could speak for myself" (p. 108).

THE BEST INTERESTS MODEL

Understanding that adults possess a great deal of power in determining students' best interests and realizing how easy it is to ignore the voices of those who literally have the most to lose, it is incumbent on school leaders to make ethical decisions that truly reflect the needs of students and not their own adult self-interests. This is not always easy. It requires a great deal of self-reflection, open-mindedness, and an understanding that making ethically sound decisions profoundly influences others' lives.

The student's best interests are at the center of the ethic of the profession, which encompasses the ethics of justice, care, and critique and is strongly influenced by the community. This model is not ideological in the sense that it follows any one theory or particular strand of reasoning. Instead, it is far-reaching, emerging from the ethic of the profession and borrowing concepts from the remaining ethical paradigms. This eclectic approach is one that, as Starratt points out, enriches educational leaders' repertoire of skills in dealing with ethical issues. Starratt (1994) describes these interconnections in this way:

> Each ethic needs the very strong connections embedded in the other: the ethic of justice needs the profound commitment to the dignity of the individual person; the ethic of caring needs the larger attention to social order and fairness if it is to avoid an entirely idiosyncratic involvement in social policy; the ethic of critique requires an ethic of caring if it is to avoid the cynical and depressing ravings of the habitual malcontent; the ethic of justice requires the profound social analysis of the ethic of critique in order to move beyond the naïve fine-tuning of social arrangements in a social system with inequities built into the very structures by which justice is supposed to be measured. (p. 55)

Nor is this model prescriptive in the sense that it needs to be followed without deviation, or worse yet, without thought. Instead, what I outline here is a way to make sense of what here-to-date has been a much used, yet amorphous, concept.

Rights

This model acknowledges rights as essential in determining a student's best interests. These include (a) rights granted to all human beings as articulated by philosophers past and present; (b) universal rights recognized by the United Nations, particularly those acknowledged under its Convention on the Rights of the Child; and (c) rights guaranteed by law, specifically those enumerated under the U.S. Constitution's Bill of Rights. In addition, this model recognizes the existence of certain fundamental rights as universal despite the fact that some countries such as the United States have not recognized them (Bitensky, 1992; Levesque, 1996).

The United Nations has, on several occasions, acknowledged the human rights of children. Although they do not expressly define the concept "in the best interests of students," they do refer to the "rights of a child." The Universal Declaration of Human Rights, adopted by the General Assembly of the United Nations in 1948, refers to children. Article 26 and Article 29 of the Universal Declaration are particularly helpful in more clearly articulating how to serve the "best interests of students" (Universal Declaration of Human Rights, 1948, p. 5).

Furthermore, the Convention on the Rights of the Child identifies the basic human rights of children who, without discrimination, "have the right to survival, to develop to the fullest, be protected from harmful influences, abuse and exploitation, and to participate fully in family, cultural and social life" (Convention on the Rights of the Child, 1989, p. 1). Standards set by health care, education, and legal, civil and social services protect these rights.

Rights characterized as fundamental under the U.S. Constitution include freedom of religion, free speech, privacy, due process, and freedom from unlawful discrimination. On numerous occasions, the United States Supreme Court has recognized that students are entitled to these basic rights but that they are limited in the school context. In addition to these rights, the "best interests" model includes a right to dignity and protection from humiliation. It also includes two rights that are not recognized as fundamental for students under the U.S. Constitution. These are the right to an education and the right to be free from bodily harm, which includes corporal punishment.

Concerning the first, the U.S. Supreme Court has stated that education is an important governmental interest but not a fundamental right (*Plyler v. Doe*, 1982). Although state constitutional language differs regarding the provision of education, the constitution of every U.S. state grants citizens some rights to an education (Bitensky, 1992; Lynch, 1998; Ozar, 1986; Thro, 1989, 1998) but only a handful see this right as fundamental (Heise, 1995; Walsh, 1993).

As to the second, the Supreme Court has maintained that the U.S. Constitution does not protect students from corporal punishment. Although the constitution's Eighth Amendment protects inmates in prisons, it does not apply to students in schools (*Ingraham v. Wright,* 1977). The Supreme Court has left both of these issues up to the states to decide. More than half of the U.S. states (29 out of 50) have passed laws prohibiting corporal punishment. And, even without the intervention of lawmakers, many school districts have passed policies protecting and affirming these rights (Rossow & Stefkovich, 2005).

Despite the fact the these rights are not uniformly viewed as fundamental in the United States, they have been recognized by other groups such as the United Nations Universal Declaration of Human Rights and the United Nations Convention on the Rights of the Child. The best interests model maintains, therefore, that all the rights mentioned are universal and fundamental to a conception of the student's best interests.

Responsibility

Individuals have rights, but these rights are not unfettered. Indeed, theorists past and present from many differing perspectives consider rights to be incomplete if viewed without consideration of accompanying responsibilities. Attention to moral responsibility is implied both in early Greek texts and later with Aristotle, who many have recognized as the first to explicitly articulate a theory of moral responsibility (Eshelman, 2004). In Book Seven of his *Nicomachean Ethics* (2002), Aristotle explains that persons who are capable of making decisions are moral agents and therefore are responsible and worthy of being praised or blamed.

Although the best interests model does not subscribe to a utilitarian approach to ethics, it does recognize merit in Mill's declaration, "Everyone who receives the protection of society owes a return for the benefit, and the fact of living in society renders it indispensable that each should be bound to observe a certain line of conduct toward the rest" (Mill, 1978, p. 73). For our purposes, Rousseau (1967) conveys a more appropriate portrayal of responsibility from this observation:

> From this we must understand that what generalizes the will is not so much the number of voices as the common interest which unites them; for, under this system, each necessarily submits to the conditions which he imposes on others—an admirable union of interest and justice, which gives to the deliberations of the community a spirit of equity ... the social compact establishes among the citizens such an equality that they all pledge themselves under the same conditions and ought all to enjoy the same rights. (p. 34)

Kant's moral imperative implies a sense of responsibility when it refers to an individual's duty (Kant, 1966). Influenced by Locke, Rousseau, and Kant, contemporary scholars have connected ethical decision making with the responsibility one has in making moral choices. For example, Rawls (1999) believes that one should make moral decisions based on issues of fairness and equality. For him, a moral decision is one that rational persons would make not knowing where they stand in a hypothetical dilemma. Herein, the just decision is one that is fair regardless of the person's social status. Kohlberg (1981) speaks of conscience as principled responsibility, one of the highest levels on his hierarchy of moral stages. Concepts of rationality and choice also underlie the basis behind Kohlberg's (1980) theory of democratic schools and Lickona's (1991) concept of students as moral philosophers.

Thus, although students may have the right to free speech, they also have the duty to exercise this right responsibly (*Bethel v. Fraser,* 1986; Diamond, 1981; Yudof, 1995, 1998). Herein lies the legal distinction of never shouting "fire" in a crowded movie theater (when, of course, there is no fire). Therefore, although nonviolent protests are clearly a student's right (given the appropriate time, place, and manner) under the Free Speech clause of the First Amendment, bullying and harassing other students is not. Recognizing that conflicts can, and do, exist between individual rights and group rights, this tension greatly diminishes when viewed through such a rights and/or responsibilities lens.

Finally, Starratt (2005), in his discussion of authenticity, notes: "Every human being has a moral responsibility to be him or herself, to be an original, to be the real thing, to author his or her own life"(p. 10). For Starratt (2004), the key factors constituting moral leadership are authenticity, responsibility, and presence (being there).

The ethic of justice provides an excellent foundation for discussions of responsibility. However, it does not exclusively control this topic. Responsibility is also an important component of the ethic of care and adds a critical dimension to this discussion. In this sense, the best interests model comports with that of Starratt (2005), who notes: "One cannot be authentic except in relationships. One's truth can only be grasped and affirmed in and by a relationship. All moral exchange is based on mutual trust in the authenticity of the other" (p. 10). Closely aligned with this theory is accountability toward others and toward society in general, which includes social responsibility.

The model also builds on Gilligan (1982), who notes the complementary nature of rights and responsibilities. For her, rights center on issues of equality and fairness, whereas responsibility emphasizes equity. "While the ethic of rights is a manifestation of equal respect, balancing the claims of other and self, the ethic of responsibility rests on an understanding that gives rise to compassion and care" (pp. 164–165).

Noddings (2002) gives us some insight into this issue in her discussion of the Golden Rule: "Do unto others as you would have others do unto you." A number of philosophers steeped in the ethic of justice see this rule as moral responsibility. On the other hand, Noddings questions this statement as a universal principle in the context of the ethic of care. "Does it mean that we should treat others exactly as we would like to be treated … we believe that people want different outcomes, treasure different values, and express different needs" (p. 149). Thus, for Noddings, context is critical as is "receptive attention" and "engrossment" (p. 149).

Another approach to this same situation comes from the counseling profession's concept of *empathy*. Unlike sympathy, feeling sorry for another's plight, empathy means the ability to put oneself in another's shoes. This concept nicely complements and overlaps with our third R, that of respect.

Respect

Philosophers have long been fascinated by the concept of *respect*. Discussion of both respect and self-respect arise in a variety of philosophical contexts. These concepts have been applied to ethics across many disciplines. There is no agreement as to a central definition, and philosophers conceptualize respect in many ways. To some, it is taught, like responsibility, through the Golden Rule. Others have constructed complicated hierarchies to elucidate the nuances between different kinds of respect (Dillon, 1992).

The concept of respect, however, is most often equated with the work of Kant. Although respect is implied throughout philosophical traditions, Kant was the first Western philosopher to place respect for persons as central to moral theory. Kant set forth: "it is morally obligatory to respect every person as a rational agent" (cited in Davis, 1993, p. 211). Central to Kant's work is the importance of treating others never simply as a means, but always at the same time as an end (Kant, 1966).

Dillon (1992) offers respect as "most generally, a relation between a subject and an object, in which the subject responds to the object from a certain perspective in some appropriate way" (p. 1). Lickona (1991), who follows Kohlberg's theory of moral development, views respect as negative obligations that we owe each other such as those delineated in the "Thou shalt nots" of the Ten Commandments, while responsibility, in contrast, emphasizes positive mandates such as loving thy neighbor. For Lickona, these are two important moral values that must be practiced in the classroom.

The best interests model agrees with Lickona's view of respect as part of the cornerstone of ethical behavior but, unlike Lickona, it conceptualizes respect as a more positive, mutual interaction, focusing on the individual. This view of respect is more akin to Martin Buber's (1958) concept of the *I–thou relationship* and theories of other existentialist philosophers such as Romano Guardini (1965), who emphasize the importance of self as well as mutuality. In this respect, Guardini tells us:

> ... it is enigmatic and inexhaustible that I am I, that I cannot be forced out of myself not even by the most powerful enemy, but only by myself, and even that not entirely; that I cannot be replaced even by the noblest person; that I am the center of existence, for I *am* that, and you are also that, and you yonder ... (p. 119)

Lawrence-Lightfoot (1999), in her book *Respect*, notes that this term has been portrayed as hierarchical, often associated with expressions of "esteem, approbation, or submission" (p. 9). For example, someone may be due respect because of his or her age, position, or accomplishments, or we respect institutions, such as the government, or symbols, such as the flag. In contrast, Lawrence-Lightfoot's (1999) approach to respect emphasizes ways in which it creates "symmetry, empathy, and connection in all kinds of relationships, even those, such as teacher and student, doctor and patient, commonly seen as unequal" (pp. 9–10).

Like Lawrence-Lightfoot, the best interests model envisions respect as mutuality. It involves treating all students with respect but also expecting students to treat others in the same manner. Here, the emphasis is on equity as well as equality, tolerance, self-respect (which includes an acceptance of one's own as well as others' frailties), an appreciation and celebration of diversity, and a commitment to finding common ground in an increasingly multicultural, pluralistic society (see Fig. 3.1).

PERSONNEL ISSUES AFFECTING STUDENTS

The best interests model emphasizes the importance of students' rights and of accepting responsibility for actions associated with these rights. One could argue that the most effective way to teach responsibility is to model it. In other words, "walk the walk." How students see supervisors treating their teacher colleagues oftentimes sends a much more profound message than any verbal communication. In addition, the degree of respect and dignity afforded teachers signals to students how adults—younger and older—should treat each other and how students as individuals will be regarded.

FIG. 3.1.   Best interests model. Illustration by Hector L. Sambolin, Jr., 2005.

Respect for teachers, or lack thereof, conveys information, whether accurate or not, to young people about how they will be treated and how they should treat others. Blase and Blase (2003, 2004), who write prolifically on mistreatment of teachers and what administrators, particularly principals, can do to either remedy or avoid these situations, identify university preparation programs as an important component in this learning process. Factors they identify as potentially related to this problem of abuse that could be included in administrator preservice programs include, among others, gender, power, law, development of norms that foster "respect and caring in the workplace" (Blase & Blase, 2003, p. 159, citing Starratt, 1991, p. 196) and ethical standards, all of which figure prominently in the best interests model.

Thus, the underlying premise here is that personnel decisions in which teachers appear to be treated unfairly have the potential to affect students in profound, and sometimes subtle, ways and that how these individuals are treated may dramatically influence the entire school community in both positive and negative directions. For these reasons, this text includes a number of personnel-related decisions in addition to the majority of cases focusing on students' rights.

CONCLUSIONS

In sum, if there is a moral imperative for educational leaders, it is to act in the best interests of student (Shapiro & Stefkovich, 2005). In the absence of any clear definition of *best interests,* this chapter presents a model that may serve as a guide in determining factors to be considered in making ethical decisions. This model relies on context, takes into account students' voices, and begins with the assumption that school officials will engage in active inquiry and self-reflection in order to make decisions that are truly in the best interests of the student rather than self-serving or merely expedient. Major aspects of the model, as depicted in Fig. 3.1, include rights, responsibility, and respect with mutuality and/or reciprocity as an intrinsic component.

4

The Courts, the Law, and Ethics

Walker (1998) asserts: "educational decisions and policies related to children must be, at the very least, grounded in applied jurisprudential and ethical considerations" (p. 300). The aim of this chapter is to acquaint the reader with the United States' legal system, to discuss what happens when the law is unclear or simply wrong, and to show the limitations of the law. Oftentimes, practices that are within the letter of the law may not necessarily follow an ethical or moral course of action. This chapter, therefore, ends with a discussion of the confluence between legal and ethical decision making.

THE U.S. LEGAL SYSTEM

Recognizing that this book may be read by a wide audience ranging from those who are quite knowledgeable about the law to those whose understanding is much more rudimentary, this section provides a brief overview of the legal system. For some readers, this discussion will serve as a quick review. For others, this chapter is designed to provide enough background in understanding the U.S. legal system so that one may be adequately prepared to grapple with the ethical issues presented by the legal cases in Parts II and III of this book. (For those persons desiring additional legal information, Appendix A [this volume] lists a number of excellent law and education textbooks that provide this information.)

In the United States, most law emanates from three major sources represented by a parallel structure at the federal and state levels. The first of these includes the U.S. Constitution as well as state constitutions. The second encompasses federal laws passed by Congress and state laws enacted by state legislatures. The third involves the judicial system.

This structure includes a balance of powers whereby the legislative branch makes the laws, the judiciary interprets the laws, and the executive branch (the Office of the President or Governor) enforces the laws. Although each branch of government has its own special domain, there is overlap. For example, in executing the law, governmental agencies under the executive branch develop and enforce rules and regulations that have the effect of law. In interpreting laws, court opinions may greatly influence those laws.

At the federal level, there are three tiers of courts where disputes may be heard. Legal cases begin at the district level, which includes either a judge only or a judge, jury, and witnesses. The remaining two levels are for appeals only. That is, if either party is unhappy with the decision rendered, he or she may appeal the decision to a federal circuit court of appeals, for example, the Second Circuit or the Eighth Circuit. There are eleven circuits in all, representing jurisdictions comprised of various states and U.S. territories. From that circuit, either party may appeal the decision to the U.S. Supreme Court. These circuits and the states they cover are outlined in Table 4.1, along with the names of the cases that are discussed later in this book.

The state level has a similar structure in that disputes must begin at the trial court level and then may be appealed to the state appeals level and then to the highest court in the state, generally, but not always, referred to as the state supreme court. State decisions may also be appealed from this highest state court to the U.S. Supreme Court. There are restrictions on what types of cases may be heard in federal court. For purposes of this discussion, most education cases heard in federal court involve a federal issue, such as violation of a federal law or violation of the U.S. Constitution.

Readers should keep in mind that the only court decisions that hold precedent for the entire country are U.S. Supreme Court decisions. Federal circuit court decisions only apply to states and territories within that circuit and are not legally binding in other circuits. Therefore, if a federal court for the Third Circuit makes a decision, it is only binding on the states and territories within the Third Circuit (Delaware, New Jersey, Pennsylvania, and the Virgin Islands) and would not apply to New York State (which is in the Second Circuit) or to Colorado (which is in the Tenth Circuit).

Of the thousands of appeals brought to the U.S. Supreme Court each year, the Court is able to hear only a small number of cases. When the Supreme Court decides not to hear a case, the lower court's decision stands. However, this is not meant to imply that the High Court agrees with the lower court's decision. It is simply a decision not to hear the case and should not be inferred as any judgment on the Supreme Court's part as to the merits of the case.

A variety of factors come into play as the Supreme Court Justices decide which cases to review. Sometimes, but not always, the Court may elect to decide a case when there is a split among the circuits. For example, the *Vernonia v. Acton* (1995) case, which addressed the legality of random drug testing of student athletes, arrived at the Supreme Court on appeal from the Ninth Circuit Court of Appeals. The Ninth Circuit court had ruled the program unconstitutional, but an earlier case

TABLE 4.1

Court Structure and Cases

Type of Court	Controlling Precedent for	Cases
U.S. Supreme Court	United States	*Kadrmas* (1988)
First Circuit	Maine, Massachusetts, New Hampshire, Puerto Rico, Rhode Island	*Hasenfus* (1999) *Timothy W.* (1989)
Second Circuit	Connecticut, New York, Vermont	*Immediato* (1996)
Third Circuit	Delaware, New Jersey, Pennsylvania, Virgin Islands	*Gruenke* (2000) *C.H. v. Oliva* (2000) *S.G. v. Sayreville* (2003) *Taxman* (1996) *U.S. v. Bd. of Ed. of Phila.* (1990)
Fourth Circuit	Maryland, North Carolina, South Carolina, Virginia, West Virginia	*Boring* (1998) *Ratner* (2001)
Fifth Circuit	District of the Canal Zone, Louisiana, Mississippi, Texas	
Sixth Circuit	Kentucky, Michigan, Ohio, Tennessee	*Boroff* (2000) *Mozert* (1987) *Seal* (2000)
Seventh Circuit	Illinois, Indiana, Wisconsin	*Billings* (2001) *Cornfield* (1993) *Nabozny* (1996) *People Who Care* (1997)
Eighth Circuit	Arkansas, Iowa, Minnesota, Missouri, Nebraska, North Dakota, South Dakota	*Davenport* (1999) *Doe v. Pulaski* (2002)
Ninth Circuit	Alaska, Arizona, California, Idaho, Montana, Nevada, Oregon, Washington, Guam, Hawaii	*Doe v. Hawaii* (2003) *LaVine* (2001) *Lassonde* (2003) *Settlegoode* (2004)
Tenth Circuit	Colorado, Kansas, New Mexico, Oklahoma, Utah, Wyoming	*Garcia v. Miera* (1987) *Fleming v. Jefferson County* (2002)
Eleventh Circuit	Alabama, Florida, Georgia	*Hearn* (1999) *Thomas* (2003)
Federal District Court	Federal courts in same state	*Beussink* (1998) *GSA v. Boyd* (2003) *Garrett* (1991) *Selman* (2005)
State Appeals Courts	State-level courts	*Hoffman* (1978) *Joye* (2003) *Prof. Standards* (2002)

on the same topic, *Schaill v. Tippecanoe* (1989), had been upheld by the Seventh Circuit court. In overruling the Ninth Circuit decision, the U.S. Supreme Court legalized random drug testing of student athletes nationwide.

Of the cases listed in Table 4.1 and reviewed in Parts II and III of this book, most represent splits in the circuits where the U.S. Supreme Court denied *certiorari*, that is the High Court refused to hear the case. Thus, what was left was a conflict in laws among various jurisdictions with some circuits deciding one way, others deciding another way, and many jurisdictions left with little or no guidance as to what actions might be legal. These cases were selected for discussion in part because the law is unclear but also because they tend to raise some serious ethical issues worthy of consideration.

WHEN THE LAW IS WRONG

Sometimes, the law is wrong. In the movie *The Pelican Brief*[1], based on a John Grisham novel of the same name, there is a powerful scene, which vividly illustrates this premise. Thomas Callahan, a law professor at Tulane University (played by Sam Shepherd) stands in front of his classroom discussing privacy rights under the U.S. Constitution in relation to the Supreme Court's decision in *Bowers v. Hardwick* (1986).

In this case, two police officers entered Hardwick's home and witnessed him and another man having sex. The act in which they were engaged was in violation of Georgia's antisodomy statute. The legal issue under the Court's consideration was whether the U.S. Constitution "confers a fundamental right upon homosexuals to engage in sodomy" (*Bowers v. Hardwick,* 1986, p. 190). If so, the laws of a number of states prohibiting such conduct would be invalidated.

Professor Callahan probes the constitutionality of this claim. After calling on several students who provide him with limited legal reasoning related to various aspects of this issue including the right to privacy, Callahan appears to want more in the way of an explanation. He spots Darby Shaw, an attractive female student (played by Julia Roberts), who also happens to be his current romantic interest. Darby's answer is intense and appears to be clearly reasoned:

Darby Shaw: If the State of Georgia can regulate Hardwick's sexuality engaged in private with consenting adults, Hardwick cannot be free. The Constitution was written to ensure limited government. If there is no right of privacy, if Georgia can enforce the statute, then we sacrifice the liberty the framers thought they guaranteed us.

Callahan: Well, the Supreme Court disagreed with you, Miss Shaw. They found that the statute did not violate the right of privacy. Now, why is that?

Darby Shaw: They were wrong.

---

[1] Excerpts from "The Pelican Brief" granted courtesy of Warner Bros. Entertainment, Inc.

Seventeen years after *Bowers v. Hardwick,* in its decision in *Lawrence v. Texas* (2003), the United States Supreme Court overruled *Bowers v. Hardwick,* stating emphatically: "*Bowers* was not correct when it was decided, and it is not correct today. It ought not to remain binding precedent. *Bowers v. Hardwick* should be and now is overruled" (p. 578).

Sometimes laws are wrong. This is one reason our form of government allows for change in the law. For example, past laws allowed Mormons to take multiple wives. Early 20th-century laws regulating women in the workforce were later overturned and criticized as being paternalist. Mandates such as the Jim Crow laws, which required separate facilities for Blacks, were widespread and then later declared illegal. A major role for the court system is to determine the legality of laws that are challenged. And, as illustrated in the aforementioned example, sometimes even the Supreme Court is wrong.

The United States Supreme Court is the highest court in this land and, unlike lower courts, any decision it renders holds precedent for the entire country. Under the doctrine of *stare decisis*, literally meaning "the decision stands," the High Court in its subsequent rulings as well as all lower courts must abide by these decisions. Only the Supreme Court can overrule itself. Although this is infrequent, as illustrated, it can and does happen.

In *Brown v. Allen* (1953), Justice Robert Jackson, in a concurring opinion, noted the inevitability of conflicts among lower courts and the finality of a Supreme Court ruling.

> Whenever decisions of one court are reviewed by another, a percentage of them are reversed. That reflects a difference in outlook normally found between personnel comprising different courts. However, reversal by a higher court is not proof that justice is thereby better done. There is no doubt that if there were a super-Supreme Court, a substantial proportion of our reversals of state courts would also be reversed. We are not final because we are infallible, but we are infallible only because we are final. (p. 533)

The finality of controversial decisions such as *Bowers v. Hardwick* and *Lawrence v. Texas* profoundly influences social policy. Other examples include the *Grutter v. Bollinger* (2003) opinion on affirmative action in college admissions. Although the Court did not explicitly overrule past precedent, it did specify clearly that diversity is a compelling state interest, a principle that a number of scholars (Eckes, 2005; Estlund, 2005; Krislov, 2004) view as a positive sign despite the challenges presented by the decision.

WHEN THE LAW IS UNCLEAR

Our legal system, like our democratic system of government, provides its citizens with generally effective ways of governance. Self-governance can be particularly effective in administering schools, but it is important to recognize that the judicial system cannot provide all the answers. It has limitations.

Courts are generally reluctant to cast a wide net when they issue opinions. In other words, their decisions often apply to the facts of the case at hand and are not always applicable to other legal issues. For example, the *New Jersey v. T.L.O.* (1985) decision involved the legality of searching a female student's purse for evidence of suspected wrongdoing (smoking cigarettes in violation of school rules). Although this court opinion applied to searching for evidence of other violations of school rules or for illegal activities, the court ruling specifically stated that it would not address a number of issues including, but not limited to, canine searches, less intrusive searches such as locker searches, searches more intrusive than a purse search (e.g., strip searches), searches without individualized suspicion (i.e., group searches), and searches involving police officers.

Thus, this decision left open many legal issues that resulted in further litigation at both the Supreme Court and lower court levels. In their research on search-and-seizure cases, Stefkovich and Torres (2006) note that in the 21 years between the time of the U.S. Supreme Court's decision in *New Jersey v. T.L.O.* on January 15, 1985, and the anniversary of the decision on January 15, 2006, there were over 270 lower court decisions recorded on LEXIS and WESTLAW, the two most widely used, comprehensive, and respected data bases of court cases. Most of these opinions were related to issues left unresolved by the *T.L.O.* Court.

In the absence of clear direction from the U.S. Supreme Court, lower courts may differ in their interpretation of the law. For example, in areas related to school prayer, the Supreme Court has deemed illegal teacher-led school prayer and Bible reading, religious speakers at graduation ceremonies, and state statutes requiring the teaching of creationism in public schools. Lower courts have subsequently grappled with the legality of related issues such as distribution of religious materials, student-led school prayers, and moments of silence, often with differing outcomes.

It is important, however, to realize that the state or the schools themselves may afford individuals more rights than those provided by the U.S. Constitution and as interpreted by the judiciary. This situation is particularly compelling when it comes to issues that the High Court has refused to decide, turning these unresolved legal issues back to the states. To illustrate this concept, in the absence of an authoritative High Court decision, 29 states have passed laws prohibiting corporal punishment in schools; and seven states have enacted statutes prohibiting school officials from strip-searching students.

Some court decisions dictate action on the part of school officials in that these opinions prohibit certain behaviors, often by ruling that they are unconstitutional. The school prayer decisions mentioned fall into this category. Teacher-led prayer and Bible reading are clearly illegal. School officials do not have a choice here; they may not engage in such behavior.

On the other hand, many court decisions do not necessarily require action on the part of school officials but state that such actions, if school officials were to undertake them, would be legal. For example, the Supreme Court has said that drug testing students involved in extra-curricular activities is legal under certain circumstances. However, this decision does not require schools to drug test students. The Court merely states that schools may legally institute such programs. Because issues of individual rights are at stake here, states (or school districts) may afford individuals more (but not less) protection of their rights.

ADMINISTRATIVE DISCRETION

U.S. courts, in issuing their opinions, often provide school officials with considerable discretion in making day-to-day decisions. It is only when fundamental rights are involved that courts are willing to interfere. In 1975, the Supreme Court in *Wood v. Strickland* clearly stated: "It is not the role of federal courts to set aside decisions of school administrators, which the court may view as lacking a basis in wisdom or compassion...." (p. 326). As illustrated later in this book, a number of lower courts have used this logic in upholding administrative actions that might seem abhorrent to many school officials.

Likewise, in the past few years, school officials have been especially reluctant to exercise their discretion. For example, school leaders often abdicate their authority by establishing and enforcing strict zero-tolerance policies or by calling in the police to handle matters, most of which were formerly typically handled on their own. One of the aims of this book is to empower school officials to use their discretion wisely in making sound ethical decisions and to encourage those who train these individuals to examine legal opinions with an eye toward ethical decision making.

ETHICS AND THE LAW

Given the considerable amount of discretion that courts generally provide school leaders and understanding that the law is often unclear and may even at times be wrong, school authorities frequently find themselves in a position where they cannot rely on the law for guidance in solving tough problems. It is then that school leaders must be particularly concerned with ethical issues.

Foster (1986), in his classic book on school administration, *Paradigms and Promises,* asserts that school leaders put beliefs into practice with every action. Whenever an administrator makes decisions "... he or she acts on an underlying philosophy of administration.... Reflections on the underlying assumptions and philosophy provide self understanding and that in turn may provide a better administration" (p. 19). As mentioned earlier, for Foster, every administrative decision is, at its heart, an ethical decision.

Acknowledging that inaction may in itself constitute a decision, it is important that school leaders be able to identify ethical dilemmas when such situations arise and that they also examine their own beliefs, values, and ethical principles in making these decisions. Inherent in this concept is the school leader's ability to distinguish between issues that can be resolved through the legal system and those that rely on administrative discretion. Either situation, but certainly the latter, may place school leaders in a position where they must make ethical decisions.

5

Applying Ethical Constructs to Legal Cases

This chapter shows how the best interests model may be applied to practical, authentic situations arising from court decisions. The analysis is not presented to give "the answer" but is rather phrased in terms that challenge readers and force them to think deeply about these issues and perhaps to understand that not all school officials or their constituents will necessarily agree on what is ethical behavior or what is in the best interests of the student.

The purpose of this chapter and of this book is not to convince the judicial system to change, perhaps to become more moral, more ethical in its reasoning. Although such discussions may have merit as well as important policy implications, these issues are well beyond the purview of our discussion and this work is best left to others who specialize in legal discourse. Rather, the purpose here is to address what is, what options school leaders have, and ethical courses of action.

Figure 5.1 illustrates different decision-making points that school leaders meet as they confront the law and approach ethical issues that may arise after legal action is taken. This chapter and the cases presented in this book focus primarily on the third category, "If the Law Permits," and how school officials use their discretion in ethical ways.

Immediately following Fig. 5.1 is a summary of the *Cornfield by Lewis v. Consolidated School District* (1993) decision. This case is used for illustrative purposes. A sample analysis is also provided. However, readers should keep in mind that there are many acceptable ways to analyze each case and that these various analyses strike at the heart of this book's reasoning and goal for the reader.

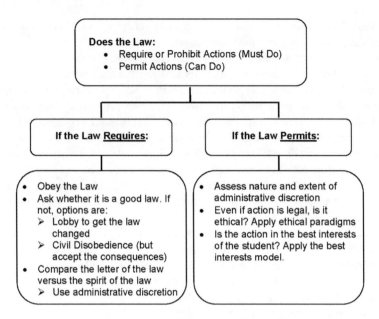

FIG. 5.1.   Legal and ethical decision points. Illustration by Marilyn Begley, 2005.

CORNFIELD BY LEWIS v. CONSOLIDATED SCHOOL DISTRICT
991 F.2d 1316 (7th Cir. 1993)

On March 7, 1991 teacher's aide Kathy Stacy found Brian Cornfield outside Carl Sandburg High School, in Illinois, during the school day in violation of the disciplinary code. She reported this incident to both his teacher, Richard Spencer, and the disciplinary Dean, Richard Frye. At the same time, she expressed to both men that she had observed an "unusual bulge" in the crotch of Brian's sweatpants. Later that day, a teacher, Joyce Lawler, and another teacher's aide, Lori Walsh, reported the same observation, that Brian seemed "too well endowed."

Brian Cornfield was enrolled in the behavior disorder program at Carl Sandburg and in recent months his name had been presented to Spencer and Frye in connection with both the sale and distribution of illegal drugs. Brian had a history of difficulty. In fact, both men understood Cornfield to have failed to complete a drug rehabilitation program and not long before, Cornfield was found with a live bullet at school. Additionally, one student reported seeing Cornfield smoke marijuana. Cornfield's bus driver had separately reported that he suspected Cornfield of smoking marijuana on the school bus. Another student claimed on a separate occasion that Cornfield had drugs on school grounds. Even Cornfield himself had repeatedly spoken about either dealing or using drugs and at one time reportedly told Kathy Stacy that he had crotched drugs in order to avoid detection when the police raided his mother's house.

With this history in mind, Spencer and Frye observed Cornfield for the rest of March 7 and again on March 8. It was this next day that Spencer and Frye observed the same "unusual bulge," as well as a pattern of suspicious behavior. Cornfield appeared to act nervous and withdrawn. Based on prior tips, Cornfield's past admissions, and current suspicious behavior, Spencer and Frye decided to take action. In the attempt to keep Cornfield from exposing other students to illegal drugs, Spencer and Frye stopped Cornfield as he was about to board the school bus for home and asked him to accompany them to Frye's office.

In Frye's office, both Frye and Spencer expressed their concerns to Brian and their belief that he was "crotching" illegal drugs. Cornfield responded by becoming extremely agitated and yelling obscenities at both men. By this time Spencer and Frye had decided that Cornfield should be searched. They decided that a pat down of Cornfield's crotch area would be too intrusive and concluded a strip search to be the more appropriate means of finding any illegal drugs on his person. Cornfield requested that his mother, Janet Lewis, be called. Cornfield's mother denied permission for Spencer and Frye to conduct the search.

Nevertheless, Spencer and Frye escorted Cornfield to the boy's locker room, made sure that the room was empty and locked the door to insure privacy. Both men stood at least 10 feet away from Brian and asked him to change into his gym clothes. While Cornfield was changing, Spencer and Frye visually inspected Cornfield's naked body and his clothing. At no time did either man touch the student. Cornfield was then allowed to change back into his street clothes. No evidence of illegal drugs was found during the search. While Spencer and Frye stressed the privacy afforded to Cornfield during the search, Cornfield later asserted that Spencer and Frye made him disrobe in a place where other students could see him. Both sides, however, agree that there were no other students who did so. After the search Frye recalled the school bus and Cornfield was brought home. Cornfield and his mother sued the school district for monetary damages, claiming that the search violated Cornfield's Fourth, Fifth, and Fourteenth Amendment rights under the United States Constitution.

THE COURT'S DECISION

Both the Federal District and Appellate courts found no basis for a claim that the search violated Cornfield's Fifth Amendment rights. Similarly, both courts found that the search conducted by Spencer and Frye was not in violation of the Fourth and Fourteenth Amendments to the United States Constitution. In particular, the courts found the search to be reasonable based on Cornfield's history of problems, including tips from others and his own past admission of drug use and possession, combined with the unusual bulge in his pants and his suspicious behavior.

The fact that school officials found no illegal drugs during the search was not at issue, because the evidence prior to the search made it reasonable to assume that Cornfield was in violation of the law. Furthermore, both the district and appellate courts found that the search was not excessively intrusive. Although both opinions stressed the possible negative impact such a search might have on a 16-year-old, given the suspicion of Spencer and Frye (that Cornfield was "crotching" drugs), the search that was conducted was far less intrusive than a pat down might have been, and involved no touching and no body cavity search.

Questions for Discussion

1. How might one view this case and the court's decision from a justice perspective?
2. Was Brian treated in a caring manner? Why or why not?
3. How might this case be viewed through the lens of critique?
4. What would the profession expect of Dean Frye or Mr. Spencer?
5. Through a best interests perspective, was Brain afforded his rights or shown his responsibilities? In this respect, how might this situation have been handled differently? Better? Was Brian afforded respect? Dignity? Why or why not?
6. What would you have done in this situation if you were Mr. Spencer? Dean Frye?

ONE POSSIBLE ANALYSIS[1]

From a legal perspective, this decision falls into the category of *law that permits, but does not require*. Thus, what the court is saying is that the school officials legally strip-searched Brian, and other cases with similar fact patterns and administrative actions in the Seventh Circuit would also likely be legal unless the state or school district prohibits it. What the court is not saying is that school officials must strip search students. School officials have great discretion in this matter.

Indeed, the school district may enact policies and the state may enact laws that prohibit strip-searching and thus grant the student greater protection. For example, the *Cornfield* decision came from the Seventh Circuit, which includes Illinois, Indiana, and Wisconsin. Strip-searching is legal in Illinois and Indiana, but not in Wisconsin, which has a state statute prohibiting these actions. Thus, if Brian had been from Wisconsin instead of Illinois, the search would not have been legal. Also, it would not have been legal if Brian's school district had had a policy against it.

Now, let us examine this case according to the four ethical frames. From a justice perspective, the school officials' actions might well be considered a moral

---

[1] This analysis is derived from an earlier article by the author. See Stefkovich and O'Brien (2004).

decision. Drugs present a real scourge to our society, destroying the lives of many young people. One could say that the ends justify the means, that we should consider the greater good for the greater number. From a caring perspective, one might note that the school administrator deeply cared for all the students in his school and believed that a student possessing drugs was a threat to the others' security. In addition, the search was conducted with care and consideration. Brian was never touched, and he stood at a distance from school authorities during the disrobing.

Critical theorists would ask who is making these rules and who enforcing them. Clearly, the student was in a powerless position as was his mother, who refused consent to the search but was ignored. From a community perspective, one might argue that searching Brian sends a message both to the school community and to the larger community that officials are determined to keep schools safe, that drugs will not be tolerated, and that the school has "get-tough policies" against such use. Community pressure, depending on the makeup of the community, may focus on these strong policies or may support student rights. Community as a process may involve others in the decision making regarding Brian's treatment.

The best interests model forces us to examine more deeply how these decisions affect students. For example, observing an adolescent boy's crotch for two days to see if his bulge is changing calls into question issues of respect, as do the disregard of his mother's refusal of consent and subjection of Brian to a total nude search by state officials (school authorities). The facts of the case show few efforts to hear Brian's voice. Indeed, the only indication we have here is that he yelled obscenities.

Some may characterize Brian as a "bad kid." Yet, within the framework of the best interests model, one must question what efforts school officials have made to assume responsibility for Brian's behavior and in turn to model responsible actions for Brian. Certainly Brian does not have the right to use drugs or to bring drugs to school, but he does have the right to be afforded help if he has a drug problem. Finally, the actions of school authorities in this case provide a valuable lesson to other students, that is, suspected drug use will result in punitive actions and serious invasion of privacy rights. And, at least in some jurisdictions, the courts will condone this invasion even if nothing is found.

The best interests model takes on added meaning when applied to real situations. What follows are summaries of a number of court decisions that carry with them significant ethical implications.

Part II

STUDENTS' FUNDAMENTAL RIGHTS

Part II of this book introduces ethical issues that relate to students' fundamental rights as articulated in the Bill of Rights, which consists of the first ten amendments to the United States Constitution. The rights specifically considered in this section, and those that are most applicable to students in public schools, fall under the First and Fourth Amendments. The First Amendment guarantees rights to free speech and freedom of religion. The Fourth Amendment prohibits unreasonable searches and seizures; it includes a wide variety of student searches, drug testing, and privacy rights. These chapters also illustrate what happens when rights collide and the ethical dilemmas that may result. In doing so, they allow us to examine important junctures such as the intersections of free exercise and establishment of religion, free speech and freedom of religion, and speech and privacy.

6

Freedom of Speech

The First Amendment to the U.S. Constitution guarantees, in part: "Congress shall make no law ... abridging the freedom of speech, or of the press...." (United States Constitution, Amendment I). This amendment covers a variety of situations that could occur in schools, ranging from dress codes to Internet use. In these instances, freedom of speech may combine with other rights, such as freedom of expression and the right to privacy.

The U.S. Supreme Court has maintained that students have First Amendment rights but these rights are limited within the context of the school. Various Supreme Court opinions have, however, conveyed what some may view as mixed messages. The law is clear that the government, in this case schools, may regulate the time, place, and manner of speech. Controversy occurs when school officials challenge the content of speech.

Although the Supreme Court has asserted that schools are a "marketplace of ideas" (*Tinker v. Des Moines Independent Community School District,* 1969, p. 512) and students do not "shed their constitutional rights to freedom of speech or expression at the schoolhouse gate" (p. 506), it has also recognized the school's responsibility to inculcate values and to maintain order and discipline. In this respect, courts allow for substantial administrative discretion. Justice Brennan captured the complexity of this situation in his concurring opinion in *Bethel School District No. 403 v. Fraser* (1986), a case dealing with a student's controversial speech at a school assembly. In this regard, he stated:

> The Court referring to these remarks as "obscene," "vulgar," "lewd," and "offensively lewd," concludes that school officials properly punished respondent for uttering the speech. Having read the full context of the respondent's remarks, I find it difficult to

believe that it is the same speech that the Court describes.[1] To my mind, the most that can be said about respondent's speech—and all that need be said—is that in light of the discretion school officials have to teach high school students how to conduct civil and effective public discourse, it was not unconstitutional for school officials to conclude, under the circumstances of this case, that respondent's remarks exceeded permissible limits. (pp. 687–688)

This chapter covers four very different cases involving the First Amendment in schools. The cases consider Internet issues, appropriateness of messages on student T-shirts, a student writing a violent poem, and a teacher who acts as a whistle-blower on behalf of students. The challenge to readers as they review these cases is to consider whether there are ethical issues beyond the actual court decision and, if so, what these issues are, and how might they be handled.

In *Beussink v. Woodland R-IV School District* (1998), Brandon, a high school student, created a Web page at home and posted it on the Internet. The content of the Web page was critical of his high school's administration and used vulgar language to describe the teachers and the principal. The viewers of the site could communicate their opinions about the high school. A teacher in the school gave permission for students to access the Web page at school and discussed the content with her students. Immediately after viewing the Web page, the principal suspended Brandon for 10 days even though the Web site had not posed any threat to the student or teacher population and there was no disruption at school.

In the *Boroff v. Van Wert City Board of Education* (2000) case, the court upheld a school district policy prohibiting a Marilyn Manson T-shirt because it had offensive illustrations. Although school authorities may exercise considerable discretion when it comes to dress codes, such cases bring forth ethical issues as to what is acceptable in the school's culture and who determines this acceptability.

LaVine v. Blaine School District (2001) focuses on an eleventh-grade student who submitted a poem on his own for his teacher to review and provide feedback. His teacher, alarmed by the content of the poem, which was written in the first person about a mass school shooting, contacted school officials. After a brief investigation and based in part on the student's record, the student was expelled. Although he was reinstated, the expulsion was part of his permanent student record. The student and his parents filed suit, alleging that the expulsion violated his right to free speech guaranteed under the First Amendment.

Settlegoode v. Portland Public Schools (2004) involves an adapted physical education teacher who questioned the safety of facilities and equipment in her school district. Ms. Settlegoode, a new teacher still on her probationary period, was subsequently disciplined for her actions.

---

[1]Fraser gave the speech in support of a candidate for student council. Among other things, he stated, "I know a man who is firm—he's firm in his pants, he's firm in his shirt, his character is firm—but most … of all, his belief in you, the students of Bethel, is firm.… Jeff is a man who will go to the very end—even the climax, for each and every one of you."

BEUSSINK v. WOODLAND R–IV SCHOOL DISTRICT
30 F. Supp. 2d 1175 (E.D. Mo. 1998)

In February, 1998, Brandon Beussink was a junior at Woodland High School in Marble Hill, Missouri, when he created and posted a public Web site on the Internet. He developed this Web site with software he obtained from the Internet and did the work on his home computer outside of school hours. This Web site used vulgar language and was highly critical of the teachers, the administration, and the Web page of his high school. Brandon's Web site had a link to the high school's own Web page and invited viewers to e-mail their comments to the principal of the high school. It is important to note that there was no link from the Woodland High School homepage back to Brandon's Web site. In his testimony, Brandon stated that the purpose of the Web site was to voice his opinion of the school administration and that he did not intend for it to be viewed at the school.

Prior to February 17, 1998, Brandon allowed a friend, Amanda Brown, to view his Web site from his home computer. He did not give Amanda the address for the Web site. Sometime later, Amanda had an argument with Brandon and he said she wanted to retaliate against him. On February 17, 1998, Amanda accessed Brandon's Web site at school and showed it to her computer teacher, Delma Ferrell. There was only one other student in the room at the time, and that individual did not see the Web site. Brandon was not with Amanda when she accessed the Web site and, in fact, was not aware that she had done so.

Ms. Ferrell was upset by the tone of the Web site and reported it immediately to the principal, Yancy Poorman. Mr. Poorman accompanied Ms. Ferrell back to the computer lab to get a firsthand look at the site. He was also upset by the content and decided to discipline Brandon, although he was not sure what measures to take. His decision to take disciplinary action was made because the Web site was displayed on a school computer. He did not know at that time if any other students had seen the site. Further testimony revealed that the Web site may have been accessed on two more occasions that day, although there were no disturbances involved with any of the viewings. One of the viewings was in the library and the other was in Ms. Ferrell's fourth-period class when she allowed three students to see the page and then discussed it with them. Another group of students in Ms. Ferrell's class accessed the Web site, but she asked them to exit the site.

Also during the fourth period, Mr. Poorman issued a notice of disciplinary action, which resulted in a 5-day suspension for Brandon. Brandon received the notice in class. Later that same day, Mr. Poorman reconsidered his initial suspension and issued a second notice of disciplinary action—a 10-day suspension—which was delivered to Brandon in his seventh-period class. In both cases, Brandon appealed to the classroom teachers to ask if they thought he deserved suspension, but they declined to comment. The teachers at the school reported that delivering these notices during the instructional period often causes disruptions in class. When he arrived home from school that day, Brandon removed his Web site from the Internet and later served his 10-day suspension. He returned to school following the 10 days and did not repost his Web site.

Woodland High School has an absenteeism policy that drops students' grades by one letter grade for each day of unexcused absence in excess of 10 days. Suspension days are considered unexcused absences for the purposes of this policy. Before the suspension, Brandon had 8.5 days of unexcused absences, which would not have resulted in any penalty in grades. After the suspension, however, his unexcused absences increased to 18.5, resulting in an 8.5 grade level drop in all subjects. Before the suspension, Brandon was failing two of his classes and had passing grades in the remaining four. After the grade drop was applied, he had failing grades in all six subjects in the second semester of his junior year.

Brandon sued the school board for a violation of his First Amendment right to free speech and filed for an injunction to prohibit using the 10-day suspension in its application of the school's absenteeism policy. Ruling against the school district, a federal district court in Missouri determined that Beussink's home page did not create a material or substantial disruption at school and that Principal Poorman disciplined Brandon because he was upset by the content, not because he feared disruption or interference with school discipline. In granting the injunction, the court determined that Brandon would likely win on the merits of the case and, without this relief, would be irreparably harmed.

The court maintained that granting this injunction would serve the public interest such as those protected by the First Amendment. In this respect, the federal judge handing down the ruling observed:

> It is provocative and challenging speech, like Beussink's, which is most in need of the protections of the First Amendment. Popular speech is not likely to provoke censure. It is unpopular speech that invites censure. It is unpopular speech which needs the protection of the First Amendment. The First Amendment was designed for this very purpose. Speech within the school that substantially interferes with school discipline may be limited. Individual student speech which is unpopular but does not substantially interfere with school discipline is entitled to protection. The public interest is not only served by allowing Beussink's message to be free from censure, but also by giving the students at Woodland High School this opportunity to see the protections of the United States Constitution and the Bill of Rights at work. (*Beussink v. Woodland R–IV School District,* p. 1182)

Questions for Discussion

1. How might one view this case and the court's decision from a justice perspective?
2. Was Brandon treated in a caring manner? Why or why not?
3. How might this case be viewed through the lens of critique?
4. What would the profession expect of Ms. Ferrell? Principal Poorman?

5. Through a best interests perspective, was Brandon afforded his rights or shown his responsibilities? In this respect, how might this situation have been handled differently? Better? Was there a teachable moment here for Brandon? Was Brandon afforded respect? Dignity? Why or why not?

6. What would you have done in this situation if you were Ms. Ferrell? Principal Poorman?

BOROFF v. VAN WERT CITY BOARD OF EDUCATION
220 F.3d 465 (6th Cir. 2000)

Nicholas Boroff was a senior at Van Wert High School, in August 1997. The school is located in west central Ohio and has a population of approximately 700 students. On August 29, Nicholas wore a Marilyn Manson T-shirt to school. Marilyn Manson is both the name of a band and the stage name of the individual who is the lead singer, Brian Warner. Each member of the band has a stage name, composed of the first name of a celebrity and the last name of a serial killer. Thus, Marilyn Manson is derived from the first name of Marilyn Monroe and the last name of Charles Manson. The individual known as Marilyn Manson is a heavy rocker who is regarded as a Satan worshiper and drug user. He denies being a Satan worshiper, but does not deny he promotes and uses illegal drugs. The members of the band dress in Goth style, wearing black clothing, black eye make-up, and lipstick when performing.

The T-shirt Nicholas wore that day had a stylized picture of a three-headed Jesus on the front. The text accompanying this picture stated, "See No Truth, Hear No Truth, Speak No Truth." Marilyn Manson's name was also displayed on the front. On the back of the shirt was the word "BELIEVE" in block letters, with the letters "LIE" within the word highlighted. Mr. Froelich, the assistant principal, told Nicholas the shirt violated the school's dress and grooming policy, which states "clothing with offensive illustrations, drug, alcohol, or tobacco slogans … are not acceptable"(p. 467). He gave Nicholas the option of wearing the shirt inside out, going home to change, or simply leaving. If he chose to leave the school, though, he would be considered truant. Nicholas chose to leave.

Nicholas's next school day after the August 29 incident was September 4 and again he wore a Marilyn Manson T-shirt. This time his mother accompanied him to school and they met with Assistant Principal Froelich, the principal, Mr. Clifton, and the superintendent, Mr. Basinger. Mr. Basinger reiterated that wearing the Marilyn Manson shirts was not allowed on school property. Despite this, Nicholas wore the band's T-shirts for the next 3 school days. Each time he was told he was not dressed appropriately and would not be permitted on school grounds unless he changed. He missed the next 4 days of school, and the following day, September 16, 1997, his mother filed the suit against the school officials.

In his testimony, Mr. Clifton reasoned that the Marilyn Manson shirts were offensive because of the perceived negative values promoted by the band. He cited some of the band's song lyrics, which contain vulgar and destructive language. He found the shirt depicting Jesus to be particularly offensive and contrary to the school's educational mission of respect for others and their beliefs. Citing his many years of experience in education, Mr. Clifton stated his belief that students are influenced by such material. On the other hand, the school did allow students to wear T-shirts from other bands, such as Slayer and Megadeth, and allowed a student to carry a backpack with three Marilyn Manson patches on it.

Nicholas filed suit, claiming a violation of his First Amendment right to free expression and his Fourteenth Amendment right to Due Process. A federal district court granted summary judgment in favor of the school district, and the federal court of appeals for the Sixth Circuit affirmed this decision. In ruling for the school district, the Sixth Circuit Court of Appeals failed to see a viable Due Process claim. As to the First Amendment claim, the court recognized the school district's authority to determine the manner of speech appropriate in the school or classroom. Accordingly, school officials do not need to tolerate speech that is inconsistent with the school's educational mission. In this case, the school prohibited the Marilyn Manson T-shirts "because this particular rock group promotes disruptive and demoralizing values which are inconsistent with and counter-productive to education" (*Boroff v. Van Wert City Board of Education*, 2000, p. 471).

Questions for Discussion

1. How might one view this case and the court's decision from a justice perspective?
2. Was Nicholas treated in a caring manner? Why or why not?
3. How might this case be viewed through the lens of critique?
4. What would the profession expect of Assistant Principal Froelich? Principal Clifton? Superintendent Basinger?
5. Through a best interests perspective, was Nicholas afforded his rights or shown his responsibilities? In this respect, how might this situation have been handled differently? Better? Was there a teachable moment here? Was Nicholas afforded respect? Dignity? Why or why not?
6. What would you have done in this situation if you were Assistant Principal Froelich? Principal Clifton? Superintendent Basinger?

LAVINE v. BLAINE SCHOOL DISTRICT
257 F.3d 981 (9th Cir. 2001),
rehearing en banc denied, 279 F. 3d. 719 (9th Cir. 2002)

In June or July of 1998, James LaVine wrote a poem called "Last Words." The subject of this poem appeared to be about the narrator going into a school and killing all of his classmates and then himself. When James first wrote the poem, a series of school shootings (Columbine, Thurston, and Springfield) had been in the news, so his mother urged him to not show it to anyone at school. James forgot about the poem until he found it in a pile of papers later that year in October.

On Friday, October 2, 1998, James turned in his homework assignment (as well as various late assignments he had made up from his absences for 3 days before) to his English teacher, Ms. Bleecker, and included the poem, "Last Words," asking her to read it and give him some feedback. He had shown the poem to a few of his friends and their opinions were mixed, so he wanted an adult's feedback. It was not unusual for James to turn in extra poems for review and he had done so in earlier years to other teachers.

When Ms. Bleecker read the poem that evening, she became concerned for James. She categorized him as a "very quiet student," and "thought the poem might be 'James' way of letting somebody know that … maybe something's hurting him, maybe he's upset about something, [or] maybe he's afraid'" (p. 984). On Saturday morning, Bleecker contacted James' guidance counselor, Karen Mulholland, who was similarly concerned, and the two set up a meeting that day with the school's vice-principal, Tim Haney.

Mulholland, who also served as the school psychologist, had spoken to James many times. She was particularly concerned because, in 1996, James had mentioned that he had thought about killing himself. After that time, Mulholland had taken extra care to look out for James and earlier that fall, James had confided that there were problems at home. On September 12, James and his father had a fight, which ended in the father throwing a rock in James' direction. James called the police and filed charges, which resulted in a no-contact order for the father. James moved out his house to temporarily live with his sister. In addition, James and his girlfriend had broken up in the preceding weeks and the girl's mother had contacted the school because she felt that James was stalking her daughter.

After Mulholland recounted these events to Mr. Haney and Ms. Bleecker, Haney reviewed James' disciplinary record. He found a few incidents including a fight in February 1998, and an episode of insubordination in May 1997. Overall, he categorized James as a "good kid, but … somewhat of a 'loner'" (p. 985).

Given James' past, Haney decided to call James' home to find out if he would be attending the school's homecoming dance that was to take place that night. Haney was told that James did not plan to attend, but he still called the Blaine Police Department for guidance. At the police's suggestion, he called Washington State's Child Protective Services, who recommended he call the Community Mental Health Crisis Line. The psychiatrist on duty that evening, Dr. Charles Dewitt, suggested that James be picked up by the police for evaluation. According to James, "eight deputies arrived with a canine unit at his family's farm outside Blaine to review the poem" (Stiffler, 2000, p. B1).

A deputy sheriff interviewed James, who told him that he had no intention of killing anyone nor did he have access to any weapons. His mother verified that there were no accessible weapons. The deputy called Dr. Dewitt and reported his findings. Dr. Dewitt concluded,

> in my professional opinion on a more probable than not basis based upon the information provided to me by the District and the law enforcement [officers] who had personally observed him, there were insufficient grounds for anyone to make a determination that James LaVine was in imminent danger of causing serious harm to himself and others. (*LaVine v. Blaine School District*, 2001, p. 985)

On Sunday, Haney met with Principal Dan Newell and filled him in on the events of the weekend. Based on the information he had been given, Newell decided to "emergency expel" (p. 985) James under Washington Administrative Code §180–40–295. Haney left a message with the LaVines requesting that they attend a meeting with the school board at 8:00 a.m. on Monday. At the meeting, board members told the LaVines that James was expelled and presented them with a letter explaining the reasons. To summarize, the letter indicated that school officials felt that James was a danger to other students.

After James' expulsion, his parents hired a lawyer, Breean Beggs, who appealed the punishment to the school board. After several conversations with the school district's attorney, Beggs told the LaVines that James would be allowed back in school after the district's psychiatrist, Dr. Watson, evaluated him. James agreed to meet with Dr. Watson, and after three visits, on October 26, 1998, Dr. Watson felt he could recommend James' return to school. After missing 17 days of school because of the expulsion, James completed the year without incident.

After James' return to school, he and his father requested that the letter be expunged from James' file because they felt it might damage James' chances at being a military pilot (Stiffler, 2000). On December 15, the school board agreed to enter a new letter, which was backdated to October 5. It explained that James had been expelled for the safety of other students as opposed to disciplinary reasons. James and his father brought this suit with the purpose of having any record of the event expunged from his file.

James and his father brought suit in a federal district court claiming that the expulsion violated James' free speech and due process rights and that no letters should be allowed in his file. This court granted summary judgment on James' First Amendment claim and ordered that the school district could neither place nor maintain any negative documentation in James' file. The school district appealed on the issue of whether the files should be kept.

The Court of Appeals for the Ninth Circuit addressed this issue but also looked to the underlying nature of this appeal. In doing so, the circuit court ruled that the district's emergency expulsion for school safety reasons was legal but that the letter recording the event should be expunged from James' record. The court determined that James was not a threat to himself or others and that keeping such records went beyond the school's documentation needs. Furthermore, the court maintained that

James' record and work opportunities should not be permanently blemished. In rendering its decision, however, the court recognized:

> In retrospect, it may appear that, as James' mother predicted, the school overreacted. James very well may have been using his poetry to explore the disturbing topic of school violence and chose to do so through the perspective of a suicidal mass murderer. In fact, James strongly contends this was all he was doing and that he had no intention of hurting himself or others. We have no reason now to disbelieve James as he did return to Blaine High School without further incident. We review, however, with deference, schools' decisions in connection with the safety of their students even when freedom of expression is involved. At the time the school officials made their determination to emergency expel James, they had facts, which might have led them to forecast a substantial disruption of or material interference with school activities.... School officials have a difficult task in balancing safety concerns against chilling free expression. This case demonstrates how difficult that task can be. (*LaVine v. Blaine School District*, 2001, pp. 991–992)

Because James and his father were concerned about this case being characterized as disciplinary rather than treatment oriented, they petitioned the court to meet as a group (*en banc*) to reconsider this issue. The court denied this hearing but, in response, Judge Kleinfeld wrote a dissenting opinion distinguishing the meaning and consequences of punishment as opposed to "examination, counseling, and exclusion for health or safety reasons based on predictions about future conduct" (*LaVine v. Blaine School District*, 2002, p. 720). Although this opinion does not hold the force of law, it stimulates important discussions related to ethical issues. Here, the judges said:

> The panel describes this case as arising "against the backdrop of tragic school shootings" and school officials' knowledge of "shootings at Columbine, Thurston, and Santee high schools." Constitutional law ought to be based on neutral principles, and should not easily sway in the winds of popular concerns, for that would make our liberty a weak reed that swayed in the winds. Nevertheless we do not perform our work in isolation from the society we live in, and there is a notion that permeates the record in this case that because of increased violence in the schools, free speech ought to give way to increased security. Both the diagnosis and the cure are probably wrong, and such constitutional law ought not to be based on this vague popular sociology. There may well be, not an increase in school violence, but rather an increase in newspaper, magazine, and television stories about school violence, which has in fact been declining or steady in its frequency. As for the cure, there is no particular reason to think that punishing speech about school violence will reduce the amount of school violence. (*LaVine v. Blaine School District*, 2002, p. 728)

Summarizing Mulvey and Cauffman's (2001) findings in *American Psychologist*, Judge Kleinfeld notes first that school crimes have not risen in the last 10 years. Second, it is very difficult to predict who a school killer might be in that these killers as well as innocent students may well exhibit the same types of behaviors and attitudes. Third, false negatives result in dire consequences for the innocent, including stigmatization and limited opportunities. Fourth, violent youth are not usually loners. Finally, other students are the best source of information as to what students are doing in schools. Disproportionate punishments such as expulsions tend to dry up information as students will remain silent rather than be punished. Thus, Judge Kleinfeld concluded:

> My purpose [in citing the Mulvey & Cauffman article] is to show that there is not necessarily any trade-off between speech and security. Suppression of speech may reduce security as well as liberty. Allowing the school to punish a student for writing a poem about a school killer may foster school killings, by drying up information from students about their own and other students' emotional troubles. If the students don't talk, the administrators and medical professionals won't find out about problems that speech might reveal. Punishment based on prediction rather than misconduct tends to be unjust, and where the predicted event is extremely rare, as in-school murders are, predictive punishment such as the school imposed is likely to punish vast numbers of innocent people for every one who would have engaged in the feared misconduct. (*LaVine v. Blaine School District,* 2002, p. 729)

This judge reasoned that it was not James' poem, but rather James, that was potentially threatening. Considering his background in conjunction with his writing the poem caused school authorities to fear that James might bring harm to himself or others. Believing this justified James' suspension for a mental examination but not punishment. As these dissenting justices observed:

> Not everyone who writes about murder and evil is an incipient murderer. There is a lot of art about homicide (e.g., the folk songs "On the Banks of the Ohio" and "Tom Dooley," Dostoevski's *Crime and Punishment*) and about homicidal maniacs who commit mass murder (e.g., *Taxi Driver*). This art sometimes inspires crime (e.g., John Hinckley shooting President Reagan to impress Jodie Foster's character in *Taxi Driver*). But the government could not properly punish Robert DeNiro for acting in *Taxi Driver,* nor the Kingston Trio for performing "Tom Dooley," no matter how many people found these artworks disturbing or threatening. We do not, under our constitution, allow the government to punish artists for making art, whether the art is good or bad, whether it makes people feel good or bad, unless the expression falls within a well established category of unprotected speech. This right too does not end at the schoolhouse gate. (*LaVine v. Blaine School District,* 2002, pp. 729–730)

Questions for Discussion

1. How might one view this case and the court's decision from a justice perspective? Was James treated fairly? Was the court's decision a fair one? Why or why not?
2. Was James treated in a caring manner? Why or why not?
3. How might this case be viewed through the lens of critique?

4. What would the profession expect of Mrs. Bleecker? Principal Newell? Mr. Haney?

5. Through a best interests perspective, was James afforded his rights or shown his responsibilities? In this respect, how might this situation have been handled differently? Better? Was James afforded respect? Dignity? Was he taught responsibility? Why or why not?

6. What would you have done in this situation if you were Mrs. Bleecker? Mr. Haney? Principal Newell?

SETTLEGOODE v. PORTLAND PUBLIC SCHOOLS
371 F.3d 503 (9th Cir. 2004)

Portland Public Schools hired Dr. Pamella Settlegoode for the 1998–1999 academic year as an adapted physical education teacher. Her probationary position involved teaching students with disabilities. As an itinerant teacher, she taught her physical education classes at two or three different schools daily. In addition to teaching the disabled students, Pamella was required by federal law to draft Individualized Education Programs (IEP) for them.

Soon after her employment, Pamella became concerned with the treatment of disabled students in the Portland schools. She found the facilities and equipment inadequate and sometimes unsafe. Pamella attempted to bring these concerns to her supervisor, Susan Winthrop, who claimed that no one had ever complained about the facilities before. Pamella said that Ms. Winthrop tried to redirect their conversations away from the topic.

Ms. Winthrop evaluated Pamella on several occasions during her first year of teaching. These evaluations were generally positive and met the minimum standards of practice for an adapted physical education teacher. Susan gave Pamella positive feedback on her teaching, planning, and her interactions with the disabled students. On the matter of IEPs and reports, Ms. Winthrop wrote that Pamella was developing skills in this area and that she had not yet written evaluation reports on students.

At the end of the school year, Pamella wrote a 10-page letter outlining her concerns to Robert Crebo, Susan Winthrop's supervisor. In the letter she said that there was evidence of "systematic discrimination, maladministration, access, pedagogy, curriculum, equity and parity" in the Adaptive Physical Education program and that it "greatly compromised" federal law (*Settlegoode v. Portland Public Schools,* 2004, p. 507). She compared the treatment of disabled students in the system to that of Black students during the Civil Rights Movement. She was also critical of Susan Winthrop in the letter, saying she ignored Pamella's concerns and was out of touch with the disabled students' needs.

Robert Crebo showed Pamella's letter to Susan Winthrop for her feedback. She expressed concern that a novice teacher would attack her character and reputation.

Mr. Crebo asked Ms. Winthrop to draft a letter to Pamella and to look into her claims. In the meantime, Susan Winthrop asked Pamella to stop writing letters, as it was not an effective way to communicate.

Mr. Crebo's letter responding to Pamella's communication defended both the school district's and the superintendent's handing of disabled students. He also wondered about the appropriateness of her comments given her inexperience. He concluded by saying, "It is unfortunate that you are so dissatisfied with your teaching position in Portland Public Schools" (*Settlegoode v. Portland Public Schools,* 2004, p. 508).

After Pamella's first letter to Susan Winthrop, her teaching evaluations became more negative. The evaluations indicated that she was performing below the minimum standard in areas such as class management, IEP writing, and personal interactions with superiors, administration, parents, and students. Ms. Winthrop went into some detail about Pamella's deficiencies in writing IEPs. She characterized Pamella as "strong, outspoken, and demanding" (p. 508) and unable to handle constructive criticism. She ended the report by stating that Pamella's contract would not be renewed if her work did not improve.

Pamella then wrote Dr. Ben Canada, the Superintendent of Portland Public Schools, claiming that she was being retaliated against as a result of her criticism of disabled students' treatment in the system. Mr. Crebo responded to Pamella's letter to Dr. Canada in writing. In his letter he reiterated that she was asked not to communicate in writing and asserted that her charges of retaliation were groundless. Mr. Crebo also sent a memo to Dr. Canada noting that it was unlikely that Pamella's contract would be renewed.

In the meantime, Pamella received her final evaluation, which stated that although there had been improvement in some areas, her IEP writing continued to be deficient. Her performance was rated below the district standards and her contract was therefore not recommended for renewal. At a subsequent board meeting, the board voted not to renew Pamella's contract. Pamella sued the Portland Public Schools, Susan Winthrop, and Robert Crebo. Her suit claimed violations of the Disabilities Act, the Oregon Whistleblowers Act, and her First Amendment right to free speech.

Ms. Settlegoode lost her case at the district court level and then appealed this decision to the Ninth Circuit Court of Appeals. In deciding against her, the district court employed a three-part inquiry that it typically applied to cases where a government employee believes that she has been retaliated against for asserting her free-speech rights under the First Amendment to the U.S. Constitution. To succeed in her claims, the employee must first prove that the conduct under question is constitutionally protected. Second, she must prove that her conduct was a substantial or motivating factor that led to the punishment. Both the district court and the appeals court agreed that Ms. Settlegoode had met her burden.

Once these first two factors are established, the employer may still escape liability if it can prove that it would have taken these actions regardless of the protected conduct. It is on this point that Ms. Settlegoode lost at the district court level. The district court agreed with the school district that, despite Pamella's objections to the school district's treatment of students with disabilities, she would have nevertheless been denied her probationary contract because of her inability to write IEPs. The Ninth Circuit Court disagreed, noting that complaints about the IEPs came to light only after Pamella began criticizing the school.

Ruling for Ms. Settlegoode, the appeals court pointed out that IEPs are written by a group, that it was not unusual for first-year teachers to have difficulties writing their portions of the IEPs, and there was no evidence to show that the district had ever fired any other teacher for this reason. In determining that the school district violated Settlegoode's constitutional rights, the appeals court maintained that her assertions were of public importance and that there was little evidence of disruption in that Settlegoode went through proper channels by conveying her concerns through internal memos and not through public means.

Questions for Discussion

1. How might one view this case and the court's decision from a justice perspective? Was the action taken against Ms. Settlegoode fair? Was the court's decision fair?

2. Was Ms. Settlegoode treated in a caring manner? Why or why not? How might school officials have treated Ms. Settlegoode in a more caring manner?

3. How might this case be viewed through the lens of critique?

4. What would the profession expect of Ms. Settlegoode? Susan Winthrop? Robert Crebo? Superintendent Canada?

5. Through a best interests perspective, was Ms. Settlegoode afforded respect? Dignity? Why or why not? What message does Ms. Settlegoode's treatment send to students? To other teachers? What message, if any, does the court's decision send?

6. What would you have done in this situation if you were Susan Winthrop? Robert Crebo? Superintendent Canada?

7

Religious Expression[1]

Socrates: Well, how would you gentlemen compose your fundamental principles, if a majority, exercising its fundamental right to rule, ordained that only Buddhism should be taught in the public schools?

[William Jennings] Bryan: I'd move to a Christian country.

[Thomas Jefferson]: I'd exercise the sacred right of revolution. What would you do, Socrates?

Socrates: I'd examine my fundamental principles.

—Lippmann, 1928, p. 22

In addition to freedom of speech, as discussed in chapter 6, the First Amendment to the United States Constitution guarantees, in part: "Congress shall make no law respecting an establishment of religion, or prohibiting the free exercise thereof..." (United States Constitution, Amendment I). Since the origins of the public school movement, the issue of religion has been a concern for public education (Yudof, Kirp, Levin, & Moran, 2002).

Starting in the 1960s, religion in public schools has clearly been among the most frequently contested of education issues to reach the U.S. Supreme Court. Ranging from aid to parochial schools, to use of school facilities for religious groups, to prayer at school football games, these decisions have provided fodder for substantial litigation at the lower court level. Moreover, the passage of the No Child Left Behind (NCLB) Act (U.S. Department of Education, 2002) and subsequent

_____
[1]Portions of this introduction are adapted from Shapiro and Stefkovich (2005), pp. 82–84.

guidelines issued from the U.S. Department of Education (USDE) via the document, *Guidance on Constitutionally Protected Prayer in Public Elementary and Secondary Schools* (U.S. Department of Education, 2003), have added to the complexity of determining what is legal.

The Supreme Court has provided some bright line law for school officials to follow. For example, it has been clear since the early 1960s that school officials may not begin the school day by leading prayers or by reading the Bible to students. Later decisions have told us that it is illegal to have religious speakers at graduation ceremonies or to lead prayers at school athletic events. All these restrictions are based on the understanding that public school officials are agents of the state and, under the First Amendment's Establishment Clause, neither the state nor its agents may endorse any religion over another religion, or religion over nonreligion. Thus, these restrictions do not apply to nonpublic (private or religious) schools.

These interpretations do not, however, mean that school officials must ignore religion. This is particularly important with regard to the curriculum. Here, the longstanding rule is that teachers may not proselytize or otherwise attempt to indoctrinate students in religious beliefs but they may certainly, when appropriate, teach about religion. Examples most commonly given are teaching comparative religion courses, recognizing the religious origins of our country's history, and understanding religion as an integral part of artistic and musical expression.

It is also generally legal for public schools to provide transportation, support services, books, and other materials to religious schools. And, if the school opens its facilities to other groups either for clubs or after-school activities, then it may not discriminate against religious groups. Finally, schools usually may, but are not required to, provide opt-outs for students when the curriculum conflicts with their religious views. An example here might be family life courses that discuss birth control methods in contradiction to some students' religious beliefs. Opt-outs may also be provided to teachers as well as students who may need to be absent from school for religious holidays.

Issues that are less clear often focus directly on students. For example, although the Supreme Court has clearly prohibited teacher-led prayer in public schools and religious speakers at graduation ceremonies, it has yet to speak on student-led prayer in these circumstances or whether students may proselytize in presenting homework assignments. Although most, but not all, lower courts confronting these issues have found such actions illegal, guidance from the federal government would appear otherwise. This possible conflict places school officials in a difficult position.

In reauthorizing the Elementary and Secondary Education Act (ESEA; 1965), NCLB requires that before school districts can receive ESEA funding, they must certify in writing that they have "no policy that prevents, or otherwise denies participation in, constitutionally protected prayer in public schools as set forth in this guidance" (U.S. Department of Education, 2003, p. 1). The Department of Education's accompanying guidelines clearly describe the prohibitions placed on religion by the High Court.

Confusion arises, however, in the student-focused gray areas (just mentioned) where the guidelines imply that such practices are legal. In reality, they are legal in some jurisdictions and are not in others. Additionally, there are more court decisions against such practices than for them. For example, reading the federal guidance, one might infer that it is appropriate to have students speak publicly on religious matters at high school commencement exercises. And, indeed, at least one federal appeals court (*Jones v. Clear Creek*, 1992) has upheld this practice.

On the other hand, the Third Circuit Court of Appeals (*American Civil Liberties Union v. Black Horse Pike Regional Board of Education*, 1996) deemed this practice illegal, asserting: "The First Amendment does not allow the state to erect a policy that only respects religious views that are popular because the largest minority can not be licensed to impose its religious preferences upon the smallest minority" (p. 1488). Accordingly, in *Lassonde v. Pleasanton Unified School District* (2003), a case discussed in this chapter, the Ninth Circuit Court of Appeals has made it clear that these types of speeches violate the Establishment Clause of the United States Constitution.

In her seminal article on this topic, McCarthy (2004) challenges the federal guidelines as representing a "conservative citizen groups' expansive interpretation of permissible religious activities in public schools" (p. 592) and warns readers of the dangers that occur when government and religion commingle. These issues present even more challenges to school leaders when one recognizes the increasing diversity, including religious diversity, in our society (Shapiro & Stefkovich, 2005). This leaves the question, which may well be an ethical inquiry, as to whether school leaders can celebrate diversity, including religious (and cultural) diversity, without violating the law.

The cases presented in this chapter represent the wide range of issues that educators must address relative to religion and public schools. In the *Mozert v. Hawkins County Board of Education* (1987) case, seven families in a Tennessee school claimed that, due to objectionable material contained in the books, the basal readers used in their children's schools violated their right to their Free Exercise of Religion. Among other things, these passages contained material that plaintiffs thought promoted secular humanism, pacifism, magic, and the occult. The court ruled that the families did not demonstrate adequately that the material they found to be objectionable was in violation of their right to free exercise of religion. Acknowledging the importance of this decision, Salomone (1996, 2000), a legal scholar who has written extensively on First Amendment issues, observes: "It is no exaggeration to state that for more than a decade *Mozert v. Hawkins County Board of Education* ... has shaped the legal and political landscape of discussion and debate on religious accommodation in the public schools" (Salomone, 2000, p. 121). Her concern, however, is that subsequent courts, rather than exploring alternative means of accommodation, have relied almost exclusively on Judge Lively's assertion in *Mozert* that mere exposure to offensive materials does not constitute a rights violation. She advises closer relationships between the schools and parents to arrive at equitable solutions.

Lassonde v. Pleasanton Unified School District (2003) involves the school eliminating parts of a student's graduation speech that appear to be proselytizing. This type of situation presents a difficult problem for school officials who want to accommodate students' religious beliefs but who also understand that in doing so, they may be endorsing one religion over another in violation of the First Amendment's Establishment Clause.

In a Philadelphia case (*United States v. Board of Education for the School District of Philadelphia*, 1990), the school district prohibited a Muslim teacher from wearing a religious headdress even though this was required by her religion. Although the court recognized that the teacher has religious rights, it determined that the state has a compelling interest in maintaining religious neutrality. This case addresses the rights of the Muslim teacher who was forced to decide between her religious obligations and continuing employment, but it also speaks directly to what is in the best interests of the student. The court contended that students, especially young students, are impressionable and may be unduly influenced by religious garb. A number of scholars believe in a strict separation of church and state and that this separation clearly applies to the wearing of religious garb (Rossow & Barnes, 1992). On the other hand, we are living in a multicultural/pluralistic society where students are increasingly exposed to other religions and cultures. It would seem logical that this type of exposure would extend to the schools (Stefkovich, 1992).

MOZERT v. HAWKINS COUNTY BOARD OF EDUCATION
827 F.2d 1058 (6th Cir. 1987)

In 1983, Hawkins County, Tennessee, Board of Education adopted a new reading curriculum that relied on a series of texts from Holt, Rinehart, and Winston. Students in Grades 1 through 4 were taught using this text during the normal school day. It was integrated in a cross-curricular method. In Grades 5 through 8, reading was taught as a separate subject and students had a class where they specifically read from the text and discussed the material. As part of the new program, the schools began to teach "critical reading" and not just word and sound recognition. Some sample tasks in the critical reading program required students to form opinions on the characters and events from the story and to compare and contrast ideas in each story with others the students had read.

In the fall of 1983, Vicki Frost, a parent of three children who attended Hawkins County Public Schools in Church Hill, Tennessee, reviewed the story her sixth-grade daughter was reading in school. She became upset because the story was about mental telepathy, a subject about which she, a self-described Born-Again Christian, did not approve. Frost then began to review the other stories in the anthology and found many of them objectionable. She spoke with the principal of Church Hill Middle School and obtained an agreement that would allow her children to be excused from reading the school's standard textbooks and instead read from an older anthology.

Mrs. Frost found numerous examples of writings, which she found objectionable for a variety of reasons. These included the poem, "Look at Anything," which presented the idea of using imagination to become part of something and understand it better. Mrs. Frost felt this encouraged children to use their imagination beyond the limitations of "scriptural authority" (*Mozert v. Hawkins County Board of Education,* 1987, p. 1062). She characterized the second passage, "Seeing Beneath the Surface," as having an occult theme because it described using imagination to see things that were not discernable with humans' physical eyes. She also objected to a story called "A Visit to Mars" because she thought it presented the concepts of *thought transfer* and *telepathy* as scientific fact. She also identified 24 passages that she considered to have evolution as a theme.

In November of 1983, the Hawkins County School Board met and voted unanimously to eliminate all alternate-reading programs and to require every student in their schools to read from the Holt series that the district had purchased. That month, nine students were suspended from Church Hill Middle School for refusing to attend reading classes where the Holt series text was being used (Associated Press, 1983). Bob Mozert, a father of one of the students who was suspended, said, "the series of grade school readers, published by Holt, Rinehart and Winston, contain stories with 'anti-gun, anti-war and anti-capitalist biases'" (Associated Press, 1983, p. B5). Mozert added that his child, 12-year-old Travis, would return to school on Friday and would continue to not read from the textbook. Most of the students whose parents objected to the series were eventually home taught, attended religious schools in the area, or transferred to other public schools outside Hawkins County.

Bob Mozert explained in his testimony that the passages he found objectionable dealt with issues such as "magic, role reversal or role elimination, particularly biographical material about women who have been recognized for achievements outside their homes, and emphasis on one world or a planetary society" (Associated Press, 1983, p. B5).

On December 2, 1983, seven families (14 parents and 17 children) filed the lawsuit against Hawkins County Board of Education, claiming that the requirement of reading set forth by the school board violated their religious beliefs and convictions. A federal district court granted summary judgment to the school district stating that although the reading series may have offended the plaintiff's religious beliefs, that on their face, these books contained no religious content. The appeals court maintained that summary judgment was inappropriate and sent the case back to the district court. This time, the district court ruled in favor of the parents, required the school district to excuse objecting students from the classes that used the contested reading series, and awarded the parents more than $50,000 in damages. The school district appealed.

Ruling for the school district, the Sixth Circuit Court of Appeals determined that the parents did not have the requisite burden on their sincere religious belief. Here, the court looked at issues of compulsion and ethical as opposed to religious concerns. Writing for the majority, Chief Judge Lively reasoned as follows:

The Supreme Court has recently affirmed that public schools serve the purpose of teaching fundamental values "essential to a democratic society." These values "include tolerance of divergent political and religious views" while taking into account "consideration of the sensibilities of others" [Citing *Bethel v. Fraser,* 1986, p. 675]. The Court has noted with apparent approval the view of some educators who see public schools as an "assimilative force" that brings together "diverse and conflicting elements" in our society "on a broad but common ground" [Citing *Ambach v. Norwick,* 1979, p. 77] ... The critical reading approach furthers these goals. Mrs. Frost stated specifically that she objected to stories that develop "a religious tolerance that all religions are merely different roads to God." Stating that the plaintiffs reject this concept, presented as a recipe for an ideal world citizen, Mrs. Frost said, "We cannot be tolerant in that we accept other religious views on an equal basis with ours" .... (*Mozert v. Hawkins County Board of Education,* 1987, p. 1068)

The "tolerance of divergent ... religious views" referred to by the Supreme Court is a civil tolerance, not a religious one. It does not require a person to accept any other religion as the equal of the one to which that person adheres. It merely requires a recognition that in a pluralistic society we must "live and let live." If the Hawkins County schools had required the plaintiff students either to believe or say they believe that "all religions are merely different roads to God," this would be a different case. No instrument of government can, consistent with the Free Exercise Clause, require such a belief or affirmation. However, there was absolutely no showing that the defendant school board sought to do this; indeed, the school board agreed at oral argument that it could not constitutionally do so.

Instead, the record in this case discloses an effort by the school board to offer a reading curriculum designed to acquaint students with a multitude of ideas and concepts, though not in proportions the plaintiffs would like. While many of the passages deal with ethical issues, on the surface at least, they appear to us to contain no religious or anti-religious messages. Because the plaintiffs perceive every teaching that goes beyond the "three Rs" as inculcating religious ideas, they admit that any value-laden reading curriculum that did not affirm the truth of their beliefs would offend their religious convictions. Although it is not clear that the plaintiffs object to all critical reading, Mrs. Frost did testify that she did not want her children to make critical judgments and exercise choices in areas where the Bible provides the answer.... (*Mozert v. Hawkins County Board of Education,* 1987, pp. 1068–1069)

In his concurring opinion, Judge Boggs took a somewhat different approach in that he recognized a possible need to change the law. In this respect, he reasoned:

Schools are very important, and some public schools offend some people deeply. That is one major reason private schools of many denominations—fundamentalist, Lutheran, Jewish—are growing. But a response to that phenomenon is a political decision for the schools to make. I believe that such a significant change in school law and expansion in the religious liberties of pupils and parents should come only from the Supreme Court itself, and not simply from our interpretation. It may well be that we would have a better society if children and parents were not put to the hard choice posed by this case. But our mandate is limited to carrying out the commands of the

Constitution and the Supreme Court. (Boggs, J. dissenting, *Mozert v. Hawkins County Board of Education,* 1987, p. 1081)

Questions for Discussion

1. How might one view this case and the court's decision from a justice perspective?
2. Were the children and parents bringing suit treated in a caring manner? Why or why not?
3. How might this case be viewed through the lens of critique?
4. What would the profession expect of the Hawkins County school officials?
5. Through a best interests perspective, were these affected students afforded their rights or shown their responsibilities? In this respect, how might this situation have been handled differently? Better? Were these students afforded respect? Dignity? Why or why not?
6. What would you have done in this situation if you were an official at the school?

LASSONDE v. PLEASANTON UNIFIED SCHOOL DISTRICT
320 F. 3d 979 (9th Cir. 2003)

In 1999, Nicholas Lassonde was a graduating senior at Amador Valley High School in California. An exceptionally bright student with a grade point average of 4.24, he was chosen as one of two co-salutatorians to address the audience at the graduation ceremony. A devout Christian, Nicholas chose to quote extensively from the Bible during his address. His intent, he said, was to encourage his fellow students to form a relationship with God through faith in Jesus Christ because he believed that this relationship would lead them to better lives.

The school's principal, Bill Coupe, controlled all aspects of the graduation ceremony, from selecting the speakers and approving their speeches, to renting and ensuring the facilities where the ceremony was to take place. When he read the draft of Nicholas' speech, he consulted with the school district's council. Together they concluded that allowing the inclusion of the overtly proselytizing comments would violate the Establishment Clauses of the United States Constitution and the California Constitution. They advised Nicholas that he could include references to God as they pertained to his own beliefs but not the proselytizing comments. The Establishment Clause's intent is to create a wall of separation between Church and State.

Some of the comments the principal and the council wanted Nicholas to remove were:

- I urge you to seek out the Lord, and let Him guide you. Through His power you can stand tall in the face of darkness and survive the trends of "modern" society.

- As Psalm 146 says, "Do not put your trust in princes, in mortal men, who cannot even save themselves. When their spirit departs, they return to the ground; on that very day their plans come to nothing. Blessed is he whose help is the God of Jacob, whose hope is in the Lord his God, the Maker of heaven and earth, the sea, and everything in them—the Lord, who remains faithful forever. He upholds the cause of the oppressed and gives food to the hungry. The Lord sets prisoners free, the Lord gives sight to the blind, the Lord lifts up those who are bowed down, the Lord loves the righteous. The Lord watches over the alien and sustains the fatherless and the widow, but he frustrates the ways of the wicked."

- For the wages of sin is death; but the gift of God is eternal life through Jesus Christ our Lord. "Have you accepted the gift, or will you pay the ultimate price?" (*Lassonde v. Pleasanton Unified School District,* 2003, p. 981)

Mr. Coupe asked Nicholas to remove these proselytizing sections of the speech but allowed him to keep other personal references to his religion. For example, he kept the dedication to his grandfather who had gone "home to be with the Lord" the previous week and the speech ending, "Good Luck and God Bless" (p. 981).

Nicholas' attorney suggested that the school district provide a "disclaimer" (p. 981) stating that the views expressed in the speech were not the views of the district. However, the district rejected the suggestion. In the end, a compromise was reached. Under protest, Nicholas agreed to the revisions in the speech but said he would hand out copies of his complete draft version outside the site of the graduation ceremony.

Amador Valley High School held its graduation ceremony on June 18, 1999 at the Alameda County Fairgrounds. Although the ceremony was held off-campus, it was entirely financed and conducted under the control of the school. Nicholas delivered his speech, pausing at the excised portions to inform the audience that sections had been censored. He informed them that the complete version of the speech would be available after the ceremony outside the facility. He also said he would deliver the full version at his church the following Sunday.

Almost a year later, Nicholas filed suit against the Pleasanton Unified School District, Superintendent Mary F. Callan, Assistant Superintendent Jim Negri, and the Principal of Amador Valley High School, Bill Coupe, citing violations of his federal and state constitutional rights to free speech and religious liberty. A federal district court granted summary judgment in favor of the school district, noting that school officials' actions were necessary to avoid an Establishment Clause violation. The Federal Appeals Court for the Ninth Circuit affirmed this decision, noting "if the school had not censored the speech, the result would have been a violation of the Establishment Clause" and that "permitting a proselytizing speech at a public school's graduation ceremony would amount to coerced participation in a religious practice" (p. 985). In addition, the school provided a less restrictive alternative to total censorship by allowing Nicholas to distribute copies of his complete speech outside the graduation location.

Questions for Discussion

1. How might one view this case and the court's decision from a justice perspective?
2. Was Nicholas treated in a caring manner? Why or why not?
3. How might this case be viewed through the lens of critique?
4. What would the profession expect of Principal Coupe? The district's council?
5. Through a best interests perspective, was Nicholas afforded his rights or shown his responsibilities? In this respect, how might this situation have been handled differently? Better? Was Nicholas afforded respect? Dignity? Why or why not?
6. What would you have done in this situation if you were Principal Coupe? A member of the district's council?

UNITED STATES v. BOARD OF EDUCATION
FOR THE SCHOOL DISTRICT OF PHILADELPHIA
911 F.2d 882 (3rd Cir. 1990)

The Pennsylvania Garb Statute (1895) prohibits any teacher performing duties in the public schools to wear any dress that indicates adherence or allegiance to a particular religious order. This law requires that any teacher found to wear such apparel shall be first suspended for 1 year from teaching duties and on the occasion of a subsequent offense, permanently removed from teaching. Furthermore, the statute holds liable public school administrators who fail to discipline teachers under their supervision who violate the aforementioned requirements, through the imposition of a fine and possibly loss of job.

In 1970, Alima Delores Reardon began teaching in the Philadelphia School District and for the next 12 years was employed at various times as both a substitute and full-time teacher. In addition to being a trained teacher, Ms. Reardon is a devout Muslim. In accordance with her beliefs, she altered her dress beginning in 1982. At that time, she started to cover her body, except for her face and hands, when in public. When she was teaching this meant that she wore a headscarf that left only her face visible, and a long dress that allowed only her hands to be shown. Reardon's dress was significantly different from the other teachers and aroused the curiosity of the children in her classes.

Although they asked questions about her dress, there was never any substantial disruption to the school day. It was not until 1984 that Reardon's dress was at issue. That year Reardon was employed as a substitute teacher throughout the district. On three separate occasions, at three different schools, she was informed that she was prohibited from wearing in the classroom the clothing that she had worn without event since 1982. Although each time she was given the opportunity to go home and change in order to be allowed in the classroom, she refused. She was barred from teaching on each of those occasions.

Upset, Ms. Reardon sought accommodation within the school district, in the hopes that some agreement might be reached in which she would be allowed to wear her religious clothing and still teach. The school district maintained its position, indicating that they had no choice but to comply with the Pennsylvania Garb Statute. According to the school district, allowing Ms. Reardon to teach in her head scarf and long dress would have placed school administrators at risk of disciplinary action. Dissatisfied with the school district response, Reardon contacted the Equal Employment Opportunity Commission (EEOC) and filed discrimination charges. The EEOC conducted an investigation into the incidents. In response, Pennsylvania's attorney general asserted the validity of the Pennsylvania Garb Statute and sided with the school district.

Eventually, the EEOC concluded that by enforcing the Pennsylvania Garb Statute, both the school board and the Commonwealth of Pennsylvania violated Title VII, which protects individuals from employment discrimination on the basis of religion. After its initial findings, the EEOC involved the Justice Department in the case. The Justice Department filed suit in federal court against both the School Board of Philadelphia and Pennsylvania. The Justice Department claimed that the School Board violated Title VII by failing to accommodate Reardon, who sought to wear clothing that was part of her legitimate and established religious observance and by failing to employ her when she was wearing the clothing in question. The Justice Department further charged both the school board and Pennsylvania with engaging in a pattern of discriminatory behavior through enforcement of the Garb Statute, which conflicts with Title VII. After a complicated history of appeals and cross-appeals from both parties, the case was brought before the Third Circuit Court of Appeals.

This court ruled that the Commonwealth of Pennsylvania was not liable under Title VII because there was no pattern of practice showing discrimination. Also, under Title VII, employers are exempt if they are unable to accommodate an employee's religious practice without undue hardship. In this case, the fact that the school district would need to violate state law in order to allow Ms. Reardon to wear her religious garb could constitute undue hardship. Moreover, the school is committed to a stance of religious neutrality. Finally, the court found irrelevant the fact that the Pennsylvania Garb Statute was passed in 1895 to bar garbed Catholic nuns and priests from teaching in public school classrooms. Here, the court reasoned:

> In this context, where the statute bans *all* religious attire and is being enforced by the Commonwealth in a non-discriminatory manner with respect to Muslim teachers as well as Catholics, we conclude that it is irrelevant whether a portion of those who voted for the statute in 1895 were motivated by a desire to bar Catholic habit from the classroom. We therefore accept that the Commonwealth regards the wearing of religious attire by teachers while teaching as a significant threat to the maintenance of religious neutrality in the public school system, and accordingly conclude that it

would impose an undue hardship to require the Commonwealth to accommodate Ms. Reardon and others similarly situated. (*U.S. v. Board of Education of Philadelphia*, 1990, p. 894)

Questions for Discussion

1. How might one view this case and the court's decision from a justice perspective? Was the action taken against Ms. Reardon fair? Was the court's decision fair?
2. Was Ms. Reardon treated in a caring manner? Why or why not? How might school officials have treated Ms. Reardon in a more caring manner?
3. How might this case be viewed through the lens of critique?
4. What would the profession expect of Ms. Reardon? The school officials?
5. Through a best interests perspective, was Ms. Reardon afforded respect? Dignity? Why or why not? What message does Ms. Reardon's treatment send to students? To other teachers? What message, if any, does the court's decision send?
6. What would you have done in this situation if you were Ms. Reardon? The school officials?

8

Censorship and Viewpoint Discrimination

Censorship, in schools, whatever its purposes, is censorship. It should be abhorrent to those who care about freedom of thought, to those who believe that minds grow sharper by contending with challenging ideas.... How weird ... to see television programs and movies that present life in all its confusing and sometimes unpleasant fullness, then to read textbooks in which language, ideas, and behavior have been scrubbed of anything that might give offense....

—Ravitch, 2003, p. 159

Diane Ravitch (2003), in her book *The Language Police: How Pressure Groups Restrict What Students Learn,* argues that political groups from both the right and the left strongly affect what is taught in schools. Some of this influence takes the form of censorship, which Ravitch says occurs when school officials fear controversy from sources such as parents or the community. While right-wing groups sought to ban books from the curriculum and from school libraries for objectionable context, the left argued just as strongly that the curriculum be politically correct. These tensions have caused great difficulties for textbook companies, which must attempt to placate both sides or risk bankruptcy. Ravitch (2003) characterizes these pressures as "pernicious and pervasive" (p. 159) in that they limit students' exposure to a world of ideas.

Justice Jackson, in his dissenting opinion in *West Virginia State Board of Education v. Barnette* (1943), a case addressing whether it is legal to require students to say the pledge of allegiance contrary to their religious beliefs, maintained: "If there is any fixed star in our constitutional constellation, it is that no official, high or petty, can prescribe what shall be orthodox in politics, nationalism, religion, or other matters of opinion or force citizens to confess by word or act their faith therein" (p. 642).

From a legal perspective, courts have concluded that schools are a "marketplace of ideas," yet school officials must also maintain order and discipline. Therefore, school officials may regulate speech, either in its pure or symbolic form, which causes a "material and substantial" disruption (*Tinker v. Des Moines Independent Community School District,* 1969, p. 512). At the same time, courts have agreed that the primary purpose of schools is to provide an educated citizenry and to inculcate values reflective of a democratic society. As with other constitutional decisions, the judiciary affords school officials considerable discretion, thus deferring to local control. It is here that the issue of "whose values?" comes into play.

It is widely recognized that school officials may place restrictions on the time, place, and manner of student speech. It is when these officials restrict content that potential ethical conflicts may arise. These concerns came to a head when the U.S. Supreme Court rendered its decision in *Hazelwood School District v. Kuhlmeier* (1988). Here, the High Court ruled that school officials have the authority to exercise reasonable restraint relative to the content of student publications. Although *Hazelwood* was a school newspaper case, its progeny extended the decision to cover other forms of speech, including "artistic expression." Basically, the *Hazelwood* Court said that school officials may exercise their judgment if the publication is presented in an open forum and is related to the curriculum. Lower courts have disagreed as to how far this standard may be extended.

In other words, may school leaders censor material because they disagree with the values the speech extols because of the potential harm to young, impressionable minds or because, as Ravitch contends, that it may be too controversial in the community? Responding to community values may reflect the work of a responsible educator or it could simply be a pretext for viewpoint discrimination. There is also the question as to whose values we are conveying. There are a growing number of scholars who point out that what we once conceived of as common values are not necessarily the case in today's society. As Salomone (2000) notes:

> At no time since the beginning of the common school movement a century and a half ago have we witnessed such a direct challenge to the purpose, content, and structure of mass compulsory schooling or to the very premise underlying the "myth of the common school," that is, that the values promoted through public education are indeed neutral or at the very least acceptable to Americans across the political and religious spectrum. (p. 8)

Coming to grips with these issues requires probing the depths of discrimination as it applies to one's own viewpoint and exploring ethical decision making from a range of perspectives. The four cases in this chapter are provided to assist the reader in such an exploration.

Addressing censorship and viewpoint discrimination, the first two cases expand on themes arising in earlier chapters by illustrating the tensions that occur when free speech rights and freedom of religion come into conflict. The remaining two cases explore how censorship and viewpoint discrimination impact rights related not only to free speech but to equal access and sexual orientation.

In the first case, *C.H. v. Oliva* (2000), kindergarten students were to make posters of things for which they are thankful. The following year, in first grade, they were asked to bring in a book to read to the other students. In kindergarten, Z.H.'s poster was moved to a less obvious place. The following year, the first grade teacher would not allow Z.H.'s book to be read. Both of these situations involved material with religious content.

Fleming v. Jefferson County School District (2002) involves students and parents from the Columbine High School who made tiles to be placed on the school's walls following the Columbine tragedy. School officials limited these tiles in that they could not include anything religious, obscene, or offensive. They were also not to include the names or initials of the victims nor could they include Columbine ribbons, in that this display was not to be a memorial. Some of the students and their parents challenged the school's authority to circumscribe the tiles' contents.

The third case, *Gay Straight Alliance v. Boyd* (2003), involves pressure to ban a club that addresses issues of gay students. While the Equal Access Act requires the school to allow this club if it opens the door to other clubs, the club was highly controversial. Hence, authorities feared that those who strongly opposed the club would cause substantial disruption in the school.

Ostensibly an employment dispute relative to a teacher's input into the curriculum, the last case in this chapter, *Boring v. Buncombe County Board of Education* (1998), provokes issues aside from its narrow legal determination. Here, we explore what appear to be school officials' censorship of a drama club play because of its controversial content and the influence of the community on what is taught in schools.

C.H. v. OLIVA
226 F. 3d 198 (3rd Cir. 2000)

In the fall of 1994, Z.H. was a kindergarten student at Haines Elementary School in Medford, New Jersey. As Thanksgiving approached, Z.H.'s kindergarten teacher asked her students to prepare a poster illustrating something they were thankful for. Z.H. drew a picture of Jesus. All of the children's posters were then displayed in a hallway outside the classroom. Soon after, on a day when Z.H.'s kindergarten teacher was away, an unnamed school board employee removed Z.H.'s poster from the hallway, because of its religious nature. When Z.H.'s teacher returned the following day, she immediately put the poster back up in the hallway, although in a less prominent location.

At that time, both Z.H. and his mother were made aware of the removal of the poster and the reason for its removal. However, neither Ms. Oliva (Z.H.'s next teacher), Ms. Pratt (the school principal), Mr. Johnson (the school superintendent) nor the Board of Education were aware of the removal of the poster. The Medford Township Board of Education did not have an established policy for removal of such items.

In February 1996, Z.H. was in Ms. Oliva's first grade class. As a reward for attaining a certain level of reading proficiency, Ms. Oliva allowed her first-grade students to bring a book to school to read to the other students. She screened the books to ensure that the length and complexity were appropriate for the grade level of the students. Z.H. qualified for this incentive. He brought in a favorite book entitled, *The Beginner's Bible: Timeless Children's Stories*. He wanted to read the story, "A Big Family," which was an adaptation of the reconciliation of Jacob and Esau from the book of Genesis.

The story reads:

> Jacob traveled far away to his uncle's house. He worked for his uncle, taking care of sheep. While he was there, Jacob got married. He had twelve sons. Jacob's big family lived on his uncle's land for many years. But Jacob wanted to go back home. One day, Jacob packed up all his animals and his family and everything he had. They traveled all the way back to where Esau lived. Now Jacob was afraid that Esau might still be angry at him. So he sent presents to Esau. He sent servants who said, "Please don't be angry anymore." But Esau wasn't angry. He ran to Jacob. He hugged and kissed him. He was happy to see his brother again. (*C.H. v. Oliva*, 2000, p. 204)

The language of the story was appropriate for young children, did not contain scriptural references, and did not mention a deity or religion. However, Ms. Oliva told Z.H.'s mother, C.H., that Z.H. could not read the story because of its religious content. She reasoned that it might influence other students. She did allow Z.H. to read the book to her privately.

Z.H.'s mother sought out the principal, Ms. Pratt, who agreed with Ms. Oliva. Ms. Pratt stated that reading the story was the equivalent of praying and, allegedly reminded of past complaints, stated that the story "might upset Muslim, Hindu or Jewish students." She added that there was "no place in public school for the reading of the Bible." She then told C.H. that she may want to take Z.H. out of public school because he does not "appear to be public school material" (p. 204). C.H. requested an appointment to talk to Z.H.'s teacher again, but this was not acknowledged. She made formal and informal requests to various Medford defendants that Z.H. be allowed to read the book and asked for a formal apology. These requests were not granted.

C.H. filed suit on behalf of her minor son, alleging that Z.H.'s First Amendment right to free speech was violated. Ruling in favor of the school district, a federal district court found no constitutional violation regarding either the kindergarten or the first-grade incident. The Third Circuit Court of Appeals ruled that the parents' complaint failed to state claims against the school. The court's majority decided not to discuss this issue further, but instead sent the case back to the trial court to give the parents an opportunity to state a claim if they so chose. (No further decisions appear on computerized databases.) Instead, the court turned to jurisdictional issues related to whether claims could be brought against the New Jersey State Department of Education.

Although the majority refrained from speaking further on this topic, Judge Alito, joined by Judge Mansmann, wrote a rather lengthy dissent. Although their opinion does not hold any legal force, it does provide a good overview of the legal and policy issues presented by this case. Here, the dissenting judges address what they characterize as the issue that the court "evades," which is "whether Zachary's constitutional right to freedom of expression was violated if, as the complaint alleges, his poster was given less favorable treatment than it would have received had its content been secular rather than religious" (*C.H. v. Oliva,* 2000, p. 209). If so, then the school discriminated against Z.H.based on his poster's religious content. As Judge Alito concludes:

> I would hold that discriminatory treatment of the poster because of its "religious theme" would violate the First Amendment. Specifically, I would hold that public school students have the right to express religious views in class discussion or in assigned work, provided that their expression falls within the scope of the discussion or the assignment and provided that the school's restriction on expression does not satisfy strict scrutiny. This conclusion follows from the following two propositions: first, even in a "closed forum," governmental "viewpoint discrimination" must satisfy strict scrutiny and, second, disfavoring speech because of its religious nature is viewpoint discrimination....

> Accordingly, viewpoint discrimination is prohibited even in a nonpublic forum if strict scrutiny cannot be satisfied, and discrimination based on the religious content of speech is viewpoint discrimination. It follows that public school authorities may not discriminate against student speech based on its religious content if the discrimination cannot pass strict scrutiny. (*C.H. v. Oliva,* 2000, p. 204)

As the dissenting judges emphasize, school officials have the authority to prevent a student from talking about the Bible when the assignment has nothing to do with religion. This, however, they maintain, is not the circumstance in this case:

> Taking down Zachary's Thanksgiving poster and replacing it in a less conspicuous location because of its religious content was plainly viewpoint, not subject matter, discrimination. The subject matter of the poster was specified by Zachary's teacher: something for which he was thankful as the Thanksgiving holiday approached. His poster fell within the specified subject matter, and it is not alleged that the poster was subjected to discriminatory treatment because of that subject. Rather, the poster was allegedly given discriminatory treatment because of the viewpoint that it expressed, because it expressed thanks for Jesus, rather than for some secular thing.... (*C.H. v. Oliva,* 2000, p. 212)

In summing up, Judge Alito rejects the possibility that the school may be endorsing religion by displaying Z.H.'s poster:

> A reasonable observer would not have viewed the exhibition of Zachary's Thanksgiving poster along with the secular posters of his classmates as an effort by the school to endorse religion in general or Christianity in particular. An art display that includes works of religious art is not generally interpreted as an expression of religious belief by the entity responsible for the display. (*C.H. v. Oliva,* 2000, p. 212)

Questions for Discussion

1. How might one view this case from a justice perspective? Was Z.H. treated fairly?
2. Was Z.H. treated in a caring manner? Why or why not?
3. How might this case be viewed through the lens of critique?
4. What would the profession expect of Ms. Oliva? Principal Pratt?
5. Through a best interests perspective, was Z.H. afforded his rights or shown his responsibilities? In this respect, how might this situation have been handled differently? Better? Was Z.H. afforded respect? Dignity? Why or why not? What issues relative to responsibility do you see in this case?
6. What would you have done in this situation if you were Ms. Oliva? Principal Pratt? Superintendent Johnson?

FLEMING v. JEFFERSON COUNTY SCHOOL DISTRICT
298 F.3d 918 (10th Cir. 2002)

Columbine High School was the sight of a multiple murder-suicide on April 20, 1999. That morning, two students, Eric Harris and Dylan Klebold, came to school with firearms. They shot and killed 12 fellow students and one teacher before turning the guns on themselves. Columbine High School was closed temporarily after the killings. In the summer of 1999, the decision was made to reopen the school. The school district recognized that returning to school could have an impact on the mental health of students. Their memories of the incident would be reawakened by visual cues in the building itself. The District made an effort to change the appearance of the school and then sought ways to reaccustom the students to the building.

Two years prior to the shootings, the art department had initiated a tile art project to decorate the hallways of the school. Art class students painted 4 × 4 inch tiles, which were then glazed, fired and adhered to the hallway walls above the molding. After the shooting, the school librarian, Elizabeth Keating, and the art teacher, Barbara Hirokawa, proposed expanding the tile art project to the greater student population. They reasoned that the project would allow the students an opportunity to visit the building and would enable them to be a part of the remodeling of the school. It would also help in the healing process. Ms. Keating and Ms. Hirokawa sought approval for the project from the District's area administrator, Barbara Monseu. Ms. Monseu consulted other school district administrators, including mental health workers who were assisting with the tragedy's aftermath.

The school officials wanted to maintain a positive learning environment and did not want the tiles to become a memorial to the events of April, 1999. There were already memorial plaques in the office area and near the library, as well as a sandstone memorial outside. Consequently, specific guidelines were drawn up for the content of the tiles. The tiles were not to include religious symbols, the names or initials of victims, the date April 20, 1999, Columbine ribbons, nor anything obscene or offensive. The guidelines stated that the tiles would be reviewed before firing and would not be fired or hung if they violated the guidelines. The Jefferson Foundation and the Columbine Memorial Account, both funded through private donations, supplied the materials for the project. The Columbine High School administration had discretion over the spending of these funds.

In the summer of 1999, the school district expanded the tile art project to include members of the affected community. They invited victims' families, rescue workers, health care workers, as well as current and new students to participate. The sessions were held outside school hours and were completely voluntary. Hundreds of participants attended the separate session that was set up for rescue workers and community members. Teachers from the school were on hand at the tile-painting sessions. Tables were set up with samples of tile designs and the participants were informed of the guidelines for the tiles, but were not given written information. Specific religious symbols that were prohibited were not identified in the samples displayed.

Some of the participants were dissatisfied with the guidelines and restrictions put on the tile art project. They told the staff who were supervising that they wanted to include the names of their children, as well as religious symbols. Some of messages on the tiles said, "Jesus Christ is Lord," "4/20/99 Jesus Wept," "There is no peace says the Lord for the wicked" (*Fleming v. Jefferson County School District,* 2002, p. 921). The teachers informed the families that while they could paint the tiles as they wished, those tiles violating the guidelines would be fired separately and not installed on the walls. These tiles would be given back to the families for their own use.

The intent was to have each tile reviewed before it was sent for firing. Teachers instructed parent volunteers who were assisting with the installation of the tiles to put aside any questionable tiles. Despite these measures, some tiles, which did not comply with the guidelines, were affixed to the walls. This was due mainly to the volume of tiles, about 2,100. When Ms. Monseu inspected the building after the tiles were installed, she observed between 80 and 90 tiles that did not conform to the guidelines. They depicted crosses, anarchy or gang symbols, a Star of David, a teacher's name, a reference to the date 4/20, the Columbine ribbon, a bloody skull, and one tile painted in red that was thought to be troubling. She had these tiles removed.

Ms. Monseu met with the victims' families in September. She relaxed some of the restrictions for the tiles so that victims' names, initials, dates other than 4/20/99 and the Columbine ribbon could be included. She kept the restrictions on religious symbols, the shooting date, and offensive or obscene material. None of the participants at the meeting returned to the school to paint another tile as "they had made their expressions previously or been denied the opportunity to paint the tiles they wanted to paint" (p. 922).

Relatives of two of the victims, Daniel Rohrbough and Kelly Fleming, brought suit against the school district and others claiming violations of their free speech rights. A federal district court found that the speech involved was private rather than school sponsored and that it occurred in a limited public forum. Also, prohibiting the religious tiles violated the doctrine of viewpoint neutrality.

Reversing this decision, the Tenth Circuit Court of Appeals maintained that the U.S. Supreme Court's decision in *Hazelwood School District v. Kuhlmeier* (1988) did not require viewpoint neutrality "given the types of decisions that the *Hazelwood* Court recognized faced educators in 'awakening the child to cultural values' and promoting conduct consistent with 'the shared values of a civilized social order'..." (*Fleming v. Jefferson County School District*, 2002, p. 928). As the court points out:

> If the District were required to be viewpoint neutral in this matter, the District would be required to post tiles with inflammatory and divisive statements, such as "God is Hate," once it allows tiles that say "God is Love." When posed with such a choice, schools may very well elect to not sponsor speech at all, thereby limiting speech instead of increasing it. The District could be forced to provide an opportunity for potentially thousands of participants to repaint their tiles without any meaningful restrictions by the District, leading to a potentially disruptive atmosphere in which to try to educate the students of Columbine High School. (*Fleming v. Jefferson County School District*, 2002, p. 934)

Applying *Hazelwood*'s (1988) public forum analysis, the Tenth Circuit Court determined that the school district was within its power to regulate the tile project in that the project was not a public forum and it did bear the imprimatur of the school because "the school permanently integrated the tiles into the school environment, and was significantly involved in the creation, funding, supervision, and screening process of the tile project" (*Fleming v. Jefferson County School District*, 2002, p. 931). In addition, the project restrictions were reasonably related to legitimate pedagogical concerns in that school officials wanted the school to remain as a positive learning environment and not as a memorial to the tragedy. As to the religious restrictions, they wanted to keep the walls from becoming a place for religious debate.

Questions for Discussion

1. How might one view this case from a justice perspective? Were the persons who provided tiles treated fairly? Was the court's decision fair?
2. Were those who submitted tiles treated in a caring manner? Why or why not?
3. How might this case be viewed through the lens of critique?
4. What would the profession expect of Ms. Monseu?
5. Through a best interests perspective, were those students who provided tiles afforded their rights or shown their responsibilities? In this respect, how might this situation have been handled differently? Better? Were these students afforded respect? Why or why not?
6. What would you have done in this situation if you were Ms. Monseu? Ms. Keating, the librarian? Ms. Hirokawa, the art teacher?

GAY STRAIGHT ALLIANCE v. BOYD
258 F. Supp. 2d 667 (E.D. Ky. 2003)

This case involves a request for an injunction against a ban of a school club, the Gay Straight Alliance (GSA), at the Boyd County High School (BCHS). The plaintiffs, seven students at the high school who formed the GSA group and their faculty advisor, Kaye King, cite violations of their rights under the Equal Access Act (EAA). The defendants in the case are the Boyd County Board of Education, five Board members, the school district superintendent, Dr. William Capehart, and the principal of Boyd County High School, Jerry Johnson.

Early in 2002, a group of students at BCHS circulated a petition to create a new club. The mandate of the club, the GSA, was to provide a safe venue to air concerns about harassment and to promote acceptance and tolerance, regardless of sexual orientation. There was a problem at the high school created by some students' intolerance of gay individuals and two students had dropped out of the school, citing antigay harassment as one of the reasons for their departure.

The testimony described several incidents of antigay harassment, including the use of epithets such as "faggot kisser," "queer," "homo," "f__ing faggot." These epithets were used in the classroom, hallways, and even via megaphone at a basketball game. During one peaceful silent protest by GSA members, other students threw things at them.

In the spring 2002 semester, Kaye King, an English teacher, became aware of the GSA petition. She discussed this with Principal Johnson, who told her that the student who was spearheading the petition had already approached him. He noted that the school would have to grant status to the club, as the students were very savvy when it came to the legal issues involved. He was concerned about the need to approve the club in order to prevent legal action against the school district. Principal Johnson discussed the issue with Superintendent Capehart, who was in favor of establishing the club because he felt it was the right thing to do. Kaye King then agreed to be the faculty sponsor of the GSA club.

Back at the high school, word of the GSA petition spread among the students. There were confrontations in the hallways, and some students wore T-shirts with slogans such as "I'm Straight" and "Adam and Eve, not Adam and Steve." Around this same time, a group of students asked to apply for club status for the GSA. This application is a requirement of the school, and submissions are made to the school's Site-Based Decision Making Council, consisting of three teachers, two parents, and the principal. School administrators encouraged the GSA to hold off on their formal application for a month to let the current dispute settle down, and the students agreed to the delay.

The Boyd County High School had another group called the BCHS Diversity Awareness Council, whose mandate was to advise on diversity and equity issues. During the month's hiatus, this council held two meetings. They discussed the proposed GSA club as well as the harassment of gay students. The council's suggestion was to change the name of the proposed club, removing the word, "gay." The GSA group refused this suggestion, saying that it would be "defeatist" to back down on the proposed name (p. 671).

In late March 2002, the GSA group made its first formal application for club status. Although Principal Johnson had made the suggestion to hold off for a month, he denied the application, saying it came too late in the school year. After the meeting he informed Kaye King that the GSA club's application would easily "slide right through" (p. 672) in the fall when there would be many club applications to consider.

In September 2002, the GSA again applied for club status. At its inaugural meeting for the 2002–2003 school year, the Site-Based Decision Making Council approved 20 applications for club status. The GSA club's application was the only one denied. Three clubs, the Drama, Key, and Pep clubs, were not accepted because their submissions were made too late. Approved clubs included the Future Business Leaders of America (FBLA), Beta Club, Future Farmers of America (FFA), Future Career and Community Leaders of America (FCCLA), Human Rights Club, 4-H, Health Occupations Students of America (HOSA), and Y-Club. The Fellowship of Christian Athletes (FCA), synonymous with Christian Fellow Club and the Bible Club, was also approved. All of the clubs except HOSA were listed in the previous year's student handbook as extracurricular activities.

In a letter to the Council on behalf of the GSA, the American Civil Liberties Union (ACLU) outlined the requirements of the Equal Access Act. The Council did not consider the ACLU letter at its September meeting; instead they put it off until October. After an executive session at the October 28 meeting, the Council announced the approval of three clubs, the Key, the Drama Club, and the GSA. Audience reaction to the announcement, in the words of the principal, was "open hostility" (p. 673). To calm fears, the school administration sent a letter to school staff and to parents in the school community, explaining the rationale for its decision.

Two days later, on October 30, there was a protest outside the school doors. The protest was directed at the Council approval and establishment of the GSA club. One hundred students, or about 10% of the population, were outside during the protest. Although the protesters taunted students by saying that if they entered the school they would be supporting "faggots," the protest did not prevent students from entering the school. GSA members were silent during the protest. Principal Johnson and Assistant Principal Richard Cyrus spoke to the crowd and encouraged them to go to class. If they did not, they could move their protest to the parking lot. Some students moved to the parking lot while others entered the school. Classes proceeded without incident. The following Monday, November 4, 2002, approximately half the students were absent.

Neither the protest nor the boycott disrupted classes significantly at the high school. There was only one incident of a disruption in class by GSA supporters or members. However, Kaye King received threatening letters, and her car was damaged. After approval of the GSA club, the Board of Education and Superintendent Capehart became the focus of anti-GSA sentiment. Parents placed many phone calls to the administration expressing concerns for the safety of the school. Although callers were irate, no parents withdrew their children from the school.

On December 20, 2002, Dr. Capehart proposed banning all noncurricular clubs for the remainder of the 2002–2003 school year. That same day, the Board met to consider Dr. Capehart's proposal of refusing recognition of all noncurricular clubs. They then wrote a closed forum policy to be implemented in July 2003, thereby avoiding EAA dictates. A closed forum policy disallows any noncurriculum related groups. A closed forum school can contravene the Equal Access Act if any of its groups are determined to be noncurricular.

At a meeting on December 17, 2002, the Council declined to vote on banning all noncurricular clubs, thereby allowing the GSA club to continue. Later, at an emergency meeting on December 20, the Board voted unanimously to suspend all curricular and noncurricular clubs at BCHS for the remainder of the school year. The Board cited the disruption that the GSA club had caused as their reasoning for the suspension. However, testimony revealed that opponents of the club, not GSA members, had caused the disruption.

According to Kaye King, Principal Johnson visited her classroom on January 2, 2003, and suggested that the GSA Club could apply to use school facilities as an outside organization. They could meet before and after school hours but not during the homeroom period. On behalf of the GSA Club, King requested permission to use her classroom once a week before school for GSA Club meetings. However, on January 7, Principal Johnson and Dr. Capehart denied the GSA Club's application. Principal Johnson said that no groups or clubs would be permitted to use school grounds. Since that time, the GSA club had not met at the school nor used the intercom or hallways for announcements. From time to time, club members gathered in Kaye King's classroom, but they did not conduct club business there. After the ban, attendance at off-campus meetings declined. Twenty to 30 students attended the on-campus meetings; attendance at off-campus meetings was down to six.

Meanwhile, many groups continued to use school facilities before and after school and during the homeroom period. These groups included the Future Farmers of America (FFA), Future Career and Community Leaders of America (FCCLA), Future Business Leaders of America (FBLA), and HOSA. In addition, the Y-club, Mock Trial and Teen Court, Academic Teams, Athletics Teams, and Cheerleading squads used BCHS facilities during non-instructional time. School officials admitted to this practice. The Boyd County Assistant Superintendent, Dr. Dawn Tackett, explained that state regulation requires students opportunities for involvement, and some courses require participation in an associated club.

A federal court for the Eastern District of Kentucky determined that the school district had allowed at least four other noncurricular clubs to meet (Bible Club, Drama Club, Beta Club, and Executive Councils), therefore, under the Equal Access Act, unless the GSA caused a material and substantial disruption (which it had not), it too must be allowed to meet. Thus, the court was able to grant the preliminary injunction requested by the GSA. The court also stressed that the club itself must cause the material and substantial disruption and not others' reactions to it:

> Assuming *arguendo* that the anti-GSA faction was sufficiently disruptive to materially and substantially interfere with the requirements of appropriate discipline, Defendants are not permitted to restrict Plaintiff's speech and association as a means of preventing disruptive responses to it. (*G.S.A. v. Boyd,* 2003, p. 690)

The court determined that GSA members would be irreparably injured without the preliminary injunction, the injunction would not harm others, and finally granting an injunction would serve the public interest. In regards to the latter, the court noted:

> While the primary teachers of tolerance should always be the parents and not the teachers and school administrators, school officials can play a vital role in fostering tolerance to its students. If, by permitting the GSA Club to meet, students are less likely to be the subject of hate crimes by fostering tolerance of the school community, the public interest is served. (*G.S.A. v. Boyd,* 2003, p. 692)

Questions for Discussion

1. How might one view this case from a justice perspective? Were the school officials fair to the GSA? Was the court's decision fair?
2. Did school officials treat the GSA in a caring manner? Why or why not?
3. How might this case be viewed through the lens of critique?
4. What would the profession expect of Kaye King? Principal Johnson? Superintendent Capehart?

5. Through a best interests perspective, were the GSA members afforded their rights? In this respect, how might this situation have been handled differently? Better? Were GSA members afforded respect? Dignity? Why or why not?

6. What would you have done in this situation if you were Kaye King? Principal Johnson? Superintendent Capehart?

BORING v. BUNCOMBE COUNTY BOARD OF EDUCATION
136 F.3d 364 (4th Cir. 1998)

Margaret Boring was a teacher for 12 years at the Charles D. Owen High School in Buncombe County, North Carolina. As a drama coach, she often entered her students in regional and state competitions. In the past, her students had won several awards, and some had gone to college on drama scholarships.

In the fall of 1991, Ms. Boring selected the play "Independence" and chose four students from her advanced drama class to perform it in a statewide competition. The play is by the Pulitzer-Prize-nominated author Lee Blessing. As was her custom, Ms. Boring gave the principal the name of the play she had chosen. She did not disclose to him the powerful nature of the play, which depicted a "dysfunctional single-parent family—a divorced mother and three daughters; one a lesbian, another pregnant with an illegitimate child" (*Boring v. Buncombe County Board of Education,* 1998, p. 366).

Margaret Boring's students performed the play at a regional competition and won 17 of 21 awards. Before going to the state competition, Margaret offered to have her students perform a scene from the play for an English class at the school. Margaret advised the English teacher about the mature nature of the play and suggested that students bring in signed parental permission slips before viewing the performance. After this in-class performance, a parent of one of the students in the English class complained to the principal, Fred Ivey. Following up on the parent's complaint, Mr. Ivey requested a script of the play from Margaret. After reading the script, Mr. Ivey informed Ms. Boring that the play would not be performed at the upcoming state competition. However, after hearing a plea from Margaret and the parents of the actresses, Mr. Ivey agreed that the play could be entered into the state competition if the offending portions were removed. Margaret entered the play in the state competition, and the performance took second place.

Mr. Ivey requested a transfer from the school for Margaret in June 1992, noting that her actions the previous school year had caused conflicts. The superintendent of the Buncombe County School District, Dr. Yeager, approved the transfer. He stated that Margaret Boring had failed to consider the provisions of the district's controversial materials policy when she produced the play. This policy was put in place to provide some parental control over what their children are exposed to at school. Margaret contended that the policy was amended only after the controversy to include dramatic productions.

Ms. Boring appealed her transfer, but it was upheld by the Board of Education at a hearing on September 2, 1992. During the public discussion at the hearing, the play was called "obscene," and Ms. Boring was accused of being immoral. She brought suit against the board, its members, the superintendent, Dr. Yeager, and the principal, Fred Ivey, citing a violation of her rights to free speech and due process.

Ms. Boring brought multiple claims in federal district court, including First and Fourteenth Amendment due process claims under the United States Constitution and state constitutional claims relative to free speech, due process, and deprivation of liberty. The district court ruled against Ms. Boring on all these claims.

On appeal, the Fourth Circuit Court rendered a decision only on the First Amendment issue which Ms. Boring had appealed, and on the narrow question of: "whether a public high school teacher has a First Amendment right to participate in the makeup of the school curriculum through the selection and production of a play" (p. 366). In ruling against Ms. Boring, the court's majority stated that the answer to this question is "no." The court maintained that selection of the play did not present a matter of public concern, which is protected by the First Amendment, that Ms. Boring's speech was a private concern only, and that the case was merely an employment dispute. The court also determined that the school administration had a legitimate pedagogical interest in regulating the curriculum.

Quoting Plato's *Republic,* a letter written by Edmund Burke, and Justice Frankfurter's discussion of a university's "four essential freedoms," this court determined that "the school, not the teacher, has the right to fix the curriculum" (pp. 370–371). Citing *Connick v. Myers* (1983, pp. 146–147), the Boring court concluded: .

> Perhaps the government employer's dismissal of the worker may not be fair, but ordinary dismissals from government service, which violate no fixed tenure or applicable statute or regulation are not subject to judicial review even if the reasons for the dismissal are alleged to be mistaken or unreasonable. (*Boring v. Buncombe County Board of Education,* 1998, p. 372, n.2)

In a strong dissent, Judge Hamilton maintained that this case is far from the "ordinary employment dispute" (p. 374) that the majority describes.

> Instead, as gleaned from a fair reading of the complaint, this is a case about a school principal, Fred Ivey, and a county school board, the Buncombe County Board of Education (the Board), who targeted Margaret Boring as a scapegoat and used her to shield them from the "heat" of the negative outcry resulting from the performance of "Independence." This is also a case about a dedicated teacher who, contrary to the implication of the majority and concurring opinions, in no way violated any aspect of an approved curriculum; who followed every previously required standard set forth for the selection and approval of the school production; who, when requested to do so, redacted certain portions of the production and only permitted its performance after that performance had been explicitly approved by her principal, Mr. Ivey; yet, who nevertheless lost her position as a result of the production, all for the sole purpose of

shielding the principal and the Board from the wrath of the public outcry.... (*Boring v. Buncombe County Board of Education,* 1998, p. 374)

Therefore, from Judge Hamilton's perspective, this case needs only to address one question and that is whether the school board can censor Ms. Boring's speech without providing a "legitimate pedagogical concern [for] justifying the restriction" (p. 374).

Addressing the concurring judges' concerns that requiring the school board to provide this justification would "consign ... to the federal judiciary the responsibility for managing our public schools," Judge Hamilton responded with this rejoinder:

Nothing could be further from reality ... any limited intrusion, whatever it may be, is precisely the intrusion required by the Supreme Court's decision in *Hazelwood*. The Supreme Court established the *Hazelwood* standard and, in doing so, clearly envisioned some minimal intrusion into public school management insofar as school administrators would be required to articulate a legitimate pedagogical concern for censoring a student's speech. The Supreme Court apparently did not believe this standard to be too ambiguous for district and appellate courts to apply, nor did it apparently believe this standard to place an unjustly onerous burden on school officials. Therefore, even if the parade of horribles feared by the concurrences came to pass, it is a parade of horribles created by a standard articulated by the Supreme Court and one to which we are bound to adhere until the Supreme Court states otherwise. (*Boring v. Buncombe County Board of Education,* 1998, pp. 374–375)

Questions for Discussion

1. How might one view this case and the court's decision from a justice perspective? Was the action taken against Ms. Boring fair? Was the court's decision fair?
2. Was Ms. Boring treated in a caring manner? Why or why not? How might school officials have treated Ms. Boring in a more caring manner?
3. How might this case be viewed through the lens of critique?
4. What would the profession expect of Ms. Boring? Superintendent Yeager? Principal Ivey?
5. Through a best interests perspective, was Ms. Boring afforded respect? Dignity? Why or why not? What message does Ms. Boring's treatment send to students? To other teachers? What message, if any, does the court's decision send?
6. What would you have done in this situation if you were Superintendent Yeager? Principal Ivey?

9

The Right to Privacy

Justice Brandeis, in his dissenting opinion in *Olmstead v. United States* (1928), a wire tapping case, characterized privacy as "the right to be let alone—the most comprehensive of rights and the right most valued by civilized men" (p. 478). Although the right to privacy, unlike other individual rights, is not expressly granted in the United States Constitution's Bill of Rights, the U.S. Supreme Court has interpreted this right as part of the Constitutions' Fourth Amendment. This amendment guarantees in part: "the right of the people to be secure in their persons, houses, papers, and effects, against unreasonable searches and seizures, shall not be violated" (United States Constitution, Amendment I). In addition, many states have laws ensuring privacy.

In 1985, the U.S. Supreme Court heard its first case addressing students' Fourth Amendment rights in schools. In rendering its decision, the court noted that although students have privacy rights in schools, these rights must be balanced against school officials' responsibility to maintain order and discipline (*New Jersey v. T.L.O.*, 1985). The latter has often been interpreted as keeping schools safe.

Therefore, students are afforded a lower standard of privacy than individuals outside the school setting. While the Fourth Amendment generally requires a warrant based on probable cause, searches by school officials require neither. Thus, searches may be conducted if the educator has a reasonable suspicion to suspect that the search will result in evidence that a student has violated either the law or a school rule. When it is unclear how this standard applies, lower courts must determine legality. For example, as mentioned earlier in this book, in the 21 years after the U.S. Supreme Court's decision in *New Jersey v. T.L.O.*, there were over 270 lower court decisions clarifying various aspects of the opinion (Stefkovich &

Torres, 2006). In the majority of these cases, school districts won (Stefkovich & Torres, 2003, 2006).

The apparent erosion of students' rights has concerned legal and educational commentators, many of whom agree with Justice Stevens' dissenting opinion in *New Jersey v. T.L.O.* (1985) where he notes:

> The schoolroom is the first opportunity most citizens have to experience the power of government. Through it passes every citizen and public official, from schoolteachers to policemen and prison guards. The values they learn there, they take with them in life. One of our most cherished ideals is the one contained in the Fourth Amendment: that the government may not intrude on the personal privacy of its citizens without a warrant or compelling circumstance. The Court's decision today is a curious moral for the Nation's youth. (pp. 385–386)

More recently, Gartner (1997) questions the price we are paying for school discipline, especially when educators use such intrusive measures as strip searching. Brooks (2004) contends: "Testing students who are not using drugs, are not likely to start using drugs, and face no special risks due to the nature of their activities hardly seems reasonable" (p. 396) while Lewis (2001) predicts: "It may be only a matter of time until a court allows schools to invade students' rights further and test for pregnancy pursuant to a 'legitimate' governmental interest" (pp. 185–186).

It is Friedelbaum (2002), however, who perhaps best captures this perspective on privacy when he concludes: "The most disappointing aspect of privacy rights, like liberty interests, is that they have been intermittently abandoned when social needs or the public good seem to require it" (p. 983). Trying to find a solution to this dilemma, he cites West (2001, pp. 1915–1919), who believes that legislators should take individual rights into account when they make laws in order to foster the "development of a moral society."

Other scholars (James & Larson, 2004; Mawdsley, 2003) take a more conservative view, maintaining that court decisions allow officials the discretion they need to keep schools safe. For example, in the area of random drug testing of students, Mawdsley (2003) asks the question: "How can school officials be opposed to drug use and not use a legal remedy in drug testing that is available to them?" (p. 621). In turn, James and Larson (2004) view the Court's reduction of students' individual rights and the granting of increased discretion to school administrators as a way to keep the student body safe and school officials accountable. They conclude:

> In its simplest form, the structure of American constitutional law assumes that public policy will yield to individual rights. The notion of a contextual exemption for public educators is both extraordinary and ironic. It is not clear, at first glance, nor under sustained observation, why this judicial reluctance to interfere with legitimate educational needs should generate such a broad departure from constitutional norms.

It is, in fact, the breadth of the model that is its most significant feature, begging the question whether judicial accommodation of local educational preferences requires such a level of deference ... (p. 90)

Russo and Gregory (1999) strike a middle ground in their approach. Observing the use of metal detectors, drug and alcohol profiles, surveillance technology, and random drug testing, the authors describe an "Orwellian milieu" on one hand and on the other hand, court decisions that support privacy rights. Regarding ethics, they come to the conclusion: "Arguments from an ethical base will be increasingly perceived as ideologically driven, civil libertarian politics, and not genuine, morally-based positions of principle" (p. 644).

Given this charge to address "morally-based positions of principle," this chapter presents four cases that illustrate the breadth, or lack thereof, of students' privacy rights and reflect the wide spectrum of court decisions addressing students' privacy issues. In the first case, *Gruenke v. Seip* (2000), a male high school swim coach suspected a female team member was pregnant and was worried for her safety. After repeated denials by the student, several other students on the swim team encouraged the young woman to take a pregnancy test that the coach had purchased for her use. The student claimed that the pregnancy test and the events surrounding it violated her Fourth Amendment rights. The court ruled in favor of the student, maintaining that the coach had violated her privacy rights.

In *Doe v. Pulaski County Special School District* (2002), the court did not recognize a valid privacy claim. This case is included in this chapter, however, because it illustrates both the limitations of students' privacy rights and how far school officials will go when they fear for the safety of students. The facts center around the expulsion of a middle school student who, influenced by rap music, wrote threatening letters aimed at an ex-girlfriend. The student was severely disciplined even though he never sent the letters (they were discovered by one of his friends who showed them to the girl), and the girl, even though initially frightened, had accepted the student's apology.

Davenport v. YMCA (1999) turns to issues of privacy and equity. Here, a middle school girls' basketball team, consisting of American Indian students, wins a tournament. The opposing team's coach suspects that the girls are really boys, and the students are subjected to a personal search to determine their gender. Representing themselves in court, the students' parents were unable to provide enough evidence to prove that these girls were the victims of discrimination.

Invasion of the privacy rights of large groups of students often manifests itself in programs such as those involving random drug testing. In 1995, the U.S. Supreme Court in its *Vernonia School District v. Acton* (1995) decision determined that public school officials may randomly drug test student athletes. Seven years later, in *Board of Education of Independent School District #92 of Pottawatomie County v. Earls* (2002), the High Court extended this authority to include random drug testing of students involved in extracurricular activities. Subsequently, some lower courts have used these decisions to justify additional drug testing (Rossow & Stefkovich, 2006). This discussion focuses on one such opinion, *Joye v. Hunterdon Central Regional High School Board of Education* (2003). Here, students driving to school and parking on school grounds are drug tested.

Thus far, courts have not upheld drug testing of an entire student body. On the other hand, if one randomly drug tests students driving to school as well as student athletes and those involved in extracurricular activities, very few remain. In essence, most students are allowed to be drug tested. This case brings up important issues as to whether schools should impose on the privacy of the vast number of students not using drugs, whether such a preventive approach actually works, and the extent to which students need to relinquish their privacy rights to feel safe.

GRUENKE v. SEIP
225 F.3d 290 (3rd Cir. 2000)

In the 1996–1997 school year, Leah Gruenke was a 17-year-old eleventh grade student at Emmaus High School in Pennsylvania. According to its Web site, the high school contains just over 2,000 students (Emmaus High School Web Site, 2005). Leah was a member of the school's varsity swim team.

In December 1996, Leah's father questioned the swim team coach, Michael Seip, about the fact that his daughter's racing times were increasing. Coach Seip had noticed a change in Leah and commented that she appeared to be heavier in the water. He did not mention to the father another suspicion he had, that Leah was pregnant. In response to Leah's apparent lack of stamina and slower racing times, Leah's mother made an appointment for Leah with her physician. Leah's doctor diagnosed a vitamin deficiency and prescribed dietary supplements. None of the tests performed were definitive in regard to pregnancy. Leah and her mother discussed the possibility of pregnancy at this time, but took no further steps to determine if she was pregnant.

In January 1997, Michael Seip began to further suspect that Leah was pregnant because, on several occasions during Christmas and New Year's practices, Leah frequently had to take breaks to go to the bathroom, complained of being nauseated and also often mentioned that her energy level was lower than normal. He also noticed her body shape changing. In February, Coach Seip spoke to his assistant coach, Kim Kryzan, about his concern and requested that she speak to Leah about "her change in performance." He also spoke with her guidance counselor about the same topic. Kryzan approached Leah to talk, but Leah did not volunteer any explanation as to why she was becoming slower.

After Kryzan's failed attempt, Seip discussed sex and pregnancy with Leah, but Leah emphatically declared that she was not pregnant. Leah was called in to talk to the guidance counselor, because of the information provided by Coach Seip, and to the school nurse because a teammate's mother asked the school nurse to talk with Leah. During this same time span, other members of the swim team and their parents also began to suspect that Leah was pregnant. At various points, Leah declared to her teammates that this was not possible as she had never had sexual intercourse but also said that it was none of their business.

After various mothers approached Seip about getting Leah to take a pregnancy test, one mother, Lynn Williams, bought a home pregnancy test and was reimbursed by the defendant for her purchase. Coach Seip kept the test at school. Around March 5, 1997, two teammates, Abby Hochella and Kathy Ritter, asked Leah to take the pregnancy test. Leah refused. The next day, the two girls approached her again.

In response to the girls' second attempt, Leah wrote a letter to Coach Seip saying that he had no right to make her take a pregnancy test because she wasn't showing any signs of being pregnant and she had never had sexual intercourse. Coach Seip either did not accept the letter or did not open it. Either way, he did not read it. On the same day, Kathy approached Leah one more time and told her, again, according to Leah, that she would have to take the test or Mr. Seip would take her out of the relay. Leah finally acquiesced and went with Kathy, Abby, and a third swimmer, Sara Cierski, to take the test in the bathroom of the locker room.

The test came back positive, so Sara suggested that Leah take another test to make sure. The girls went to the parking lot to get money from their parents and bought two more tests. Leah took them, and both came back negative. When Leah returned home that evening, she discussed the day's events with her mother, who became upset. Leah also received a phone call from Abby, who suggested she take a fourth test and, if Leah wanted, Abby's mother would take her to see a doctor. Leah went to school the next morning and took the fourth pregnancy test, which had been purchased by Abby's mother, and that test came back negative.

After learning about the test results, Coach Seip asked a volunteer assistant coach, Dr. Meade, an orthopedist, whether it was safe for pregnant swimmers to compete. Dr. Meade said there was no medical reason why a pregnant swimmer should not race, so Coach Seip did not pull Leah from racing because of his suspicions. On March 10, 1997, Leah had an appointment with Dr. Greybush. At that appointment, Leah found out that she was almost 6 months pregnant. She did not tell her mother or her teammates because she wanted to compete in the state's tournament.

After giving birth, Leah next saw Coach Seip at a summer swim meet where she was swimming independent of a team and Coach Seip was present as the coach of Emmaus Aquatic Team, a private swimming league. Leah claims that Coach Seip told his swimmers not to sit near Leah or to talk with her. During the next school swim season, Leah said that she felt alienated because the coach never spoke with her and took her out of several swim meets.

Leah's mother, Joan Gruenke, sued Michael Seip in August 1997, claiming four violations of Leah's and her own rights: Being forced to take the pregnancy test violated Leah's Fourth Amendment rights; Leah's and Joan's right to familial privacy had been violated; Leah's right to privacy had been violated; Leah's right to free speech and association had been violated when the coach allegedly told his swimmers not to associate with her.

A federal district court granted summary judgment for the school district, stating that because pregnancy tests had not been mentioned in any previous case as a violation of Fourth Amendment rights, it was not a violation. Therefore, Coach Seip did not violate any rights by persuading Leah to take the test. The Third Circuit Court of Appeals overturned the district court's opinion, maintaining that the law against illegal search and seizure provided a framework for what can be declared a breach of privacy; just because no previous case had dealt with pregnancy tests specifically did not mean they were automatically allowable. Thus, the appeals court found for Leah in that her Fourth Amendment rights had been violated, however the court found that she had no basis for a First Amendment claim. Leah and Seip settled the case in November 2001, with Leah receiving $21,500 in damages under 42 U.S.C. § 1983 (Civil Rights Act, 1871).

As to Leah's familial rights' claim, the appeals court ruled that even though there is a right at stake, Coach Seip is immune from §1983 damages on this claim in that the law as applied to the facts of this case was not clearly established at the time of the incident. In making this determination, the court noted:

> Public schools must not forget that "in loco parentis" does not mean "displace parents." It is not educators, but parents who have primary rights in the upbringing of children. School officials have only a secondary responsibility and must respect these rights. State deference to parental control over children is underscored by the Court's admonitions that "the child is not the mere creature of the State," [citing *Pierce v. Society of Sisters,* 1925, p. 535] and that it is the parents' responsibility to inculcate "moral standards, religious beliefs, and elements of good citizenship" [citing *Wisconsin v. Yoder,* 1972, p. 233]. (*Gruenke v. Seip,* 2000, p. 307)

Questions for Discussion

1. How might one view this case and the court's decision from a justice perspective?
2. Was Leah treated in a caring manner? Why or why not?
3. How might this case be viewed through the lens of critique, especially taking gender equity into consideration?
4. What would the profession expect of Coach Seip? Assistant Coach Kim Kryzan?
5. Through a best interests perspective, was Leah afforded her rights or shown her responsibilities? In this respect, how might this situation have been handled differently? Better? Was Leah afforded respect? Dignity? Why or why not?
6. What would you have done in this situation if you were Coach Seip? Kim Kryzan?

DOE v. PULASKI COUNTY SPECIAL SCHOOL DISTRICT
306 F.3d 616 (8th Cir. 2002)

J.M. and K.G. were considered a "couple" during their seventh-grade year at Northwood Junior High School. Like most middle school romances, J.M. and K.G. went through a series of break-ups, finally ending their relationship during the summer vacation between their seventh- and eighth-grade years when K.G. turned her attentions to another boy.

J.M. reacted with anger and frustration. A White boy from rural Arkansas, J.M. liked to put forth a "tough guy" persona and even made claims to be a member of the Bloods gang. In spite of his bravado, he received a chamber of commerce award, did well in school, and was not a disciplinary problem. Influenced by rap music such as the lyrics of Eminem, J.M. wrote a letter, of which there were two copies, to K.G. The letter was filled with obscenities and violent references, including a desire to rape, murder, and sodomize her. The letter was graphic in its account of how J.M. wished to hide under K.G.'s bed and kill her with a knife. After writing these letters, J.M. stored them in his bedroom. J.M. did not make any attempt or express any desire to mail the letters. They remained in his bedroom for months untouched until his best friend, D. M., found them during a visit. When D.M. discovered the letters, J.M. immediately grabbed them from D.M.'s hands. After some prompting however, he let D.M. read the letters. At that time, J.M. refused to give D.M. a copy to take home.

Sometime during the summer, K.G. learned that J.M. had written a lewd and violent letter to her. She confronted J.M., who eventually admitted that he wrote a letter that discussed her murder. K.G. wanted the letter and, at her request, D.M. stole a copy of it from J.M.'s bedroom at the end of summer vacation.

On the second day after the start of the new school year, D.M. gave K.G. the letter during gym class. She read it and immediately started to cry and express her fear of J.M. There were other students around K.G., and one of those students, on learning of the contents of the letter, immediately reported the incident to the school resource officer. The officer went to the gym, and after seeing K.G. greatly disturbed, conducted an investigation. He then informed the school principal of his findings. Hearing about the school officer's report, the principal conducted his own inquiry. Even though he was aware that D.M. had stolen the letter from J.M.'s bedroom without his consent, he recommended that J.M. be expelled for the remainder of the school year, based on a school policy that prohibits terroristic threats from one student to another.

After an appeal by J.M. and his parents, a hearing officer recommended that the expulsion be changed to a suspension for 1 year, and that J.M. be permitted to attend the district alternative school for the duration of the suspension. Thinking this punishment still too harsh, J.M. and his parents appealed the decision to the school board. Before his appearance in front of the board, J.M. had the opportunity to apologize to K.G. and her mother at the church they attended. At that time,

K.G.'s mother and K.G. hugged J.M. in response to his apology. The school board followed the principal's recommendation and meted out a harsher punishment. The board ordered J.M. expelled for the entire school year with no opportunity for any alternative educational placement. Even though a police report was filed at some point, the county refused to press charges.

J.M. and his mother filed suit, claiming that the school violated J.M.'s First Amendment free speech rights when the board voted to expel him for the unsent letter. Ruling for the student, a federal district court concluded that J.M.'s letter was protected speech in that it was not a true threat because the student never intended to communicate the information in the letter. A divided panel of the federal circuit court agreed with the district court, but on appeal, the entire Eighth Circuit Court of Appeals heard the case and decided for the school district.

This appeals court determined that, despite J.M.'s claim to the contrary, the case was not moot because the student had already been expelled and that there remained a live controversy between the parties. In regard to the free speech claim, the court first determined the standard for a true threat, which is "a statement that a reasonable recipient would have interpreted as a serious expression of an intent to harm or cause injury to another" (*Doe v. Pulaski County Special School District*, 2002, p. 624). Next, the court looked to whether J.M. intended to communicate his alleged threat. In making its decision, the court stressed the importance of privacy issues, noting that the government has no business regulating what persons may view or read in the privacy of their homes. As to this specific case, the court contended:

> The government similarly has no valid interest in the contents of a writing that a person, such as J.M., might prepare in the confines of his own bedroom. After all, "our whole constitutional heritage rebels at the thought of giving government the power to control" the moral contents of our minds. [Citing *Stanley v. Georgia*, 1969, p. 565]. It is only when a threatening idea or thought is communicated that the government's interest in alleviating the fear of violence and disruption associated with a threat engages. (*Doe v. Pulaski County Special School District*, 2002, p. 624)

Based on the facts of the case, particularly that J.M. permitted K.G.'s best friend to read the letter and then discussed the contents of the letter in a phone conversation with K.G., the court determined that there was intent to communicate. The court then turned to the question of whether "a reasonable recipient would have perceived the letter as a threat" (p. 625). Here, the court determined that K.G. did feel threatened and that even though J.M. apologized, it came only after the school board expelled him. Thus, K.G. perceived this letter as a serious expression of J.M.'s threat to harm her.

Rendering judgment in favor of the school district, the appeals court, in its majority opinion, made the following observation:

> Had we been sitting as the school board, we might very well have approached this situation differently, for it appears to us that the school board's action taken against

J.M. was unnecessarily harsh. Other options have occurred to us that could have furthered the district's interest in protecting its students, as well as have punished J.M., but also have aided him in the severity and inappropriateness of his conduct. However, "it is not the role of federal courts to set aside decisions of school administrators, which the court may view as lacking a basis in wisdom or compassion...." [Citing *Wood v. Strickland,* 1975, p. 326]. Those judgments are best left to the voters who elect the school board. (*Doe v. Pulaski County Special School District,* 2002, p. 627)

Questions for Discussion

1. How might one view this case and the court's decision from a justice perspective?
2. Was J.M. treated in a caring manner? Why or why not?
3. How might this case be viewed through the lens of critique?
4. What would the profession expect of the principal? The school board?
5. Through a best interests perspective, was J.M. afforded his rights or shown his responsibilities? In this respect, how might this situation have been handled differently? Better? Was J.M. afforded respect? Dignity? Why or why not?
6. What would you have done in this situation if you were the principal? A member of the school board?

DAVENPORT v. YMCA
1999 U.S. App. LEXIS 29864 (8th Cir. 1999)

In December 1995, the YMCA in Rapid City, South Dakota hosted a girls' basketball tournament for area schools. One of the teams was from the Loneman School. The Loneman School team advanced to the semifinals and beat the team from the Hermosa School. This meant the Loneman team would be playing for the championship title. However, when the players returned for the championship game, they were told of a complaint against the team by the Hermosa School's coach. The coach had complained to officials that the Loneman team included boys. In order to resolve the dispute, a female YMCA volunteer and a female chaperone from the Loneman School took the eight girls into a nearby restroom. There, each of the girls demonstrated that she was indeed a female. All of the girls on the Loneman team were 10- to 12-year-old Oglala Sioux Native Americans from the Pine Ridge Reservation where the school was located. Following the restroom incident, the Loneman School team played in the championship game and the tournament ended.

Two years later, the parents of the girls on the basketball team sued the Loneman School, the Custer School District where the Hermosa School is located, the YMCA, and the tournament director. The parents acted on their own behalf and as guardians of the girls. They stated that the incident had humiliated the girls and caused depression and embarrassment. The parents brought forth state tort liability claims for invasion of privacy, negligence, intentional infliction of mental distress, mental anguish, and unlawful imprisonment and federal claims based on race, sex, and age discrimination. A Federal Court of Appeals for the Eighth Circuit granted summary judgment in favor of the school district, maintaining that the tort claim should have fallen under federal law because the Loneman School was operated under the auspices of the Bureau of Indian Affairs. As to the discrimination claims, the court maintained that the students lacked enough evidence to support a claim.

Questions for Discussion

1. How might one view this case and the court's decision from a justice perspective?
2. Was the Loneman team treated in a caring manner? Why or why not?
3. How might this case be viewed through the lens of critique?
4. What would the profession expect of the Loneman school officials? The Hermosa School coach?
5. Through a best interests perspective, were these students afforded their rights? Were they afforded respect? Dignity? Why or why not? What message did the school's actions and the court decision send to these students?
6. What would you have done in this situation if you were the Hermosa coach? An official from the Loneman School?

JOYE v. HUNTERDON CENTRAL REGIONAL HIGH SCHOOL BOARD OF EDUCATION
826 A.2d 624 (NJ 2003)

Hunterdon Central Regional High School, located in Flemington, New Jersey, has a population of 2,500 students in Grade 9 through Grade 12. School officials take the matter of underage drinking and the use of illegal drugs seriously. Since 1987, they had undertaken measures to deter these illegal activities and to support students with substance abuse problems. At the time of this incident, they had employed three counselors through a Student Assistance Program (SAP) to assist students and their families.

In the past, school officials occasionally searched student lockers and conducted sweeps of the school, using canines to sniff for drugs. These sweeps were conducted in cooperation with the county prosecutor. In 1996, the school began a suspicion-based program of drug testing, targeting students suspected of illicit drug or alcohol use. These searches and testing were not challenged in this case.

Despite the abovementioned measures, Lisa Brady, the school's principal, continued to have concerns about illicit drug and alcohol use by the student population. She based these concerns, in part, on anecdotal evidence from coaches, teachers, and administrators. She claimed to have firsthand knowledge of two students snorting heroin on school property. The results of the suspicion-based testing indicated that 90% of those tested were positive.

Principal Brady engaged the Rocky Mountain Behavioral Science Institute, Inc. (RMBSI) of Fort Collins, Colorado, to conduct a survey of the student population, using a questionnaire. This survey, conducted in 1996–1997, revealed that over 40% of students in Grade 10 through Grade 12 had "been drunk" in the past year and 33% had used marijuana. Over 89% of all students had experimented with alcohol. Use of drugs such as cocaine, hallucinogens, and inhalants ranged from 12% to 29%, depending on the grade and substance.

Based on the results of the survey, the Board instituted its first random drug-testing program in July 1997. This program was conducted only on students participating in the school's athletic programs and required parental or guardian consent. Between 1998 and 2000, over 1,000 students were eligible for the test. The school randomly selected 100 students a year for actual testing and, of these, approximately 5% tested positive for drug or alcohol use.

After the random drug-testing program was implemented, the Board held a public meeting to respond to questions from students and their parents. David Evans, a parent and an expert on teen substance abuse, answered questions. Evans suggested that the Board establish a task force to look at the current testing program and make recommendations for any necessary revisions. The Board appointed David Evans as the task force's chair and Joan Greiner as its vice chair. Joan Greiner was a parent, a drug-testing opponent, and later a plaintiff in this case. The task force also included representatives from stakeholder groups such as parents, students, the booster club, the SAP, school administrators, teachers, coaches, and drug testing experts.

The task force held meetings between January and November 1998. During these meetings, they investigated research and police data on alcohol and substance use by teens, and heard comments from various members of the school staff, including coaches, administrators, and the school nurse. They also solicited feedback from parents through letters and at a public meeting held in October 1998.

The school board received the task force's report and also held public meetings. The board engaged RMBSI to conduct a follow-up survey in the 1999–2000 school year. This second survey indicated that drug use was down in most categories and it was the board's belief that the random drug-testing program was partly responsible. However, marijuana use among senior students was up slightly, and the board believed that there continued to be unacceptable levels of drug use among the general student population.

In September 2000, at the recommendation of the task force, the school board implemented an expanded drug-testing policy, which allowed for random drug testing of all students engaged in extracurricular activities and those with school parking permits. It defined as "extracurricular" noncredit activities in which students participate. The policy required both the student and his or her parent or guardian to sign a consent form. The form authorized the Hunterdon Central Regional High School District to conduct a urine and saliva or breath specimen test on site and to release the test results to designated school district personnel. As of January 2001, 866 consent forms had been signed.

The policy set out the consequences for students who test positive for drugs or alcohol. For a first infraction, the student would be suspended from participating in the sport or extracurricular activity and from parking privileges. The student must attend a 5-day education program and resubmit a specimen for testing, which must not indicate the presence of drugs or alcohol.

For a second infraction, the student would be suspended from the sport or activity for 60 days and would lose parking privileges. The student must again attend the 5-day education program and a minimum of ten counseling sessions. He or she must also test negative for drugs and alcohol at the end of the suspension period. The student would also be subject to periodic, unannounced testing in the future. Hunterdon Central's policy was to treat students' test results as health records, which are kept confidential. Results were not to be shared with law enforcement.

Joan Greiner contended that the policy interfered with her rights as a parent to raise her daughter as she thinks best and to "teach her the personal responsibility she needs as a young adult" (*Joye v. Hunterdon Central Regional High School Board of Education,* 2003, p. 632). She also indicated that there was no evidence of drug or alcohol problems in the school, specifically applying to those students participating in sports, extracurricular activities, or those with parking permits. The school board's president responded that the board had taken the steps necessary to ensure that the policy fairly balanced students' privacy rights with school officials' obligations to protect students.

In August 2000, three sets of parents, including Joan Greiner, filed suit, challenging the constitutionality of the school's policy according to the Fourth Amendment of the United States Constitution and Article I, paragraph 1, of the New Jersey Constitution, which has language almost identical to the federal law. A New Jersey state trial court ruled for the parents and thus invalidated the program. A state appeals court reversed the decision, ruling for the school district and upholding the program as legal. Parents appealed to the New Jersey Supreme Court, which also upheld the program as legal.

In rendering its decision, this court looked to the need for individualized suspicion. To justify the intrusions of students' privacy without having individualized suspicion, the drug-testing program had to pass a special-needs analysis. Here the court determined: "the 'special need' in this case derives from the unique public-school environment that already results in a relaxed set of search-and-seizure rules" (*Joye v. Hunterdon Central Regional High School Board of Education,* 2003, p. 641). Accordingly, the court stressed the duty of school officials to maintain order and a safe environment in the schools. Having said this, the *Joye* court also emphasized:

No part of our analysis is intended as an endorsement of the Board's decision on policy grounds. Whether the Board's program reflects a wise or appropriate expenditure of resources is for the Board and its local constituents to determine. Our sole task is to evaluate the Board's action within the special-needs framework as articulated by our federal counterpart and as applied by this Court.... Having considered the affected students' diminished expectation of privacy, the sufficient limitations on the obtrusiveness of the testing, and the substantial governmental interest in maintaining a school environment free of drugs and alcohol, we find that Hunterdon Central's program passes muster under Article I, paragraph seven of the New Jersey Constitution. (*Joye v. Hunterdon Central Regional High School Board of Education,* 2003, p. 607)

Agreeing with Justice Breyer's concurring opinion in *Earls* as to the importance of wide community support for school-based drug and alcohol testing programs, the New Jersey high court added a disclaimer:

We do not, however, suggest that a majority of citizens in any one community can bend the constitution to their collective will. Rather, we merely follow prior case law that instructs us to consider society's viewpoint when evaluating whether an expectation of privacy is entitled to enhanced protection in a given circumstance.... According to the Board's president, no parents of students eligible for testing (aside from plaintiffs) have expressed opposition to the school's program. Although parental sentiment is not controlling, we accord it some weight, especially within the public-school context in which school officials often assume a parent-like role.... (*Joye v. Hunterdon Central Regional High School Board of Education,* 2003, pp. 651–652)

The court saw no legal problem with testing such large numbers of students. On the other hand, it also did not see its decision as permission for all school districts to adopt similar practices. As to concerns about the message sent to students, the court notes:

The dissent further contends that upholding Hunterdon Central's program somehow reflects bad civics. So long as its program is reasonable, we leave it to the Board and its local constituents to determine what "lesson" the program might convey to students. It might well be that this case will instill in students an appreciation of the rule of law, namely, that officials are permitted to maintain a testing policy not on some whim, but only after they have justified it under constitutional standards. Or the lesson might be that there are consequences to illegal drug and alcohol use, both in terms of a student's health and his or her ability to participate in selected activities. In any event, our only task is to evaluate the program's constitutionality, not to substitute our value system for that of the Board in respect of the broader public policy underlying its program. (*Joye v. Hunterdon Central Regional High School Board of Education,* 2003, p. 616)

Questions for Discussion

1. How might one view this case and the court's decision from a justice perspective?

2. Were these students treated in a caring manner? Why or why not?

3. How might this case be viewed through the lens of critique?

4. What would the profession expect of Principal Brady? The board president?

5. Through a best interests perspective, have school officials afforded students their rights? Shown them their responsibilities? In this respect, how might this situation have been handled differently? Better? Were the students who were tested afforded respect? Dignity? Why or why not? Do you agree with the court regarding the lessons students may have learned from this situation?

6. What would you have done in this situation if you were Principal Brady? The board president?

10

School Safety and Zero Tolerance

Tough love now translates into zero tolerance policies that turn public schools into prison-like institutions, as students' rights increasingly diminish under the onslaught of military-style discipline. Students in many schools, especially those in poor urban areas, are routinely searched, frisked, subjected to involuntary drug tests, maced, and carted off to jail.... Children are no longer given a second chance for minor behavior infractions, nor are they simply sent to the guidance counselor, the principal, or detention. They now come under the jurisdiction of the courts and juvenile justice system.

—Giroux, 2004, pp. 94–95

Certainly, violence and drugs are a concern in our society and a threat to school safety. One of the ways the legal system and, hence, schools have chosen to address this problem is through the use of zero tolerance policies. First instituted in response to problems with drug dealers, federal and state governments later passed zero tolerance laws applying to students possessing drugs and weapons in schools. Some school districts' policies and procedures expanded this scope to include more trivial offenses (Shouse, 2005).

Zero tolerance policies and practices emerge from a very strict interpretation of the law and the ethic of justice. They emphasize equality, treating everyone exactly the same. The rule is the rule. Although zero tolerance speaks to issues of evenhandedness and equality, a number of scholars have pointed out the inequities resulting from zero tolerance policies, particularly the disparate impact on African American males (Reyes, 2001).

At the same time, zero tolerance practices raise other pedagogical and ethical concerns. Zero tolerance literally means "no tolerance." Whether this is a message that school officials want to convey to students is critical to the concept of *best interests*. Indeed, Hanson (2005), a legal scholar, asks this question:

What has happened to the "best interests of the child" approach that recognizes that at least some children need treatment and not necessarily punishment for delinquent and antisocial acts? ... [T]he courts apparently disregard the best interests of the children, or in deference to administrative authority, find these policies and actions acceptable. (pp. 324–325)

Hyman and Snook (1999), in their book *Dangerous Schools,* refer to schools as places where students may suffer both psychological and physical abuse, often from those they should trust the most, school officials. Although such abuses occur, they are not necessarily intentional or widespread. When they do happen, it is important that students have advocates at the school. Being a moral leader requires this type of advocacy. However, determining what actions are in the best interests of a student is not always easy. As emphasized earlier in this book, context is critical both to the work of school leaders and to the court system, both of which make decisions in a larger arena. The cases in this chapter illustrate how some school officials have coped with competing interests, often to the detriment of individual students.

In *Ratner v. Loudoun County Public Schools* (2001), a student was expelled for violating the school's zero tolerance policy on weapons when school authorities found a knife in his locker. Ratner had taken the knife from a friend who had threatened suicide. Although the court expressed concern over the harsh result of the zero tolerance policy, it found no constitutional violation and stated that courts are not in a position to make judgment on the wisdom of zero tolerance policies or their application.

Seal v. Morgan (2000) involved a student who was expelled for having a knife in the glove compartment of his car, even though he did not know the knife was there. The student was eventually exonerated, but the administrative and legal processes were so stressful that, according to the student's father, they led to his son's suicide. In the third case, *S.G. v. Sayreville Board of Education* (2003), a federal appeals court upheld the suspension of a 5-year-old kindergarten student for playing a game with another student where they pretended to shoot each other. This behavior was in violation of school policy.

In the final case, *Hearn v. Board of Public Education* (1999), a high school constitutional law teacher was fired for refusing to take a drug test in violation of the district's Safe School Plan, which calls for zero-tolerance of drugs, alcohol, and weapons and a Drug-Free Workplace Policy. Even though Hearn was found to be drug free and despite a public outcry in her favor (over 100 teachers and students appeared at the board hearing in her defense), the school board terminated Ms. Hearn who had only a few years left until retirement.

RATNER v. LOUDOUN COUNTY PUBLIC SCHOOLS
No. 00–2157 (4th Cir. 2001)

The Safe and Gun Free Schools and Communities Act mandates that states require schools to adopt zero tolerance policies for guns or risk losing federal funding. As a direct response, schools throughout the country adopted zero tolerance policies that often moved beyond firearms and encompassed other weapons, including knives and sometimes drugs and mandated automatic suspension or expulsion for such infractions. Loudoun County School District offered no exception. In 1999, when Benjamin Ratner was 13 years old and in the eighth grade at Blue Ridge Middle School, the zero tolerance weapon policy of the district was in full force.

On October 8 of that year, Ratner arrived at school as any other day. Upon arrival, he engaged in conversation with a fellow student who was distressed. She revealed to him that she had thought about committing suicide the previous evening by slitting her wrists. Ratner had known this girl for 2 years and knew that she had tried to kill herself several times before. Based on his knowledge of her past history, Ratner had no reason to believe that she was not telling the truth. He expressed concern for her safety.

The student also told Ratner that she had brought the knife to school that she planned to use to kill herself and that it was in her binder. In an effort to save the life of his schoolmate, Ratner confiscated the binder and put it in his locker. At no time during his exchange with the other student did he see the knife. Ratner continued with his school day and although he did not plan on telling school officials of the incident, he decided to tell both his and the girl's parents later that day.

As the school day progressed, Roberta Griffith, assistant principal at Blue Ridge Middle School, became aware that Ratner had a knife. She discussed the matter with the school dean, Fanny Kellogg, who called Ratner into her office. When questioned, Ratner readily admitted to possessing the knife. Kellogg sent Ratner alone to his locker to get the binder and deliver it to her office, evidence that Kellogg never perceived Ratner to pose any type of threat with the weapon. At no time was there any question as to whether Ratner intended to use the knife.

Regardless of the lack of danger Kellogg perceived in this matter and in spite of her belief that Ratner acted in a way to protect his fellow student, Griffith suspended Ratner for 10 days for possessing a knife. The school principal, Joseph Mauck, supported Griffith's decision and delivered written notice to Ratner regarding the suspension. Several days after Mauck's letter, Edgar Hatrick, division superintendent, gave notice to Ratner that he was under long-term and indefinite suspension, pending a school board hearing. Hatrick specifically recommended that the suspension last until February 2000, or the remainder of the academic semester, a length of almost 4 months. An administrative hearing panel upheld Hatrick's recommendation and even after appeal to the school's discipline committee, the suspension was upheld.

Ratner and his mother filed suit in federal court claiming that the school district's enforcement of the zero tolerance policy in this matter violated Ratner's Fourteenth Amendment Equal Protection and Due Process rights as well as his Eighth Amendment right to be free from cruel and unusual punishment under the United States Constitution. Both the federal district court and the Fourth Circuit Court of Appeals found that Ratner did not have enough facts to prove that his rights had been violated under any of these claims. Both courts concluded that, in essence, Ratner's claims involved due process and that school officials gave Ratner "constitutionally sufficient, even if imperfect" (*Ratner v. Loudoun County Public Schools,* 2001, p. 4) process in his notices and hearings. Speaking for the majority Judge Widener concluded:

> However harsh the result in this case, the federal courts are not properly called upon to judge the wisdom of a zero tolerance policy of the sort alleged to be in place at Blue Ridge Middle School or of its application to Ratner. Instead, our inquiry here is limited to whether Ratner's complaint alleges sufficient facts which if proved would show that the implementation of the school's policy in this case failed to comport with the United States Constitution. We conclude that the facts alleged in this case do not so demonstrate. (*Ratner v. Loudoun County Public Schools,* 2001, p. 4)

Judge Hamilton, agreeing with the majority, wrote a separate opinion, "to express … compassion for Ratner, his family, and common sense" (p. 4). Recognizing that school officials are rightfully concerned about safety issues and that many schools adopted strict policies in reaction to a series of tragic shootings nationally, Judge Hamilton, nonetheless, maintained:

> The panic over school violence and the intent to stop it has caused school officials to jettison the common sense idea that a person's punishment should fit his crime in favor of a single harsh punishment, namely, mandatory school suspension. Such a policy has stripped away judgment and discretion on the part of those administering it; refuting the well-established precept that judgment is the better part of wisdom…. Ratner's nearly four-month suspension from middle school is not justifiable. Indeed, it is a calculated overkill when the punishment is considered in light of Ratner's good-faith intentions and his, at best, if at all, technical violation of the school's policy. Suffice it to say that the degree of Ratner's violation does not correlate with the degree of his punishment. Certainly, the oft repeated maxim, "there is no justice without mercy" has been defiled by the results obtained here. But, alas, as the court explains, this is not a federal constitutional problem. (*Ratner v. Loudoun County Public Schools,* 2001, pp. 5–6)

Questions for Discussion

1. How might one view this case and the court's decision from a justice perspective?
2. Was Benjamin Ratner treated in a caring manner? Why or why not?

3. How might a critical theorist view this situation?

4. What would the profession expect of Principal Mauck? Superintendent Hatrick?

5. What message did the school's actions send to Benjamin? To the other students in the school? What message, if any, did the court's decision send to school officials?

6. What would you have done in this situation if you were Principal Mauck? Superintendent Hatrick?

SEAL v. MORGAN
229 F.3d 567 (6th Cir. 2000)

In the fall of 1996, Dustin ("Dusty") Seal was a junior at Powell High School in Knox County, Tennessee. Dustin played saxophone in the band and was a "B student who plan[ned] to attend college" (Mayshark, 1996, p. A1). On October 30, 1996, Dustin and his friend Ray Pritchert, also a student at Powell High School, became entangled with another student in an out-of-school dispute over Pritchert's ex-girlfriend. As a result, Pritchert began carrying a hunting knife.

The next day, Seal, Pritchert, and another friend, David Richardson, went to pick up Seal's girlfriend, Allison Reardon (Lawson, 2003). They were driving Seal's mother's car because his was not running. On the ride over, Pritchert placed the knife on the floor of the car. When he went into the house to get Allison, Richardson took the knife and placed it in the glove compartment. It is not disputed that Seal knew Pritchert had the knife in the car that day.

The next day, November 1, 1996, Seal, again using his mother's car, drove to the high school where he, Pritchert, and Allison Reardon were to play in the band for the football game. They had worn their uniforms to the event, but were informed when they got there that uniforms were not required that night, so Seal and Pritchert returned to Seal's car to change. When they returned to the band room, the director, Gregory Roach, pulled them aside and asked if they had been drinking. They said no. The director smelled their breath and did not detect any alcohol so he let them enter the band room.

About 15 minutes later, Roach called Seal and Pritchert into his office where they were joined by the school's vice-principal, Charles Mashburn. Mashburn told them that four students had reported seeing Seal and Pritchert drinking. Although Mashburn searched both students' instrument cases and coats, he found nothing and announced that he needed to search Seal's car. He then told them that an assistant band director had seen the two with a flask, and chewing gum and checking each other's breath. Seal agreed to the search and Mashburn began his inspection. He found a bottle of amoxicillin pills (for which Seal had a prescription), two cigarettes in a crumpled pack on the back seat, and Pritchert's knife in the glove compartment.

Mashburn had Seal accompany him to his office where he directed Seal to write out a statement about what had happened. When Seal asked what he was supposed to say, Mashburn told him to explain why the knife was in the glove compartment. Seal wrote:

> Went to Roach's office because he thought or had been told that we had a flask and had been drinking, so we went and Mr. Mashburn searched the car. He found a knife and two cigs. The knife was there because Ray's ex-girlfriend's boyfriend had been following us around with a few of his friends so we were a little uneasy. (*Seal v. Morgan*, 2000, p. 571)

Mashburn began the preparation of a form for Notice of Disciplinary Hearing for Long-Term Suspension from school because of the knife, pills, and cigarettes found in the car on school property. On November 6, 1996, Principal Vicky Dunaway conducted a disciplinary hearing where Mashburn and Seal recounted the events of the night before. After hearing the evidence, she suspended Seal pending expulsion for having the knife on school property. Seal appealed the decision. On November 14, 1996, the Board of Education's disciplinary hearing authority, Jimmie Thacker, Jr., heard Seal's appeal.

Seal, his parents, his girlfriend, Principal Dunaway, and David Richardson all attended the hearing. Seal testified that he knew Pritchert had the knife on October 31, but that he did not know it was still in the car when he drove to school the next day. Richardson testified that Seal had not been in the car when the knife was placed in the glove compartment and, as far as he knew, Seal did not know it was still in the car. Seal's girlfriend also testified to Dusty's lack of knowledge about the knife.

On November 18, 1996, Mr. Thacker notified Seal's mother by letter that he had decided to uphold Principal Dunaway's decision and that Seal was to be suspended pending expulsion. Seal's mother called the school and indicated that she wanted to appeal the decision. She received a certified letter saying that the school's board of education would consider the appeal at its next meeting.

At the hearing, Seal, represented by counsel, argued that he had no knowledge that the knife was in the car when he drove it to school that day. School board member Sam Anderson asked Seal whether he had ever seen the knife in his car. Seal responded that he knew Pritchert had a knife on him on November 1, 1996, but that he had thought Pritchert had taken it with him and had not realized that it had been left in his mother's car. Anderson responded by saying that he felt that a clear message had to be sent and said to Seal, "You are responsible for what's in your car and that's where I'm torn but I would have to say that you have to be held responsible as a driver for what's in your car" (*Seal v. Morgan*, 2000, p. 572).

After a unanimous vote, the board supported the principal's decision and upheld Seal's expulsion. The transcript of the board's hearing was three pages long (as opposed to the 50-page transcript that came out of Thacker's hearing).

Seal's father initiated, on Dustin's behalf, a lawsuit claiming violation of his son's rights under the Equal Protection and Due Process clauses of the Fourteenth Amendment and also violation of the Fourth Amendment when his car was searched. A federal district court granted summary judgment to the school district on Seal's Fourth Amendment and Fourteenth Amendment Equal Protection claims, but ruled in favor of Dustin on his Due Process claim. The Sixth Circuit Court of Appeals also decided in favor of Seal on his Due Process claim.

Defending the school district, counsel argued: "The Board's policy requires 'Zero Tolerance,' and the policy does not explicitly say that the student must know he is carrying a weapon" (*Seal v. Morgan,* 2000, p. 576). This logic, the court noted, opposes basic tenets of criminal law, which require that contraband possession must be "conscious or knowing" (p. 577). The court maintained that the school district's policy to expel Seal for something he did not know about was inappropriate. In rendering its decision, the court reflected:

> We understand full well that the decision not to expel a potentially dangerous student also carries very serious potential consequences for other students and teachers. Nevertheless, the Board may not absolve itself of its obligation, legal and moral, to determine whether students intentionally committed the acts for which their expulsions are sought by hiding behind a Zero Tolerance Policy that purports to make the student's knowledge a non-issue. We are also not impressed by the Board's argument that if it did not apply its Zero Tolerance Policy ruthlessly, and without regard for whether students accused of possessing a forbidden object knowingly possessed the object, this would send an inconsistent message to its students. Consistency is not a substitute for rationality. (*Seal v. Morgan,* 2000, p. 582)

In a separate opinion, Judge Suhrheinrich argued otherwise, stating that the school board's interpretation of the policy was rational:

> In addition to their duty to educate, schools act *in loco parentis.* Given this enormous responsibility, and the potentially devastating consequences of weapons on campus, a strict weapons policy is rationally related to a legitimate government interest—protecting our children from the very threat of violence. (*Seal v. Morgan,* 2000, p. 582)

The case was sent back to the district court to decide on damages. In fall 2001, Dustin was awarded $30,000 under his 42 U.S.C. §1983 claim. Dustin Seal never returned to school after the expulsion and worked for a while laying floors and then installing cable. On June 21, 2002, Dustin Seal committed suicide by sitting in the bathtub and shooting himself in the head. Dusty's father said that he could still hear his son's words each night as he lays down to sleep: "Dad how can [I] be so right and they be so wrong and they be allowed to get by with ruining my life?" (*The Dustin Seal Story,* 2003, p. B3). Dusty's father told the press that his son's expulsion and the legal battles that followed broke Dusty's spirit and started his son on a slide downward that ended with his eventual suicide (Satterfield, 2003).

Questions for Discussion

1. Were the school's actions toward Seal just? Were they fair?
2. Was Dusty treated in a caring manner? Why or why not?
3. How might this case be viewed through the lens of critique?
4. What would the profession expect of Principal Dunaway? Vice Principal Mashburn? What would you have done if you had been in their place?
5. What message did the school officials' actions send to Dusty?
6. Through a best interests perspective, was Dusty afforded his rights? Was Dusty afforded respect? Dignity? Why or why not?
7. Do you believe school officials had any responsibility for Dusty's ultimate suicide? Why or why not?

S.G. v. SAYREVILLE BOARD OF EDUCATION
333 F.3d 417 (3rd Cir. 2003)

A.G. was a 5-year-old kindergarten student at Wilson Elementary School in Sayreville, New Jersey. In March 2000, three incidents took place within 5 days that provide the context for the case. In one incident, a student told another student that he was going to shoot a teacher. That same day, a student threatened to kill another student by putting a gun in his mouth. The following week, a student claimed his mother allowed him to bring guns to school. In each of these incidents, the principal suspended the offending student for 3 days. The first two students met with the school psychologist and were recommended for additional outside counseling. The principal also reported the second incident to police. These three incidents took place within 2 weeks of a high-profile killing of a 6-year-old by another 6-year-old at a school in Flint, Michigan.

On March 10, the principal of Wilson Elementary, Georgia Baumann, decided to visit all of the classes in the school to discuss the seriousness of making threats involving a weapon. In a letter sent home to parents, Ms. Baumann suggested parents should discuss the issue with their children. The letter also stated that disciplinary action would be taken against any student who threatened to harm another student. A.G. was not at school on March 10, and his parents did not receive the letter.

On March 15, A.G. and three friends were playing a game at recess. According to A.G., they were "playing guns," pretending to shoot each another. A.G. told one of his playmates, "I'm going to shoot you" (*S.G. v. Sayreville Board of Education*, 2003, p. 419). A student who was an onlooker reported the game and the comment to a teacher who said that some of the students were upset. However, there was some dispute over whether any children other than the child who reported the incident were upset or even witnessed the game. Nonetheless, the boys were taken to the principal's office.

After notifying Assistant Superintendent Dennis Fyffe and Superintendent William Bauer, Ms. Baumann gave the students 3-day suspensions. Ms. Baumann could not reach A.G.'s parents by telephone. She did contact A.G.'s grandmother to explain the situation, and sent a letter home with A.G. Superintendent Bauer supported the suspensions when contacted by the father, S.G. A.G. served the suspension and returned to school to finish the year. The suspension was not part of A.G.'s permanent record, although Ms. Baumann maintained her own personal records, which she shared with other principals when asked.

S.G. brought suit on behalf of his son. Legal claims included violation of A.G.'s rights to free speech under the First Amendment of the United States Constitution and Equal Protection and procedural Due Process under the Fourteenth Amendment. A federal district court granted summary judgment in favor of the school district. The Court of Appeals for the Third Circuit agreed that the school district should prevail.

The appeals court maintained that the school was within its authority to restrict A.G.'s free speech rights, noting:

> ... a school's authority to control student speech in an elementary school setting is undoubtedly greater than in a high school setting ... [and] the school's prohibition of speech threatening violence and the use of firearms was a legitimate decision related to reasonable pedagogical concerns and therefore did not violate A.G.'s First Amendment rights ... the determination of what manner of speech is appropriate properly rests with the school officials. (*S.G. v. Sayreville Board of Education*, 2003, p. 423)

As to the Due Process claim, S.G. argued that his son's rights were violated in that A.G. was not in school when Principal Baumann discussed the issue of drugs and weapons, that the parents had not received the letter the school sent, and that A.G. did not understand the process. The court denied the claim, asserting that Principal Baumann met with A.G. and his friends before imposing the sentence. The court concluded:

> Contrary to S.G.'s argument, the record does not reflect that A.G. did not understand the meeting with Baumann. Baumann had sought to inform A.G.'s parents, but her inability to reach them does not signify that A.G. was deprived of procedural due process. She asked each of the boys to explain to her what he had said and done. The boys admitted that they were "playing guns," [citation omitted] and that they had made statements regarding shooting a gun. The discussion fulfilled the requirements of Due Process, which can be satisfied in a case like this by informal procedure. (*S.G. v. Sayreville Board of Education*, 2003, p. 424)

The Equal Protection claim rested on S.G.'s assertion that the suspension relied solely on a school policy that lacked a rational basis. The court saw no Equal Protection violation and maintained that a policy deterring violent threats constituted a rational basis.

Questions for Discussion

1. How might one view this case and the court's decision from a justice perspective?
2. Was A.G. treated in a caring manner? Why or why not?
3. How might this case be viewed through the lens of critique?
4. What would the profession expect of A.G.'s teacher? Principal Baumann?
5. Through a best interests perspective, was A.G. afforded his rights or shown his responsibilities? In this respect, how might this situation have been handled differently? Better? Was A.G. afforded respect? Dignity? Why or why not?
6. Do you agree with the court's decision? Why or why not?

HEARN v. BOARD OF PUBLIC EDUCATION
191 F.3d 1329 (11th Cir. 1999)

In 1992, the Chatham County Board of Education adopted a zero tolerance policy for drugs, alcohol and weapons in its schools. The following year, the school board adopted a Drug Free Workplace Policy, which required drug testing of an employee within 2 hours if an incident arose in which there was a reasonable suspicion of a drug or alcohol violation. The policy stated that an employee who failed to submit to the drug test would be disciplined, possibly leading to termination.

Sherry Hearn was a high school teacher in Savannah and an employee of the Chatham County School Board. A popular teacher, who was the 1994 Teacher of the Year, Hearn was 3 years away from retirement, having been employed as a teacher for 27 years. A teacher of constitutional law, Hearn was critical of the Chatham County School District's practice of lockdowns and drug sweeps. She conveyed her dissatisfaction in the classroom and was out of favor with school officials because of this practice. In spite of her disagreement, she was under contract with the Chatham County School Board and subject to its policies.

In April 1996, a search for illegal drugs was conducted at the high school where Hearn taught. Campus police in tandem with a Chatham County Deputy used a drug-sniffing dog to search automobiles parked in the school's parking lot. That day, Hearn's car was parked in the school lot with the doors unlocked and the windows open. That was how the County Deputy found the vehicle when the dog alerted. The officer had the dog enter the vehicle through the driver's side window, at which point the dog smelled something in the closed ashtray of Hearn's car. The dog alerted correctly. The school officer entered the automobile, opened the ashtray and found a partially burned marijuana cigarette. The officer obtained neither a warrant nor Hearn's consent before entering the car.

The officer brought the evidence obtained during the search to the high school principal, Linda Herman. Herman called Hearn into her office and informed her of the search results. Hearn denied knowledge of the drug. Nevertheless, a County Police Officer told Hearn that she would likely be charged with possession of marijuana. Herman then asked Hearn to submit to the urinalysis drug test within the next 2 hours as required by the school board's policy. Hearn refused. In response, Herman issued a warning letter and requested for a second time that Hearn take the drug test or face disciplinary measures. Hearn again refused to take the urinalysis until she could contact her attorney. Hearn took the drug test the following day and the results were negative.

Even though Hearn had taken the urinalysis in ample time to determine if marijuana was actually used, the superintendent recommended that she be suspended and eventually terminated. A school board hearing took place, during which time it was decided that the termination should be upheld because Hearn failed to take the required drug test within the 2-hour time frame.

Hearn filed suit against the district in federal court, claiming that her rights under the Fourth and Fifth Amendments to the United States Constitution were violated, as well as her due process rights. She also charged the district with breach of contract and sought both damages and reinstatement. After losing at the district court level on summary judgment, Hearn appealed to the Eleventh Circuit Court of Appeals.

Hearn argued that both her contract with the district and board policy prohibited the search of her car. The court agreed but stated that these prohibitions applied only to searches by school authorities. Law enforcement officers conducted the search; therefore they were not bound by either board policy or Hearn's employment contract. Moreover, the search was legal in that the dog alerted to an odor emanating from the car. This alert constituted probable cause that there were drugs in the car, and a warrant was not necessary as justified under the automobile exception to the warrant requirement. The court determined that by refusing to consent to a drug test, Hearn was subject to possible termination under board policy. Thus, her subsequent termination violated neither her contract nor board policy. Finally, there was no violation of Hearn's Fifth Amendment right to remain silent in that this right involves testifying, not submitting to a drug test.

In a dissenting opinion, Judge Ferguson pointed out that Ms. Hearn had been in her class for the entire morning and could not have lit the cigarette found partially burned in her car. In addition, law enforcement officers did not bring criminal charges against Ms. Hearn. Thus, this judge characterized the case as a civil dispute rather than a criminal offense. In arguing for a jury hearing, Judge Ferguson identified important policy implications arising from the majority's decision:

> No argument can be made that the delay in submitting to the test was intended to conceal the use of drugs or that the school board was hindered in its investigation. Clearly this case is not about drug possession or use by a high school teacher. Mrs. Hearn was fired because she challenged an unlawful school board action and delayed submission to a drug test while seeking the advice of counsel.

Legally, the plaintiff's position is unassailable. But there are relevant factors beyond principles of contract law, which have chilling ramifications. The plaintiff had been very critical of the School Board's policy of campus lockdown searches for drugs, which she likened to police state tactics. Because of her classroom criticism of the practice as unconstitutional, she was not in favor with the employer. Expectations of privacy guaranteed by the policy were ignored and the penalty imposed was the professional equivalent of the death penalty. The 27-year stellar career of a 1994 "Teacher of the Year" is shattered with only three years remaining to retirement with benefits.

By the holding here the majority has recognized, implicitly, an illegal drugs exception to the law that the court will not rewrite private contracts between parties who are on equal footing.... It is widely recognized that in the nation's zealous war on drugs, rights secured by the Fourth Amendment have shrunk.... This may be the first case to hold that courts will not enforce private contract rights between an employer and employee, hammered out after negotiations to govern conduct of the parties in areas of privacy, where the employer has a suspicion, no matter how insubstantial, that the employee violated a drug policy. Not only is an outstanding high school teacher a casualty in this episode; so, incidentally, are basic contract principles. (*Hearn v. Board of Public Education*, 1999, p. 1336)

Questions for Discussion

1. How might one view this case and the court's decision from a justice perspective? Was the action taken against Ms. Hearn fair? Was the court's decision fair?

2. Was Ms. Hearn treated in a caring manner? Why or why not? How might school officials have treated Ms. Hearn in a more caring manner?

3. How might this case be viewed through the lens of critique?

4. What would the profession expect of Ms. Hearn? Principal Herman? Hearn's superintendent? The school board members?

5. Through a best interests perspective, was Ms. Hearn afforded respect? Dignity? Why or why not? What message does Ms. Hearn's treatment send to students? To other teachers? What message, if any, does the court's decision send?

6. What would you have done in this situation if you were Hearn's Superintendent? Principal Herman? A member of the school board?

Part III

SCHOOL GOVERNANCE, THE CURRICULUM, AND THE STUDENT

This part of the book focuses on legal and ethical implications of school governance and the curriculum and how administrative decisions impact students. Here, the issues are broader than those portrayed in Part II. They include an examination of academic standards, assessment, and the right to an education; various aspects of teaching, learning, and the curriculum, including what some have characterized as a "hidden curriculum"; and whether students should be able to recover money damages from school districts when their rights have been violated. The final chapter complements earlier discussions of equity, equality, and equal protection by focusing on specific cases related to disability, poverty, gender, and race.

11

Academic Standards, Assessment, and the Right to Education

With the tightening of academic standards and an emphasis on high-stakes testing as the primary assessment tool, some students, often poor and often minorities, may be excluded from an education. Moran (2000) points out important ethical implications of this strategy when she observes:

> High-stakes testing is popular because it offers a way to identify and blame individuals without acknowledging a collective unwillingness to invest in public schools, particularly those in low income, often minority areas. The tests have taken on the dimensions of a morality tale. Failure is located in low-performing schools and failing pupils, not in systems of public education that suffer from serious inequities in the allocation of resources. (p. 132)

Passage of the U.S. Department of Education's No Child Left Behind (NCLB) Act (2002) has exacerbated these concerns about equity and equality. Although some assert that proficiency testing is a good strategy for raising standards in schools, others note dangers in the misuse of standardized testing particularly when it influences administrative decisions related to the tracking, promotion, and graduation of individual students, especially those who are poor or minority (Heubert & Hauser, 1999). Discussing assessment of knowledge and the evaluation inherent our educational practices, Freire (1993) observes:

> The evaluation criteria the school uses to measure students' knowledge—intellectualism, formal, bookish—necessarily helps these children from the so-called privileged social

111

classes, while they hurt children from poor and low socioeconomic backgrounds. And in the evaluation of the knowledge base of children—evaluated when they first arrive in school and during the time they stay in school—the mechanism in general never takes into consideration any "knowledge from life experiences" the children bring with them to school. (p. 16)

High-stakes testing also raises issues of equality. Because educational governance, including the institution of academic standards and assessment, is left primarily to state and local governments, students might possibly fail competency exams in one state but could well pass them in another. Moreover, pressure to pass the exam extends to teachers and administrators, whose wage stability and job security might be jeopardized if their students fail to perform on these exams. It is certain, therefore, that these tests carry with them high stakes for many parties in addition to students. These may include parents, teachers, administrators, and citizens who either benefit from an educated workforce or suffer from a lack thereof. Accordingly, O'Neill (2003) questions the utility of this means of assessment, noting:

Increased pressure to perform does not necessarily translate into improved performance. Indeed, it could be argued that making additional threats for failure to schools that already seem to have demonstrated that they do not adequately stimulate student achievement can be counterintuitive and may lead to increases in cheating at all levels. Reliance on high stakes alone, without offers of guidance and other assistance, may serve to widen the gap between schools that work and schools that don't. (p. 662)

Interest in, and concerns about, high-stakes testing did not, however, begin with NCLB. Our country has a long history of testing and sorting children. Beginning in the early 1900s with the development of the Stanford-Binet IQ test, schools began to track students. In 1962, Raymond Callahan in his classic book, *Education and the Cult of Efficiency,* questioned applying business models to public schools and their students.

This issue also made its way into the courts. In the *Hobson v. Hansen* (1971) decision, a District of Columbia court maintained that academic tracking, which has a disproportionate impact on African Americans, is legal as long as there is no intent to discriminate. Starting in the 1980s, there were a number of important lower court decisions that argued for multiple measures of success in making decisions related to academic issues such as special education placement (*Larry P. v. Riles,* 1984) and awarding of state-based scholarships (*Sharif v. New York,* 1989). In the first case, where students were placed in classes for the mentally retarded based solely on IQ test scores, there were disproportionately larger numbers of African Americans. In the latter case, a larger portion of males received state fellowships to college when the selection criterion was based solely on Scholastic Aptitude Test (SAT) scores.

Guinier and Torres (2002) point out the high relationship between SAT scores and family income. In other words, high SAT scores are more greatly equated with family income than with any other variable. In proposing ways for administrators to audit equity (or inequities), Skrla, Scheurich, Garcia, and Nolly (2004) observe: "persistent achievement gaps by race and class in U.S. public schools are educationally and ethically deplorable" (p. 135).

People Who Care v. Rockford (1997), the first case in this chapter, addresses the complexities, both legal and ethical, of a court decree that requires racial quotas and the elimination of tracking as remedies for segregation as well as the appeals court decision that declared these strategies illegal.

In *Hoffman v. Board of Education* (1978), a New York student was placed in classes for the mentally retarded for 11 years, based on the assessment of one psychologist, in spite of a test score one point from the normal range. Thirteen years after the initial placement of this child, who had a serious speech impediment, professionals determined that he was of average intelligence. The state trial court ruled against the student's family, but a state appeals court overturned the decision.

In *Professional Standards Commission v. Smith* (2002), a Georgia middle school teacher was suspended from his job because he taught vocabulary items from a 1990 standardized test that was reissued to his students in 1998. The teacher said that another teacher gave him the 1990 test in 1995 for diagnostic purposes. He had told his principal, who did not object, and had openly used information from this test for several years, not knowing that this was not allowed. Perry Zirkel, an education law scholar, writes about this case and several others relative to proficiency testing, asserting that such litigation is inevitable (Zirkel, 2003). He quotes Smith's attorney, who states: "To make matters worse, the school authorities made my client start his suspension in the middle of the school year, rather than in June—is that in the best interest of his students?" (p. 712).

PEOPLE WHO CARE v. ROCKFORD
111 F.3d 528 (7th Cir. 1997)

In 1994, a district judge found that the Rockford Board of Education had discriminated against Black and Hispanic students. At that time, there were significant differences in achievement between White and non-White students and the school board had failed to prevent schools from becoming either all White or all minority. The discrimination was found by the district court to be intentional on the part of the board. The board accepted liability in the case and the parties agreed to enter a remedial phase, presided over by a magistrate judge. The judge appointed an assistant in the form of a special master and, in 1996, entered a detailed decree (the "comprehensive remedial order"). The decree consisted of several provisions regarding the Rockford School District's operation. Both the school district and employee unions appealed many of these provisions. This case is a consolidation of nine appeals against the Rockford Board of Education concerning the implementation of this remedial order.

The 1994 judgment found that the Rockford school district had an underrepresentation of non-White teachers at 8.7%. The magistrate judge ordered that the percentage of non-White teachers be at least 13.5% and that minority teachers be given seniority so that they would not lose their jobs in the event of layoffs.

The decree forbade ability grouping of students (tracking) with some exceptions, notably for gifted students. The remedial order stipulated that the racial composition of every nonelective class in the district reflect the racial composition of the school, within 5%. The appeals judge, Posner, stated that using race as the sole determination of class composition can have detrimental effects on both brighter and slower students, regardless of race. He also found the 5% tolerances too rigid. Objective and nonracist tracking based on achievement scores, the judge maintained, is common in most public schools. When used this way, tracking could relieve some of the policing of the school districts' class composition being done by the special master. In this discussion of tracking, Judge Posner noted:

> Tracking is a controversial educational policy, although just grouping students by age, something no one questions, is a form of "tracking." Lawyers and judges are not competent to resolve the controversy. The conceit that they are belongs to a myth of the legal profession's omnicompetence that was exploded long ago. To abolish tracking is to say to bright kids, whether White or Black, that they have to go at a slower pace than they're capable of; it is to say to the parents of the brighter kids that their children don't really belong in the public school system; and it is to say to the slower kids, of whatever race, that they may have difficulty keeping up, because the brighter kids may force the pace of the class....

> Were abolition of tracking the only means of preventing the school district from manipulating the tracking system to separate the races, it might be a permissible remedy. It is not the only way—as we take the plaintiffs implicitly to concede by accusing the school district of having placed White kids in higher tracks, and Black kids in lower tracks, without always complying rigorously with objective criteria, such as scores on achievement tests. (*People Who Care v. Rockford,* 1997, p. 536)

The decree ordered the Rockford School District to reduce the achievement gap between White and minority students by one half in 4 years. This, the appeals court found, was an unreasonably short length of time. In addition, Judge Posner found that many of the factors contributing to the achievement gap were out of the school board's control. For example, up to 30% of the achievement gap could be attributable to family poverty, not discrimination. The education level of parents and parental involvement were factors in student achievement, yet none of these variables were accounted for in the one statistical study used in the original case. The appeals court observed that if the school district knew how to close the achievement gap, it would already have done so.

The decree also forbade the school district's teachers from referring a large number of minority students for discipline. Judge Posner found this practice to be arbitrary and unacceptable in that it could result in innocent students being disciplined and guilty students not being disciplined, based on a quota system.

Racial disciplinary quotas violate equity in its root sense. They entail either systematically overpunishing the innocent or systematically underpunishing the guilty. They place race at war with justice. They teach schoolchildren an unedifying lesson of racial entitlements. And they incidentally are inconsistent with another provision of the decree, which requires that discipline be administered without regard to race or ethnicity. (*People Who Care v. Rockford,* 1997, p. 538)

The order limited the number of minority students who can receive remedial education. This was also found to be illegal on appeal, as it might deprive minority students from receiving compensatory education when they require it simply because of an arbitrary quota system. Under the original order, the racial makeup of the cheerleading squads had to reflect the racial composition of the school. Finding this requirement to be arbitrary and possibly discriminatory against nonminority students, Judge Posner observed:

Of course the school district may not discriminate against minority aspirants for the cheerleading squads. But to fix a racial quota for cheerleaders demeans the remedial process in school desegregation litigation and cannot possibly be justified in the absence of evidence (of which there is none) that any current cheerleaders owe their position to past discrimination against Blacks or Hispanics by the school district or its agents.... To prevent children who are not beneficiaries of past discrimination from becoming cheerleaders, because of their race, is, on this record, a barefaced denial of equal protection. (*People Who Care v. Rockford,* 1997, p. 538)

Questions for Discussion

1. How might one view this case and the court's decision from a justice perspective?
2. Are the Rockford children treated in a caring manner? Why or why not?
3. How might this case be viewed through the lens of critique?
4. What would the profession expect of Rockford's school officials?
5. Through a best interests perspective, were these students afforded their rights? In this respect, how might this situation have been handled differently? Better? Were the students afforded respect? Why or why not?
6. What message does the way this situation was handled send to students? To teachers?
7. What would you have done in this situation if you were a Rockford school official?

HOFFMAN v. BOARD OF EDUCATION
64 A.D.2d 369 (N.Y. App. Div. 1978)

Daniel Hoffman was born in 1951 in Queens, New York. Daniel had started walking and talking at an early age, but he stopped both when he was 13 months old after his father's death. Daniel's mother, who had emigrated from Germany when she was 3 years old and had only a junior high school education, went to work full-time as a bottle washer at Pfizer & Co. Daniel's paternal grandmother cared for him during those working hours.

During the next several years, Daniel's speech failed to progress. When he was almost five, Daniel was still not talking intelligibly, so his mother took him to the National Hospital for Speech Disorders to be evaluated. As part of the hospital's evaluation, Daniel was given a nonverbal intelligence test. He scored 90, which was within the normal intelligence range. It was no surprise, though, that he was diagnosed with a severe speech problem. As a result, his mother began bringing him to the New York Speech Institute for weekly therapy sessions, which lasted several years.

When Daniel was 5, he entered kindergarten at the local elementary school. Shortly thereafter a school psychologist tested him. This psychologist, Monroe Gottsegen, administered the Stanford-Binet, a highly verbal test. Given Daniel's speech deficiencies, his IQ based on this test was determined to be 74. The cutoff score for placement in the class for Children with Retarded Mental Development (CRMD) was 75. Dr. Gottsegen also observed "Mongolian tendencies" (*Hoffman v. Board of Education,* 1978, p. 372), features associated with a certain type of mental retardation. This diagnosis was subsequently found to be incorrect in that it did not apply to Daniel; also, there is no such thing as "Mongolian tendencies." Either a person is diagnosed as Mongoloid or they are not.

Daniel was assigned a CRMD placement. Because of Daniel's speech issues, Dr. Gottsegen questioned the validity of the results and recommended that a retest be given 2 years later. Daniel's mother was not interviewed during the testing process and the school never learned of the results of the test given to Daniel that placed his IQ at 90. When placement was determined, Mrs. Hoffman was not told that Daniel had missed the cutoff for a regular classroom by one point. She was also not informed of her right to request a retest.

Subsequently, Daniel was enrolled in the CRMD class for the next 12 years, during which time the district transferred him to six different schools. Daniel eventually ended up at the Queens Occupational Training Center as a young adult. During his time in CRMD classes, Daniel consistently tested low on standardized achievement tests. The low test scores, coupled with his continued severe speech impairment, gave school officials reason to believe that the CRMD placement was appropriate. As a result, Daniel did not have his intelligence retested until he was 18.

When he was 18, Daniel was tested at his mother's request after he had been denied Social Security payments. After being in classes for mentally retarded children since kindergarten, Daniel was given an IQ test by William Garber. The results of the Wechsler Intelligence Scale for Adults given to Daniel indicated an IQ of 94. After being tested by Dr. Garber, Daniel continued to attend the Occupational Training Center. However, he was soon told that his score on the intelligence test made him ineligible to attend the Center and he was denied further enrollment. Once out of school, Daniel was depressed and despondent. He had not known any other setting and was lost. As a response, his mother hired a lawyer, who requested Dr. Lawrence Kaplan to provide an additional evaluation of Daniel.

Dr. Kaplan noted that Daniel's years of being labeled as *retarded* had a marked psychological effect on him. Daniel was referred to another doctor, Lawrence Abt, who conducted more psychological tests and determined that Daniel possessed a full-scale IQ of 100, which is squarely within the average range. Furthermore, Dr. Abt determined that Daniel was actually above average, and that the score of 100 was lower than it might have been, given the lack of education and stimulation Daniel encountered during his years of CRMD placement.

Daniel did not enroll in school again, though he did receive speech therapy services and made some improvement in his ability to talk. Though it was determined that Daniel was able to train for a skilled vocation, by the time he was 26, he had not done so. In one of the first educational malpractice cases, Daniel sought damages in a New York state court for psychological injury. The Hoffmans won at the trial court level and the school district appealed.

Affirming the lower court judgment but reducing monetary claims from $750,000 to $500,000, Judge Shapiro, speaking for the majority (which included three of the five presiding judges), reasoned:

> Defendant's [the school board's] rhetoric constructs a chamber of horrors by asserting that affirmance in this case would create a new theory of liability known as "educational malpractice" and that before doing so we must consider public policy ... and the effects of opening a vast new field which will further impoverish financially hard pressed municipalities. Defendant, in effect, suggests that to avoid such horrors, educational entities must be insulated from the legal responsibilities and obligation common to all other governmental entities no matter how seriously a particular student may have been injured and, ironically, even though such injuries were caused by their own affirmative acts in failing to follow their own rules.

> I see no reason for such a trade-off, on alleged policy grounds, which would warrant a denial of fair dealing to one who is injured by exempting a government agency from its responsibility for its *affirmative* [duty].... This does not mean that the parents of the Johnnies who cannot read may flock to the courts and automatically obtain redress. Nor does it mean that the parents of all the Janies whose delicate egos were upset because they did not get the gold stars they deserved will obtain redress....

> As Professor David A. Diamond noted [citing Diamond, 1978, pp. 150–151], when discussing this very case after the judgment at Trial Term ... "the thrust of the plaintiff's case is not so much a failure to take steps to detect and correct a weakness in a student, that is a failure to provide a positive program for a student, but rather, affirmative acts of negligence which imposed additional and crippling burdens upon a student" and that "it does not seem unreasonable to hold a school board liable for the type of behavior exhibited in *Hoffman*." I agree. (*Hoffman v. Board of Education*, 1978, pp. 385–386)

The court also pointed out that this type of problem should not reoccur in that after 1968, both the State and the City of New York required periodic retesting of students in CRMD classes. The appeals court concluded its opinion with this observation: "Not only reason and justice, but the law as well, cry out for affirmance of plaintiff's right to a recovery. Any other result would be a reproach to justice. In the words of the ancient Romans: *'Fiat justitia ruat coelum'* (Let justice be done though the heavens fall)" (*Hoffman v. Board of Education,* 1978, p. 387).

Questions for Discussion

1. How might one view this case and the court's decision from a justice perspective? Do you agree or disagree with the courts' application of the justice paradigm? Why or why not?
2. Was Daniel treated in a caring manner? Why or why not?
3. How might this case be viewed through the lens of critique?
4. What would the profession expect of school officials? Of Monroe Gottsegen, the first psychologist who tested Daniel?
5. Through a best interests perspective, were Daniel and his mother afforded their rights? In this respect, how might this situation have been handled differently? Better? Was Daniel afforded respect? Dignity? Why or why not?
6. What would you have done in this situation if you were Daniel's teacher? His principal?

PROFESSIONAL STANDARDS COMMISSION v. SMITH
571 S.E.2d 443 (Ga. Ct. App. 2002)

In 1998, Charles Smith, a fifth-grade teacher at East Lake Elementary School in McDonough, Georgia, was disciplined for unfairly preparing his students for the Iowa Test of Basic Skills (ITBS) by giving them questions from previous tests. The ITBS is a national achievement test that assesses students in several subject areas. The same test is used for several years before the questions are changed. Copies of the test are kept under lock and key at the school except during the hours when the test is being administered, and teachers are not allowed to keep copies in their classrooms.

Ms. Calvin-Thomas, a fifth-grade teacher, testified that while administering the vocabulary portion of the test, she overheard a student say "Yes!" when she saw the words on the test. After the test, another student reported that the test was easy because Mr. Smith supplied copies of the test beforehand. Further questioning of her students revealed that Mr. Smith had given the class an identical test. Some of the students even produced the vocabulary lists that Mr. Smith had distributed.

Ms. Calvin-Thomas went to the principal and the instructional teacher with the information. Jeffrey Meyers, the instructional teacher, was responsible for distributing the test to the teachers and securing them when not in use. At the principal's request,

Meyers went into Charles Smith's classroom and found individual student files that contained exact copies of the vocabulary portion of the test, some with comments and grades on them. The names on the files corresponded with the names of the students in Mr. Smith's science class. The principal, Dr. West, also found an unmarked copy of the test that was used in Mr. Smith's classroom. Copies of the reading comprehension portion of the test were also found in Mr. Smith's room. Dr. West questioned Mr. Smith as to why a science teacher would be interested in vocabulary tests. Mr. Smith told him that subjects are all interrelated.

Mr. Smith claimed that the test found in his classroom was an old copy, which he had obtained from a colleague in 1995. He said he found another test on the floor and thought that another teacher at the school had given it to the students. He also claimed to have told Dr. West that he had a 1990 test and that Dr. West did not tell him not to use it with students.

Reversing a lower court decision, Georgia's state court of appeals ruled that the evidence was admissible. This court concluded that there was enough evidence to find: "Smith had improperly coached his students" (*Professional Standards Commission v. Smith,* 2002, p. 446).

Questions for Discussion

1. How might one view this case and the court's decision from a justice perspective?
2. Was Mr. Smith treated in a caring manner? Why or why not?
3. How might this case be viewed through the lens of critique?
4. What would the profession expect of Mr. Smith? Ms. Calvin-Thomas? Mr. Meyers? Principal West?
5. Through a best interests perspective, was Mr. Smith afforded his rights? In this respect, how might this situation have been handled differently? Better? Was Mr. Smith afforded respect? Why or why not?
6. What message does the way this situation was handled send to students? To other teachers?
7. What would you have done in this situation if you were Mr. Smith? Ms. Calvin-Thomas? Mr. Meyers? Principal West?

12

Teaching, Learning, and the Curriculum

A major role of schools is to socialize students and make them "good citizens." In other words, intentional or not, schools inculcate certain values. As mentioned in earlier chapters, courts have recognized that schools represent a "marketplace of ideas" (*Tinker v. Des Moines Independent Community School District,* 1969, p. 512). This concept implies that students should be encouraged to think for themselves through a wide exposure to various ideas and philosophies. On the other hand, the curriculum as such is not only what is taught in schools. As Arons and Lawrence (1980) note in their seminal article on this topic:

> Even when a school bends over backwards (as it almost never does) to provide all points of view about ideas and issues in the classroom, it barely scratches the surface of its system of value inculcation. A school must still confront its hidden curriculum—the role models teachers provide, the structure of classrooms and of teacher–student relationships, the way in which the school is governed, the ways in which the child's time is parceled out, learning subdivided and fragmented, attitudes and behaviors rewarded and punished. Even in those areas concerned with basic skills it is clear that teaching is never value-neutral, that texts, teachers, subject matter and atmosphere convey messages about approved and rewarded values and ideas. (p. 310)

Accordingly, students learn lessons by observing how they and others are treated. The cases included in this chapter vividly illustrate this concept and the points that Arons and Lawrence make and, in turn, raise important ethical questions as to the inculcating of beliefs on young minds, which beliefs should be imparted, how this should be done, and who determines these beliefs. Thus, this chapter looks at the curriculum in the broadest sense of that word, including what Arons and Lawrence (1980) characterize as the "hidden curriculum" (p. 310).

Many school districts require students to participate in community service as a requirement for graduation. In *Immediato v. Rye Neck School District* (1996), students claimed that this requirement violated their rights to be free from involuntary servitude. Yet, a federal court ruled that such a requirement is constitutionally permissible. Here, an important issue is whether it is in the best interests of students to require them to take certain actions that some feel would make them good citizens.

Yudof et al. (2002) use the *Nabozny v. Podlesny* (1996) case to illustrate how the curriculum may manifest itself in the way school personnel treat students. In this Wisconsin case, an openly gay student was both verbally and physically harassed for years by his fellow students. In spite of the student's attempt to get help from the school administration, and the intervention of both a guidance counselor and his parents, the harassment escalated until it resulted in the student's physical attack. The high school's assistant principal laughed and supposedly told this student that he "deserved such treatment because he is gay" (*Nabozny v. Podlesny,* 1996, p. 452) and that he should look for an alternative educational setting. After the boys in his class performed a mock rape witnessed by some 20 students, Nabozny stated that the school's female principal told him that "boys will be boys" and he should expect such treatment from his classmates if he is "going to be so openly gay" (*Nabozny v. Podlesny,* 1996, p. 451).

In *Billings v. Madison Metropolitan School District* (2001), parents challenged the policy of their third-grade daughter's elementary school, which used race and other factors to determine classroom assignment. The parents further challenged the seating assignment of their daughter, since it was race based, by claiming that both practices were discriminatory even though the teacher believed that such strategies would improve the student's ability to learn.

Mead, a legal scholar on educational issues, uses *Billings* as an example of how entangled courts can become in instructional delivery. Raising an issue similar to that in *Billings*, she questions what would happen legally if a school administrator wished to divide students by race to ensure diversity. Based on some lower court decisions, this practice could be unconstitutional, yet school authorities have postulated that there could well be compelling pedagogical reasons for such a practice, viewing diversity as critical in providing students with a balanced education in today's society (Mead, 2002). Mead concludes by presenting educational leaders with this challenge:

> Public elementary and secondary educational institutions exist for no reason other than to transmit to students what others have learned, inspire students to new learning, and inculcate the values held dear by our democracy. Student assignment or selection policies also teach. Schools can either turn a blind eye to the ramifications of racial isolation and enduring racial stereotypes, thereby becoming complicit in their

perpetuation; or schools can accept the mantle that has defined them as public institutions since the Supreme Court's decision in *Brown*. (p. 148)

Finally, the last case in this chapter, *Selman v. Cobb County School District* (2005), addresses scientific theories of evolution and what happens when school districts try to accommodate the religious beliefs of students and their parents when there is a conflict between religion and the curriculum. In this case, the district school board approved a disclaimer sticker to be placed on students' science books. The court decided that even though this disclaimer had a secular purpose, it nonetheless had the effect of endorsing religion.

IMMEDIATO v. RYE NECK SCHOOL DISTRICT
73 F.3d 454 (2nd Cir. 1996)

While he was a student at Rye Neck District's public high school in Mamaroneck, New York, Daniel Immediato was required to complete 40 hours of community service in order to graduate. He disagreed with this policy on several grounds. He felt that by its very nature, community service is voluntary and cannot be mandated. He also wanted any community service in which he chose to participate to remain private. His parents, also parties in the suit, believed that the volunteer spirit should come from within the individual and not from the government and that they had tried to instill this attitude in their son.

The Rye Neck School District put the mandatory community service program in place as a graduation requirement in 1990. Starting with the 1992 graduating class, the program stipulates that all students complete 40 hours of community service during their 4 years of high school. The program also includes a classroom component in the senior year where students discuss their service. Because it is a mandatory program, there are no exceptions or provisions for opting out. There are also rules for the type of service that is allowable. For example, no more than 20 hours may be served at the school during the school day, and the student must not receive any payment for the service. The school provides an extensive list of acceptable organizations, such as secular and nonsecular charities, political organizations, not-for-profit organizations, and public agencies.

Students are allowed to contribute service to a religious organization only as it relates to providing charitable assistance, and not proselytizing, for the group. Students may also nominate their own organizations and activities for approval. The school demonstrates significant latitude in granting these special requests. Over the course of the program, only two student-nominated projects were rejected. In cooperation with the service organization, the students establish their own work hours, including during the summer break if they choose, and provide their own transportation.

During their senior year, students must take a required course, Managing Your Future. In this course, they complete a short form documenting their community service and reflecting on what they gained from the experience. They are also asked if there was a career connection in the service they provided. The students then discuss the experience with their teacher and the other students. The program is graded as pass/fail, and a pass is required to graduate.

Daniel and his parents claimed that the mandatory community service requirement violated Daniel's rights under the Thirteenth Amendment, which provides freedom from involuntary servitude. In addition, Daniel's parents claimed that their Fourteenth Amendment rights to due process and to direct the upbringing and education of their son were violated. Determining that the program violated neither Daniel's nor his parents' constitutional rights, a federal district court granted summary judgment in favor of the school district.

As to the Thirteenth Amendment claim, the court determined that Rye Neck's program did not rise to the level required to meet a violation of students' rights. The program's requirement of 40 hours in 4 years is not onerous, and students enjoy considerable freedom in arranging their work schedules. The program is coupled with classroom experiences and is not exploitive. As the court concluded:

> The level of coercion is not so high as to compel a finding of involuntary servitude. Although students who forego their required service will not graduate, they may avoid the program and its penalties by attending private school, transferring to another public high school, or studying at home to achieve a high school equivalency certificate. While these choices may be economically or psychologically painful, choices they are, nonetheless. They might not render the program voluntary, but they contribute to the conclusion that it is not involuntary servitude....
>
> Considering all these factors, we find that the program is not constitutionally infirm. That is not to say that any and every service program that a public school district may devise would survive constitutional scrutiny. If, for instance, the students were required to spend their Saturdays at the homes of their teachers, washing their cars, painting their houses, and weeding their gardens, the extent, nature, and conditions of "service," and the more obviously exploitative purpose of the program, might indeed warrant a finding of "involuntary servitude." But this is not our case. (*Immediato v. Rye Neck School District,* 1996, p. 460)

As part of their Fourteenth Amendment due process complaint, Mr. and Mrs. Immediato claimed that the Rye Neck program interfered with their rights as parents to direct Daniel's education and upbringing. To overcome this claim, the school needed only to provide a rational basis for its program, which according to the appeals court, it has easily done.

> We are aware that Daniel's parents object because of their "values" or "morals," as opposed to a general objection to the educational wisdom of the program, but we do not find this difference to be of constitutional significance. While the Constitution does indeed distinguish between religious objections and secular objections ... it makes no similar distinctions among purely *secular* objections based on values, morals, or other firmly-held beliefs.... The District's mandatory community service program easily meets the rational basis test. Education is unquestionably a legitimate

state interest.... The state's interest in education extends to teaching students the values and habits of good citizenship, and introducing them to their social responsibilities as citizens [Citing *Ambach v. Norwick,* 1979, p. 80].

Furthermore, the mandatory community service program rationally furthers this state objective. The District reasonably concluded that the mandatory community service program would expose students to the needs of their communities and to the various ways in which a democratic system of volunteerism can respond to those needs. In doing so, the program helps students recognize their place in their communities, and, ideally, inspires them to introspection regarding their larger role in our political system. (*Immediato v. Rye Neck School District,* 1996, p. 462)

The Immediatos also brought liberty claims under the Fourteenth Amendment as well as privacy claims, both of which, according to the appeals court, lacked merit.

Questions for Discussion

1. How might one view this case and the court's decision from a justice perspective?
2. Was Daniel treated in a caring manner? Why or why not?
3. How might this case be viewed through the lens of critique?
4. What would the profession expect of the school officials at Rye Neck?
5. Through a best interests perspective, was Daniel afforded his rights or shown his responsibilities? In this respect, how might this situation have been handled differently? Better? Was Daniel afforded respect? Dignity? Why or why not?
6. What would you have done in this situation if you were a school official at Rye Neck?

NABOZNY v. PODLESNY
92 F.3d 446 (7th Cir. 1996)

Matthew Nabozny was a student in Ashland, Wisconsin from the time he was of school age. He attended elementary school in the district, largely without event. However, about the same time he became a seventh-grade middle school student in 1988, he realized that he was gay. Nabozny chose to be open about his sexuality and as a result faced the abuse of his classmates.

Other students verbally harassed Nabozny on a regular basis. Throughout seventh grade, the verbal assaults escalated to physical abuse, at which time Nabozny contacted the school guidance counselor, Mr. Peterson. Mr. Peterson took quick action to discipline the students involved. Mr. Nowakowski soon replaced Mr. Peterson. When Nabozny approached Mr. Nowakowski about the abuse he received from his fellow students, the guidance counselor contacted Mary

Podlesny, the school's principal. Even though Nabozny continued to express his fear and concerns, neither adult took action.

The harassment continued to worsen, and two students in particular habitually abused Nabozny. These students, Jason Welty and Roy Grande, physically assaulted Nabozny on numerous occasions. One such incident included performing a mock rape on him in a science classroom in front of 20 other students. When Nabozny told the principal about this incident, Principal Podlesny dismissed the behavior of the two boys, telling Nabozny that his openness about being gay should lead him to expect such behavior. Nabozny left school early that day, and even though Welty and Grande did not receive punishment for their behavior, the next day Nabozny was forced to explain why he left school without permission. The abuse continued throughout the rest of the school year and continued into the eighth grade.

In the eighth grade, Welty and Grande again attacked Nabozny, this time in the boy's restroom. These boys were not disciplined even though Nabozny and his parents had met with Principal Podlesny to discuss the matter. Again, Nabozny was told that he should expect such behavior. There was no relief for Nabozny; the harassment reached such a level of intensity that he attempted suicide. Nabozny completed the remainder of eighth grade at a Catholic school.

After eighth grade, Nabozny returned to the Ashland School District, enrolling in Ashland High School. The abuse started as soon as the school year began. At one point a group of students attacked Nabozny, again in the restroom. After Nabozny was struck by student Stephen Huntley, Roy Grande urinated on him [Nabozny]. No action was taken against the attackers, and Nabozny was referred to another school guidance counselor, Mr. Reeder. Again, Nabozny attempted suicide. He then ran away. His parents tried to keep him out of the Ashland Schools, but because they could not afford private school tuition, the Department of Social Services forced him to return to Ashland High School.

In tenth grade, there was no improvement in the treatment Nabozny received. Only one school official, Ms. Hanson, a guidance counselor, attempted to advocate for Nabozny and get school officials to discipline the harassing students. One day, a group of eight boys attacked Nabozny, including Stephen Huntley, who kicked him repeatedly in the stomach over a period of several minutes. With the desire to press charges, Nabozny was ultimately directed to the assistant principal in charge of discipline, Thomas Blauert. Instead of helping Nabozny, Mr. Blauert "laughed and told him he deserved such treatment because he is gay" (*Nabozny v. Podlesny*, 1996, p. 452). In spite of both his parents' and Ms. Hanson's pleadings, school district officials failed to grant Nabozny relief. Weeks later, Nabozny collapsed from internal bleeding as a result of the attack by Huntley and the other boys.

By eleventh grade, both Ms. Hanson and Nabozny's parents agreed that school officials would do nothing to help him, and he left school. Upon leaving, he was diagnosed with posttraumatic stress syndrome. Nabozny brought suit against the school district and several school officials, claiming monetary damages under 42 U.S.C. §1983 for violation of his Fourteenth Amendment rights to Equal

Protection and Due Process. A federal district court granted summary judgment for the school district.

Nobozny appealed this decision to the Seventh Circuit Federal Court of Appeals. This court ruled that Nabozny's Equal Protection rights had been violated based on gender discrimination or sexual orientation—the court combined the two claims—and that the law was clearly enough established to support Nabozny's §1983 claims. In rendering its decision, Judge Eschbach, speaking for a unanimous three-judge panel stated:

> The defendants ask us to affirm the grant of qualified immunity because "there was no clear duty under the Equal Protection Clause for the individual defendants to enforce every student complaint of harassment by other students the same way." The defendants are correct in that the Equal Protection Clause does not require the government to give everyone identical treatment. Nothing we say today suggests anything to the contrary. The Equal Protection Clause does, however, require the state to treat each person with equal regard, as having equal worth, regardless of his or her status. The defendants' argument fails because they frame their inquiry too narrowly. The question is not whether they are required to treat every harassment complaint the same way; as we have noted, they are not. The question is whether they are required to give male and female students equivalent levels of protection; they are, absent an important governmental objective, and the law clearly said so prior to Nabozny's years in middle school. (*Nabozny v. Podlesny,* 1996, p. 456, n.7)

At the same time the court denied Nabozny relief on his due process claims. Making this determination, the court concluded:

> However untenable it may be to suggest that under the Fourteenth Amendment a state can force a student to attend a school when school officials know that the student will be placed at risk of bodily harm, our court has concluded that local school administrations have no affirmative substantive due process duty to protect students. (*Nabozny v. Podlesny,* 1996, pp. 458–459)

Questions for Discussion

1. How might one view this case and the court's decision from a justice perspective?
2. Was Matthew treated in a caring manner? Why or why not?
3. How might this case be viewed through the lens of critique?
4. What would the profession expect of Matthew's guidance counselor? Mr. Blauert? Principal Podlesny?
5. Through a best interests perspective, was Matthew afforded his rights or shown his responsibilities? In this respect, how might this situation have been handled differently? Better? Was Matthew afforded respect? Dignity? Why or why not?
6. What would you have done in this situation if you were Matthew's guidance counselor? Mr. Blauert? Principal Podlesny?

BILLINGS v. MADISON METROPOLITAN SCHOOL DISTRICT
259 F.3d 807 (7th Cir. 2001)

B.B. was a student at John Muir Elementary School in Madison, Wisconsin from kindergarten until the middle of third grade in the 1999–2000 school year. In the spring of 1999, the second-grade teachers at the school met several times to discuss third-grade class placements for their students for the following year.

The school district did not have a policy on student placement in elementary classes, so the teachers relied on a memo from the principal, John Burmaster, which stated, in part, "to the extent possible we should attempt to balance classes according to gender, ethnicity, academic abilities, and special needs while also considering the Parent Input sheet" (*Billings v. Madison Metropolitan School District,* 2001, p. 810).

The teachers, Sue Perry, Annie Keith, and Sue Berthouex, prepared an index card for each student to make the assignment of students easier. Each of these cards contained the student's academic data, such as reading and math levels, behavioral issues, special education requirements, as well as gender, neighborhood, and ethnicity. In creating the individual classes for the third grade, the teachers tried to reflect the overall third-grade population at John Muir. They used the academic information to create balanced classrooms with respect to high and low achievers and students with special needs. They considered ethnicity only to ensure that there were not disproportionate numbers of minority students in any one classroom. The teachers did not want any of the students isolated from friends in their own neighborhood and so took this into consideration as well.

Ms. Perry assigned B.B. to Ms. Zabel's class for the following year. (Ms. Perry shared teaching responsibilities with Ms. Mueller, who did not attend any of the placement meetings.) She based this decision on input from the parents, who wanted B.B. placed with a teacher with high academic expectations. Ms. Perry was also aware that B.B. had some negative interactions with special education students who were assigned to the other two classes, to be taught by Mary Bostrom and Lesley Wilke-Nadler.

Near the beginning of the 1999–2000 school year, Ms. Zabel divided her class into five groups. Two of the groups had six students and three of the groups had four students. In these latter groups of four, she indicated that she would put two African American students together. She did the same for Hispanic students. When asked why she did this, she replied, "I think in my education training sometimes we were told that African American students need a buddy, and sometimes it works well if they have someone else working with them because they view things in a global manner" (*Billings v. Madison Metropolitan School District,* 2001, p. 811).

Evidence presented at the hearing indicated that B.B. was the only student in her class from Wexford Ridge, a neighborhood where many African American students lived. The Billingses came to believe that B.B., who performed well academically, was placed in the class to be a role model for the other African

American students, who were all at the low achievement level. They cited a comment made by Principal Burmaster to Mrs. Billings, in which he said that he hoped B.B. could be a role model for other children.

The Billings parents claimed violations of the Wisconsin Constitution and the Equal Protection Clause of the United States Constitution. A federal district court granted summary judgment in favor of the school district. The federal court of appeals for the Seventh Circuit Court agreed with the district court that B.B. was not assigned to Ms. Zabel's class because of race, nor was she considered a role model for the other children. The appeals court contended that Ms. Perry made her decision based on two reasons, both of which were race-neutral. First, B.B.'s parents wanted her to have a teacher with high expectations, and Ms. Zabel fit that criterion. Second, the other two classrooms contained students with whom B.B. had had problems. Moreover, B.B.'s class did not have a disproportionate number of African American students as compared to the other classes.

There was also no evidence to support the contention that Ms. Perry ever saw B.B. as a role model for other students. This claim was based on Principal Burmaster's remark, "he hoped B.B. could be a role model for these other children" (*Billings v. Madison Metropolitan School District*, 2001, p. 813). This comment was made offhand following a disciplinary incident in B.B.'s class, and it was Ms. Perry, not the principal, who made the placement decision. As the court noted:

> Principal Burmaster's remark is ambiguous as to the children for whom he hoped that B.B. could be a role model; the Billings have provided no evidence justifying their assumption that the principal was referring only to African American students. Additionally, the principal's offhand remark is irrelevant to our review of the assignment process because it is undisputed that Principal Burmaster did not participate in making the classroom assignments. (*Billings v. Madison Metropolitan School District*, 2001, p. 813)

The appeals court also agreed with the lower court that the Billings parents failed to provide evidence to support their claim that B.B. was denied educational opportunities equal to those of White students. Where these two courts depart is on the Fourteenth Amendment Equal Protection claim relative to Mrs. Zabel's classroom seating arrangement. Ruling in favor of the Billingses on this claim, the Seventh Circuit Court observed that Ms. Zabel freely admitted to arranging minority students in her classroom in pairs. Even if Ms. Zabel had good intentions, her decision, nonetheless, was based purely on race. Here, the court points out that such racial classifications by government officials are highly suspect and likely illegal unless they are employed as an attempt to remedy past discrimination.

> This record provides no basis for justifying the racially based seating arrangement other than Ms. Zabel's reliance on a stereotypical notion that African American students "view things in a global manner." No evidence of record indicates that this arrangement was implemented to rectify past discriminatory conduct that had left its

effect on these students. On this record, without any justification other than Ms. Zabel's stereotypical notion as to how African American children learn, her action cannot be justified, and, consequently, summary judgment is inappropriate. It may be that, in further proceedings, Ms. Zabel will be able to explain in a more satisfactory manner the reasons for her adoption of the racially based buddy system seating plan. Perhaps her decision was based on her professional assessment that, because of past discriminatory practices, students in this particular school had difficulty in adjusting to a racially diverse educational environment. However, we cannot accept as adequate her conclusory explanation. We must decide the case on the record before us. (*Billings v. Madison Metropolitan School District*, 2001, p. 815)

Questions for Discussion

1. How might one view this case and the court's decision from a justice perspective?
2. Was B.B. treated in a caring manner? Why or why not?
3. How might this case be viewed through the lens of critique?
4. What would the profession expect of Ms. Zabel? Principal Burmaster?
5. Through a best interests perspective, was B.B. afforded her rights or shown her responsibilities? In this respect, how might this situation have been handled differently? Better? Was B.B. afforded respect? Dignity? Why or why not?
6. What would you have done in this situation if you were Ms. Zabel? Principal Burmaster?

SELMAN v. COBB COUNTY SCHOOL DISTRICT[1]
390 F. Supp. 2d 1286 (2005)

Since 1979, the Cobb County School District had maintained a policy, revised several times, which acknowledged a conflict between the scientific account of the origin of human species and the family teachings of a significant number of Cobb County residents. The policy directed the instructional program to respect these family teachings while preserving the constitutional principle of separation of church and state. In 1995, a more specific statement was issued. It prohibited school officials from compelling any student to study about the origin of human species. It also forbade the teaching of this topic in elementary and middle schools. The statement provided for electives and material to investigate theories of the origins of human species that would include, but not be limited to, creation theory. Any course including this topic was to be noted in course selection materials provided to students and parents.

---

[1]This opinion was appealed to the Eleventh Circuit Court, which heard oral arguments on December 15, 2005. As this book went to press, no decision had been rendered. Thus, readers are strongly advised to check on the status of the latest ruling.

Although the policy and statement made no reference to evolution, both implied that enough parents had beliefs conflicting with evolution to merit the district's actions. Even though the state curriculum mandated the teaching of evolution, it was common practice for textbook pages with material on evolution to be removed. In addition, teachers were asked not to discuss human evolution in courses required for graduation.

In the fall of 2001, the school district began the process of adopting new science textbooks. The textbook committee raised concerns that an adopted textbook would conflict with existing policy. Following a legal review of the issues, school administrators recommended revisions to the policy that would strengthen evolution instruction and bring the district into compliance with state curriculum requirements.

In accordance with school board regulations, parents could review and comment on the recommended textbooks. Only three parents reviewed the books, with only one criticizing the presentation of evolution without any mention of alternate theories involving a creator. Several other parents complained about the textbooks but did not submit official comment forms. One parent organized a petition containing 2,300 signatures of Cobb County residents. The petition requested the school board to "clearly identify presumptions and theories and distinguish them from fact" (*Selman v. Cobb County School District*, 2005, p. 1291). Legal counsel recommended the following language to be placed on a sticker to be placed in the textbooks: "This textbook contains material on evolution. Evolution is a theory, not a fact, regarding the origin of living thing[s]. This material should be approached with an open mind, studied carefully, and critically considered" (*Selman v. Cobb County School District*, 2005, p. 1295).

On March 28, 2002, the school board unanimously adopted the recommended textbooks with the condition that a sticker with the abovementioned information be placed in certain science textbooks. There were no minutes from school board meetings about any discussions regarding the sticker, nor did the school board issue any statement about the purpose of the sticker at the time of its adoption. A majority of the school board members stated that they did not intend the sticker to promote or benefit religion and that they were aware that the district policy was being revised to strengthen the teaching of evolution. In September 2002, Mr. Lindsay Tippins, chair of the school board, issued a statement that the sticker "was not intended to interject religion into science instruction but simply to make students aware that a scientific dispute exists" (*Selman v. Cobb County School District*, 2005, p. 1293).

Various school board members had several different reasons for deciding to adopt the sticker. Mr. Tippins believed that a scientific dispute regarding the origin of life existed; he wanted students to be able to critically consider information regarding evolution. Another member was concerned that the textbooks did not address the controversy from an evidentiary standpoint and wanted to facilitate open discussion in classes about issues of a scientific nature. Another member wanted the board to find a constitutional way to guide discussion in the classroom, encourage students to think critically, and get teachers to adhere to the state curriculum guidelines on the origin of species, which included only evolution. Still others saw the sticker as a notice to parents that evolution would be taught. A veteran educator on the board wanted the science classroom to be safe enough for students to express their different views. Two board members testified by affidavit (but not at the trial) that they wanted to promote tolerance and acceptance of a diversity of opinions.

The school board did not seek expert opinion on scientific theories of origin, nor did they conduct research outside of the board meetings before voting on the sticker. However, at the trial, George Stickel, the district's science curriculum supervisor, and Wes McCoy, a science teacher at the high school, joined by both a biology textbook coauthor and a university assistant professor of genetics and molecular biology, acknowledged: "Evolution is the dominant *scientific* theory regarding the origin of the diversity of life and is accepted by the majority of the scientific community" (*Selman v. Cobb County School District*, 2005, p. 1309).

Dr. McCoy, who opposed placing stickers in the textbooks, nevertheless proposed an alternative version of the sticker that the administration favored. It read:

> This textbook contains material on evolution, a scientific theory, or explanation, for the nature and diversity of living things. Evolution is accepted by the majority of scientists, but questioned by some. All scientific theories should be approached with an open mind, studied carefully and critically considered. (*Selman v. Cobb County School District*, 2005, p. 1295)

Even though this suggestion was made before the stickers were printed, the school board gave only minimal consideration to the alternative language because it was presented after the vote on the sticker. After the school board adopted the sticker, numerous citizens, organizations, churches, and academics contacted the members to both praise and express their dismay at the inclusion of the sticker in the textbooks.

Following the placement of the stickers in the textbooks, the school board revised its policy on the teaching of the origin of species. The revised policy recognized the controversy surrounding this subject and emphasized that related teaching should be done in a manner to promote tolerance and acceptance of a diversity of opinions, and to ensure neutrality toward religion. A revised regulation specified that theories of origin "shall be taught as defined within the Quality Core Curriculum (QCC)" (*Selman v. Cobb County School District*, 2005, p. 1296). It also cautioned teachers to set limits on discussions of theories of origin "in order to respectfully focus discussion on scientific subject matter" (*Selman v. Cobb County School District*, 2005, p. 1296), while at the same time recognizing that such instruction could conflict with some students' belief systems. "Under no circumstances should teachers use instruction to coerce students to adopt a particular religious belief or set of beliefs or to disavow a particular religious belief or set of beliefs" (*Selman v. Cobb County School District*, 2005, p. 1296).

In the 2 years after adopting the new science textbooks with the sticker, neither the district superintendent nor the school board members received any complaints about the teaching of religion or religious theories of origin in science classes.

Additionally, students had not mentioned religion as it relates to evolution any more frequently than before the sticker. One science teacher testified that the board's misuse of the word "theory" required him to spend more time trying to distinguish "fact" from "theory" for his students.

Nonetheless, the stickers alarmed some parents, who feared that they promoted a religious view of origin and questioned the science in the textbooks. One of the plaintiffs in this case, Jeffrey Selman, felt that because the stickers only singled out evolution, their intent was to disparage evolution and was, therefore, "obviously religious" (*Selman v. Cobb County School District,* 2005, p. 1297).

Jeffrey Selman, as well as several other parents, sued the school district and its board of education, claiming that the stickers violated the Establishment Clause of the First Amendment to the United States Constitution as well as Georgia's state constitution. The essence of their claim was that the stickers endorsed religion. A federal court for the northern district of Georgia found in favor of the parents and ordered that the stickers could not be disseminated in any form and that the stickers currently on textbooks must be removed.

In deciding the legality of the stickers, the court applied the *Lemon* test, a standard first articulated in the *Lemon v. Kurtzman* (1971) Supreme Court decision. Applied to the facts at hand, the test would first determine whether the sticker had a secular (nonreligious) purpose. Here, the court identified two purposes for the sticker, both of which it deemed secular. One purpose was that the sticker supported critical thinking about evolution, encouraging students to individually assess its merits. Next, it attempted to reduce the offensiveness of teaching this theory to parents and students with religious beliefs that were antithetical to the theory.

Where the constitutionality of the sticker fell short was on the second prong of the *Lemon* test. Here, the court examined whether the effect of the sticker was one of either support for or hostility toward religion. In making its determination, the court found that the purpose of the sticker went well beyond religious accommodation in that it showed preference toward the Christian fundamentalists and creationists who pushed for the disclaimer. Moreover, by stating that evolution was a mere theory rather than *the* dominant scientific theory that it is, the court downplayed the importance of this theory and in effect endorsed alternative theories such as creationism. In this respect, the federal district court decided:

> In sum, the Sticker in dispute violates the effects prong of the *Lemon* test and Justice O'Connor's endorsement test, which the Court has incorporated into its *Lemon* analysis. Adopted by the school board, funded by the money of taxpayers, and inserted by school personnel, the Sticker conveys an impermissible message of endorsement and tells some citizens that they are political outsiders while telling others that they are political insiders. Regardless of whether teachers comply with the Cobb County School District's regulation on theories of origin and regardless of the discussions that actually take place in the Cobb County science classrooms, the Sticker has already sent a message that the School Board agrees with the beliefs of

Christian fundamentalists and creationists. The School Board has effectively improperly entangled itself with religion by appearing to take a position. Therefore, the Sticker must be removed from all of the textbooks in which it has been placed. (*Selman v. Cobb County School District,* 2005, p. 1312)

Questions for Discussion

1. How might one view this case and the court's decision from a justice perspective?
2. Were Mr. Selman and the other concerned parents treated in a caring manner? Why or why not?
3. How might this case be viewed through the lens of critique?
4. What would the profession expect of the school board's chairman, Mr. Tippins? The administrators at the school? Mr. McCoy? Mr. Stickel, the district's science curriculum supervisor?
5. Through a best interests perspective, were the students afforded their rights or shown their responsibilities? In this respect, how might this situation have been handled differently? Better?
6. What would you have done in this situation if you were Mr. Tippins? Mr. McCoy? Mr. Stickel?

13

Governmental Immunity

Many of the cases discussed in this book are based on claims that students' constitutional rights have been violated. When students bring forth such complaints, they may also claim money damages for violation of their rights under the Civil Rights Act of 1871, 42 U.S.C. §1983. In such cases, plaintiffs must first prove that either their constitutional rights or their rights guaranteed by federal law have been violated. In addition, the persons who violated these rights must be government agents working in their official capacity. This category would include public school personnel, but would not apply to private or religious school officials. If plaintiffs' rights were not violated or if the persons depriving the plaintiffs of their rights are not government officials, then the plaintiff cannot receive money damages under §1983.

Even if there is a violation of a constitutional or federal right, plaintiffs may not be able to recover monetary damages. Over the years, federal courts have crafted a presumption that governmental officials are immune from such damages. Only if government officials accused of rights violations knew or should have known that such actions were illegal, may plaintiffs overcome this presumed immunity. This is a very high standard to prove. Often, courts look to whether previous decisions have clearly shown that similar actions were violations of individual rights. One rationale for requiring such a high standard is that schools and other government agencies are publicly supported and do not have "deep pockets." Accordingly, courts do not wish to tie educators' hands as they make day-to-day decisions, so they are very careful to give school authorities ample discretion and protect them from liability.

I present four cases that serve as illustrations of how far the courts will go in granting school officials immunity. Even when school officials are legally protected, these cases raise important ethical questions. For example, in *Thomas v.*

134

Roberts (2003), a teacher strip-searched an entire classroom of students for a missing $26. Although the court found this type of search to be illegal, school authorities were immune from liability. The court maintained that because there had been no laws or other cases showing that such actions were illegal, the school could not be held financially responsible for the damage occurring as a result of the strip searches.

Hasenfus v. LaJeunesse (1999) addresses the extent to which school authorities are legally responsible for students who commit suicide. In this case, a 14-year-old student failed at a suicide attempt, which took place at school, but was left permanently disabled. Shortly before the attempt, this student's teacher reprimanded her in front of the class and sent her alone to the locker room, ignoring the fact that the student was raped the year before, had been depressed, and was frequently teased by the other students because of the incident and her testimony in court. *Hasenfus* is representative of a litany of court opinions addressing student suicides, most of which have held school officials immune from liability. Fossey and Zirkel (2004), in their law review article detailing these cases, call attention to the role of ethics in administrative discretion.

> The conclusion is inescapable that the courts—both state and federal—are inhospitable to plaintiffs seeking to hold educators legally responsible for a student's suicide death. This conclusion does not mean that educators should ignore suicidal behavior by students. Rather, school policies and programs to reduce the tragedy of student suicide are more a matter of professional discretion and ethical imperative than a necessary precaution against litigation. (p. 439)

In another case, this one dealing with corporal punishment (*Garcia v. Miera,* 1987), a teacher held a 9-year-old female student upside down by her ankles while another teacher struck the student on the front of her leg with a split wooden paddle. Even though the child's parents ultimately prevailed, the victory was bittersweet. At the district court level, the majority declared that the school district was immune from monetary damages because this action did not "shock the conscience." The appeals court reversed this part of the lower court's decision, but only by a 3–2 vote. Even then, the majority sent the case back to be reheard at the trial court level and cautioned the parties that, despite their decision: "These claims may not survive the crucible of the trial" (*Garcia v. Miera,* 1987, p. 658).

Finally, in *Doe v. State of Hawaii Department of Education* (2003), a vice principal taped a student to a tree for misbehaving. The school official released the student when a fifth grader pointed out the impropriety of these actions. Here, the administrator was held liable in that there was a rights violation and the law was clearly established at the time of the incident.

Regardless of whether one believes that state-supported schools should have to literally pay for their transgressions, there is a deeper issue here when one considers the best interests model. Students clearly have rights to privacy and dignity, and school authorities have the obligation both to act responsibly and to teach students to assume responsibility. As Thimmig (1998) points out relative to teachers' immunity in strip searching cases:

> The United States Courts of Appeal are heading in a dangerous direction for both students and teachers. Students are taught that teachers do not have to accept responsibility for their actions and that constitutional rights are not to be taken seriously. Teachers, on the other hand, are given a sense of absolute authority over their students. (p. 1414)

Accordingly, Ingrassia (2004) agrees with this sentiment that school officials must be held responsible, especially in cases such as *Thomas v. Roberts,* which deal with mass strip searching of students. She suggests, however, that training programs be required so that school officials will know the law.

Conducting highly intrusive searches on entire groups of students for a relatively small amount of money, making examples of students who misbehave by humiliating them, as in the *Miera* and *Hawaii* cases, and blaming the victim, as in *Hasenfus,* shows disrespect toward those students and denies them their dignity as well as the opportunity to assume and accept responsibility. Perhaps even more importantly, these actions teach all students that disrespect toward others is acceptable behavior.

THOMAS v. ROBERTS
323 F.3d 950 (11th Cir. 2003)

Ms. Tracey Morgan was teaching fifth grade at the West Clayton Elementary School in Georgia in the fall of 1996. Many of the students in her class were poor and could not afford their own lunches. On the morning of October 31, a student in her class brought $26 in an envelope to class. The money was proceeds from a fund-raising project for a school trip. The student put the money on a table near the teacher's desk, after telling her that he had left it there. A few minutes later, the envelope and the money were missing. Ms. Morgan questioned the students about the whereabouts of the money.

Meanwhile, a male police officer, Zannie Billingslea, arrived at Ms. Morgan's room to begin a presentation on drug awareness as part of the Drug Abuse Resistance Education (DARE) program. Ms. Morgan left him in charge of the class while she removed the trash containers to a workroom to search for the money. At that point the assistant principal, R. G. Roberts, came into the workroom with another member of the staff. Ms. Morgan told her about the incident and requested permission to search the students for the money. Ms. Roberts, who was acting as principal that day, agreed to the search although she was not a party to it.

Back in the classroom, Officer Billingslea remained in the room while the teacher searched the students' desks, bookbags, purses, pockets and shoes in an attempt to locate the money. Billingslea suggested to Ms. Morgan that children, especially boys, sometimes wore two pairs of pants and they could have hidden the money in between the layers of clothing. Offering to assist with the search of the boys, he took groups of four to five boys at a time into the restroom and asked them to drop their pants. He demonstrated to the boys by lowering his own pants and underpants to his ankles. Some of the boys reported that he told them they would be taken to jail or suspended if they did not comply. Some of the boys lowered both their pants and their underpants and Officer Billingslea conducted a visual search of the underwear for the money.

Following the search of the boys, Ms. Morgan lined the girls up in the hall and escorted small groups of four to five to the bathroom, where she conducted the search. She asked the girls to lower their pants and lift their shirts or dresses. She also requested most of the girls to lift their brassieres and expose their breasts to prove that the money was not hidden there.

Officer Billingslea and Ms. Morgan also conducted searches of a boy and girl, respectively, who were not in the classroom when the money went missing. The boy was not Ms. Morgan's student and informed the officer of that fact. Nevertheless, he was subjected to a limited search. In contrast, three students were allowed to leave the classroom after the money went missing, and before the searches began, yet they were never questioned or searched. The searches did not turn up the missing money. The school day then proceeded as usual.

The following day, three sets of parents contacted Principal Ralph Matthews, who promised to investigate the matter. He asked the students in question to write an account of the incident and questioned Ms. Morgan. The school district conducted its own investigation into the allegations. Their investigator interviewed Ms. Morgan, Ms. Roberts, and Mr. Matthews and read the students' written statements. The district found that there had been no strip search. The Clayton County Police Department conducted an internal investigation of Officer Billingslea, who received a written reprimand and a loss of a pay increase.

The parents brought suit in federal district court claiming violation of their children's Fourth Amendment rights and monetary damages under 42 U.S.C. §1983. The district court granted summary judgment in favor of the school district. The federal Court of Appeals for the Eleventh Circuit ruled that even though school officials violated students' Fourth Amendment rights to be free from unreasonable searches and seizures, they were immune from monetary damages in that existing case law did not "give a school official fair, much less clear, warning that the search conducted here would be unlawful. Furthermore, the search did not rise to a level so egregious as to alert the school officials that such conduct is unconstitutional...." (*Thomas v. Roberts,* 2003, p. 956).[1]

---

[1]This case had been appealed to the U.S. Supreme Court, which sent it back to the Eleventh Circuit Court of Appeals to review in light of a new decision on another related case. These quotes are from the most recent Eleventh Circuit decision.

Questions for Discussion

1. How might one view this case and the court's decision from a justice perspective?
2. Were the students treated in a caring manner? Why or why not?
3. How might this case be viewed through the lens of critique?
4. What would the profession expect of Ms. Morgan? Principal Matthews? Officer Billingslea?
5. Through a best interests perspective, were these students afforded their rights or shown their responsibilities? In this respect, how might this situation have been handled differently? Better? Were the students afforded respect? Dignity? Why or why not?
6. What would you have done in this situation if you were Ms. Morgan? Principal Matthews? Officer Billingslea?

HASENFUS v. LAJEUNESSE
175 F.3d 68 (1st Cir. 1999)

In spring 1996, Jamie Hasenfus was a 14-year old eighth-grade student at Winthrop Middle School in Maine. On May 2, Jamie's class was outside on the softball field for their physical education period. Jamie's teacher, Carlo Kempton, reprimanded Jamie in front of the class and told her to go back to the locker room inside the school. The locker room was unsupervised at the time. When she returned to the locker room, Jamie attempted to commit suicide by hanging herself. Jamie's classmates found her and called for emergency help. Jamie was rushed to the hospital, where she remained for several weeks, initially in a coma. She survived the suicide attempt, but was left permanently impaired.

Jamie had been raped the previous year, when she was 13 years old. Testifying in court against the rapist was a further traumatizing experience for her. Officials at the Winthrop Middle School were aware of this past experience. In fact, the school nurse, Jackie Kempton (the teacher's wife), and a guidance counselor had each provided Jamie with counseling support. Fellow students harassed Jamie about the incident and her decision to testify. Indeed, on the day of the suicide attempt, some students were harassing her again and Jamie had lashed out verbally. Mr. Kempton sent her into the school because of her outburst. Jamie's parents felt that Mr. Kempton knew or should have known about Jamie's past and that she was depressed. They believed that he should not, therefore, have allowed Jamie to be alone and unsupervised.

In the 3 months leading up to May 2, seven other Winthrop students had attempted suicide. Several of these attempts had taken place either on school property or at school events. Jamie knew at least two of these students. Her parents believed that the school stood by and did nothing during the rash of suicide attempts.

Jamie's parents sued the town, the school board, the superintendent, the principal, and the teacher for damages under 42 U.S.C. §1983 due to violations of substantive due process under the U.S. Constitution and under state law pertaining to tort negligence and negligent infliction of emotional distress. They claimed that the school should have done more to counter the epidemic of attempted suicides (e.g., by offering counseling or monitoring programs and communicating with the parent community) and specifically could have done more to prevent Jamie's suicide attempt, citing their failure to discover her in a timely fashion and their failure to act reasonably when they did find her. They alleged wrongful acts on the part of Jamie's teacher, Mr. Kempton, in that he reprimanded Jamie in front of her classmates and sent her alone to be alone in the locker room. A federal district court ruled that the Hasenfus parents had failed to state a claim under § 1983. The parents appealed.

The First Circuit Federal Court of Appeals found no grounds to support a claim of negligence on the part of any school officials and also asserted that school officials have no constitutional duty to protect students. As to this duty, the court explained:

> The federal courts have no general authority to decide when school administrators should introduce suicide prevention programs, or whether an unruly or upset school child should be sent out of class, or what should be said to other parents about a tragic incident at school. Substantive due process is not a license for judges to supersede the decisions of local officials and elected legislators on such matters. (*Hasenfus v. LaJeunesse,* 1999, p. 74)

Questions for Discussion

1. How might one view this case and the court's decision from a justice perspective?
2. Was Jamie treated in a caring manner? In this respect, was there a better way for school officials to handle this matter? If so, what was it?
3. How might this case be viewed through the lens of critique?
4. What would the profession expect of Carlo Kempton? Jackie Kempton? Jamie's guidance counselor?
5. Through a best interests perspective, was Jamie afforded her rights? Was Jamie afforded respect? Dignity? Why or why not?
6. What would you have done in this situation if you were Mr. Kempton? Jamie's guidance counselor? The school nurse?

GARCIA v. MIERA
817 F.2d 650 (10th Cir. 1987)

Teresa Garcia, a third-grade student at Penasco (New Mexico) Elementary School, was called to the school principal's office after an altercation with a fellow student. The teacher reported that Teresa had hit a boy in her class after the boy had kicked her. The principal, Mrs. Miera, told Garcia that as part of the punishment for hitting, she would be paddled. Nine-year-old Teresa vehemently resisted, telling Miera that her father had said, "Mrs. Miera had better shape up." The comment attributed to Mr. Garcia was ill received by Mrs. Miera and later indicated on a disciplinary form as reason why corporal punishment was given to Teresa that day.

After Teresa failed to comply with Miera's request that she go to her chair to be paddled, Miera sought help. Teacher, J. D. Sanchez was called in to provide assistance. At Miera's request, Sanchez picked up Teresa and held her upside down by her ankles while Miera hit her five times on her thighs with a split wooden paddle. When Teresa returned to her classroom, her classroom teacher noticed that her leg was bleeding through her pants. The teacher took Teresa into the restroom and upon examination discovered a 2-inch cut on her leg. The cut was severe enough to leave a permanent scar. This event took place in February 1982.

After this incident, Teresa's parents requested that Mrs. Miera call them to obtain their permission before paddling Teresa again. In May, however, Teresa was called to the principal's office after claiming that she had seen a teacher kiss a student's father on the school bus during a class trip. Teresa further claimed that she knew the father had sent love letters to the teacher on more than one occasion through his son. Miera decided to punish Teresa for expressing her observations, even though it was later revealed that the teacher and parent were engaged in a relationship.

This time Teresa's punishment was to be two hits on the buttocks with a paddle. Once again, Teresa refused punishment. Miera called in Edward Leyba, an administrative associate, to assist with the paddling. Leyba was charged with pushing Teresa toward the chair over which she was to bend to receive three more paddles. When Leyba pushed Teresa, a struggle ensued, during which time Teresa hit her back on Miera's chair. As per her parents' request, Teresa asked Miera to contact her mother. Miera refused. Teresa stopped struggling and Mrs. Miera administered the three remaining blows. Teresa's back hurt for several weeks and her buttocks were bruised extensively.

When Teresa's parents brought her for medical treatment, both a doctor and nurse noted the severity of the bruises. Photographs were taken after the paddling that showed the extent of the injury. After the second beating, the Garcias secured an attorney who filed suit in federal court, claiming that the punishment Miera meted out to Teresa denied the child due process in violation of the United States Constitution. The Garcias also filed a claim for monetary damages under 42 U.S.C. §1983 for violation of Teresa's constitutional rights. The federal district court hearing this case granted summary judgment in favor of the school district.

The Garcias appealed to the Tenth Circuit Court. In order to violate substantive due process, the punishment must be excessive, so much so that it "shocks the conscience" in that the force is "brutal" or "offensive to human dignity" (*Garcia v. Miera,* 1987, p. 654, citing *Rochin v. California,* 1952, pp. 172–174). Reversing the summary judgment, the appeals court remanded the case to the lower court for further proceedings. In making this determination, the appeals court concluded:

The threshold for recovery on the constitutional tort for excessive corporal punishment is high. But the allegations with respect to the first beating, that this nine-year-old girl was held up by her ankles and hit several times with a board of substantial size on the front of her legs until they bled—supported by evidence of a permanent scar—are sufficient. The allegations with respect to the second beating, that the punishment was severe enough to cause pain for three weeks—supported by pictures of the injured buttocks, an affidavit from an examining doctor that in his long experience he had not seen bruises like that from routine spankings, and an affidavit from an examining nurse that if a child had received this type of injury at home she would have reported it as child abuse—are also sufficient. These claims may not survive the crucible of the trial, but they overcome defendant's motion for summary judgment. (*Garcia v. Miera,* 1987, p. 658)

Questions for Discussion

1. How might one view this case and the court's decision from a justice perspective?
2. Was Teresa treated in a caring manner? Why or why not?
3. How might this case be viewed through the lens of critique?
4. What would the profession expect of Principal Miera? Mr. Leyba?
5. Through a best interests perspective, was Teresa afforded her rights or shown her responsibilities? In this respect, how might this situation have been handled differently? Better? Was Teresa afforded respect? Dignity? Why or why not?
6. What would you have done in this situation if you were Principal Miera? Mr. Leyba?

DOE v. STATE OF HAWAII DEPARTMENT OF EDUCATION
334 F. 3d 906 (9th Cir. 2003)

In February 1998, Plaintiff John Doe was an 8-year-old second grader at Pukalani Elementary School. Doe's teacher sent him to the vice principal, David Keala, to be disciplined for fighting, along with some other boys. Doe refused to stand still with his nose against the wall for his time-out punishment. Keala threatened to take Doe outside and tape him to a nearby tree if he did not stand still. Doe still kept "horsing around," so Keala took him outside and taped his head to a tree using 1-inch wide masking tape.

There was no indication that John Doe was fighting or posing a danger to others. He remained taped to the tree for about 5 minutes until a fifth-grade girl told Mr. Keala that she did not think he should be doing that. The vice principal then instructed the girl to remove the tape.

The district court denied the Mr. Keala's motion for summary judgment on §1983 claims of qualified immunity because there was enough evidence to conclude that Keala's conduct violated the Fourth Amendment. Hearing this case, the Ninth Circuit Court of Appeals agreed that Mr. Keala's actions constituted a seizure under the Fourth Amendment. For purposes of this case, "a seizure occurs when there is a restraint on liberty to the degree that a reasonable person would not feel free to leave" (*Doe v. State of Hawaii Department of Education*, 2003, p. 909. Citing *United States v. Summers*, 2001, p. 686).

In determining whether Vice Principal Keala's actions were entitled to qualified immunity, the court noted: "A public official is not entitled to qualified immunity if his conduct violates 'clearly established constitutional rights of which a reasonable person would have known'" (*Doe v. State of Hawaii Department of Education*, 2003, p. 908, citing *P. B. v. Koch*, 1996, p. 1301, and *Harlow v. Fitzgerald*, 1982, p. 818). Applying this standard, the appeals court first examined whether there had been a Fourth Amendment violation. According to *N.J. v. T.L.O.* (1985), a seizure must be justified at its inception and not excessively intrusive in light of the nature of the infraction and the age and gender of the child. Determining that this seizure was illegal, the court reasoned:

> At the time that Keala taped him to the tree, Doe's only offense had been "horsing around" and refusing to stand still. There is no indication that Doe was fighting or that he posed a danger to other students. Doe was eight years old. Taping his head to a tree for five minutes was so intrusive that a fifth grader observed it was inappropriate. There is sufficient evidence for a fact finder to conclude that Keala's conduct was objectively unreasonable in violation of the Fourth Amendment. (*Doe v. State of Hawaii Department of Education*, 2003, pp. 909–910)

Accordingly, the court determined that the school official's actions were excessive. Previous court decisions support the conclusion that there is clearly established law, which indicates that use of excessive force in a seizure is unconstitutional. Thus, Vice Principal Keala was not granted qualified immunity for his actions.

Questions for Discussion

1. How might one view this case and the court's decision from a justice perspective?
2. Was John Doe treated in a caring manner? Why or why not?
3. How might this case be viewed through the lens of critique?
4. What would the profession expect of Vice Principal Keala?
5. Through a best interests perspective, was John Doe afforded his rights or shown his responsibilities? In this respect, how might this situation have been handled differently? Better? Was John afforded respect? Dignity? Why or why not?
6. What would you have done in this situation if you were Vice Principal Keala?

14

Equity, Equality, and Equal Protection

As early as 1954, the United States Supreme Court, in *Brown v. Board of Education* (1954), recognized the importance of education with these words:

> Education is perhaps the most important function of state and local governments. Compulsory school attendance laws and the great expenditures for education both demonstrate our recognition of the importance of education to our democratic society. It is required in the performance of our most basic public responsibilities, even service in the armed forces. It is the very foundation of good citizenship. Today it is a principal instrument in awakening the child to cultural values, in preparing him for later professional training, and in helping him to adjust normally to his environment. In these days, it is doubtful that any child may reasonably be expected to succeed in life if he is denied the opportunity of an education. (p. 493)

In striving for equality, sometimes we deprive the very students who need the most help. This chapter focuses on the tension between issues of equality (treating everyone alike) and issues of equity (understanding that some individuals need more assistance than others). This tension is accentuated when two or more very deserving groups must compete against each other for scarce resources.

Timothy W. v. Rochester School District (1989) involves a multiply handicapped and profoundly mentally retarded student who suffers from complex developmental disabilities, spastic quadriplegia, cerebral palsy, seizure disorder, and cortical blindness. In this case, the school wanted to deny Timothy access, claiming that he could not benefit from educational services. The court ruled that the law mandates the education of all children with disabilities and does not require that the child demonstrate "benefit." This case was particularly controversial

143

because of the high expenses it incurred for the school district. It calls into question the tension between serving students with severe disabilities and a district's responsibilities to other types of disadvantaged students when budgets are tight.

In *Kadrmas v. Dickinson Public Schools* (1988), the U.S. Supreme Court found that a school district, in assessing a fee to an indigent child who lived 16 miles from the nearest school, did not deny that student equal protection because the statute did not discriminate against a suspect class such as race or ethnicity. According to the U.S. Supreme Court, the government needs a compelling state interest to pass laws that discriminate on the basis of race or ethnicity. To discriminate against the poor, only a rational basis is needed. Although a number of commentators (e.g., Bitensky, 1992; Smith, 1997) have argued that poverty should be considered at a higher level of scrutiny, the High Court has yet to agree. The Court would also apply a higher standard of review if education was a fundamental right, but as mentioned early on in this book, this is not the case.

Aware of research indicating that African American males learn better in single gender classrooms, the school district of Detroit, Michigan, established a school solely for young, Black men. A Michigan court, in *Garrett v. Board of Education of the School District of Detroit* (1991) determined that establishing this school constituted gender discrimination in that it was an all-male school. Yet, as Green and Mead (2004) note some 20 years later, a number of states support the establishment of single-gender schools, many of which are charter schools. Focusing on equity issues, these authors caution us that charter schools need to adhere to legal constrictions the same as other public schools in that there must be a justification for the school to serve only one gender, and the benefits for that particular sex must be comparable to benefits provided to the opposite sex.

Providing another twist to the gender equity argument, Salomone (2003) cites both legal and social science research to focus on the individual rights and needs of students, asserting that there are times when students of each gender would clearly benefit from attending a single-sex school. Her conclusions frame the equity argument this way:

> Over the past three decades, the equity ideal has come to mean not just "same is equal" but sometimes "different is equal" and even "more is equal" when applied to various groups, including the economically and educationally disadvantaged, linguistic minorities, and the disabled. The ultimate goal has been to develop each student's full potential by initially leveling the playing field to accommodate individual needs. Why should gender be any different? Girls and boys appear largely the same at the core, but also slightly different within a narrow range at the margins, while some within each group depart from the norm. (p. 244)

Finally, in *Taxman v. Board of Education of the Township of Piscataway* (1996), we turn to an important personnel issue related to equity and equality. In this case, school authorities used race as a factor in deciding to lay off one of two teachers. The teachers had equal seniority and were equally qualified. The district chose to lay off Ms. Taxman, the White teacher, instead of Ms. Williams, the Black teacher, because there were no other Black teachers in the business department where the cut was taking place even though the district had a racially diverse faculty. The Supreme Court agreed to review this case, however the parties settled before the High Court had time to hear the appeal. This was a particularly controversial case at the time, in part because affirmative action advocates pushed for a settlement, believing that if the High Court heard the case, the justices might use this opportunity to strike down affirmative action policies in employment situations.

TIMOTHY W. v. ROCHESTER SCHOOL DISTRICT
875 F.2d 954 (1st Cir. 1989)

Born prematurely in 1975 in Rochester, New Hampshire, Timothy W. had numerous problems that left him severely handicapped and profoundly mentally retarded. He also suffered from blindness, a seizure disorder, cerebral palsy, and spastic quadriplegia. Timothy's family sought treatment for him at an early age. Before he was 5, he received limited services from the Rochester Child Development Center.

In 1980, when it was time to enroll Timothy in school, he was denied admission. The Rochester School District refused to provide him with educational services. The officials at the school district determined that Timothy was not entitled to educational services because he was not considered educationally handicapped. The school district explained this as meaning that the nature of Timothy's handicap was so "severe" as to make him unable to benefit from any kind of educational program.

The decision to deny the boy services took place after the district held a determination meeting. During this meeting, several medical professionals, as well as Timothy's mother, testified that he was able to benefit from an educational program of the type that Rochester was able to provide. However, one medical professional present at the meeting testified that there was no service available that would be of benefit to Timothy.

In 1982, during a review of the Rochester School District's special education program, the New Hampshire Department of Education found the district to be noncompliant, because of their use of "capable of benefiting" as a criterion for providing educational services. In response, 1 year later, the school district met to consider Timothy's case. The district heard the testimony of various medical professionals, including those who worked closely with Timothy. These professionals confirmed that Timothy had made progress in recent years, and they gave recommendations as to what they believed would be a suitable educational program. Once again, the school district denied services.

In 1984, Timothy's attorney contacted the school district, and as a result, the placement team met to discuss the case. Additional expert testimony was gathered, and suggestions were again made. The placement team followed the ideas offered and recommended that an education program for Timothy begin at the Rochester Child Development Center. Such a program would have incurred considerable expense to the school district. The school board rejected the placement team's findings, and the district sought more information including both an additional neurological evaluation and a CAT scan. Timothy's mother refused the district's requests.

Shortly thereafter, Timothy's attorney requested, through a complaint to the New Hampshire Department of Education, that an educational program for Timothy start without further delay. By October of 1984, the Department of Education ordered the school district to immediately place Timothy in an educational program. The school district refused. District officials once again determined during a meeting on November 8, 1984, that Timothy was ineligible for special education services.

A little over a week later, Timothy's attorney filed suit in federal court, alleging that Timothy's rights under the federal Education for All Handicapped Children Act (EAHCA; 1975) and New Hampshire state law had been violated. The suit also alleged that Timothy was denied his right to Equal Protection and Due Process as guaranteed by the Fourteenth Amendment to the United States Constitution.

Timothy's mother wanted the school district to be ordered to provide Timothy with educational services immediately. She also sought $175,000 in monetary damages. Reviewing the federal EAHCA and New Hampshire law, a federal district court determined that the school district was not bound to provide Timothy W. with special education services because the student was not capable of benefiting from these services.

Timothy's parents appealed. Focusing on the interpretation of the EAHCA, the First Circuit Court of Appeals ruled in favor of Timothy. In making its determination, the court noted that the legislative history of the EAHCA not only guarantees services for students with disabilities, but gives priority to those with the most severe disabilities. Furthermore, a benefit/eligibility test is not necessary to determining services. In its concluding remarks, the court noted:

> The statutory language of the Act, its legislative history, and the case law construing it, mandate that all handicapped children, regardless of the severity of their handicap, are entitled to a public education. The district court erred in requiring a benefit/eligibility test as a prerequisite to implicating the Act. School districts cannot avoid the provisions of the Act by returning to the practices that were widespread prior to the Act's passage, and which indeed were the impetus for the Act's passage, of unilaterally excluding certain handicapped children from a public education on the ground that they are uneducable.

> The law explicitly recognizes that education for the severely handicapped is to be broadly defined, to include not only traditional academic skills, but also basic functional life skills, and that educational methodologies in these areas are not static,

but are constantly evolving and improving. It is the school district's responsibility to avail itself of these new approaches in providing an education program geared to each child's individual needs. The only question for the school district to determine, in conjunction with the child's parents, is what constitutes an appropriate Individualized Education Program (IEP) for the handicapped child. We emphasize that the phrase "appropriate individualized education program" cannot be interpreted, as the school district has done, to mean "no educational program." (*Timothy W. v. Rochester School District,* 1989, pp. 972–973)

Questions for Discussion

1. How might one view this case and the court's decision from a justice perspective?
2. Was Timothy treated in a caring manner? Why or why not?
3. How might this case be viewed through the lens of critique?
4. What would the profession expect of the Rochester school officials?
5. Through a best interests perspective, was Timothy afforded his rights or shown his responsibilities? In this respect, how might this situation have been handled differently? Better? Was Timothy afforded respect? Dignity? Why or why not?
6. What would you have done in this situation if you were an official at the Rochester schools?

KADRMAS v. DICKINSON PUBLIC SCHOOLS
487 U.S. 450 (1988)

In North Dakota, the population is sparse and widespread, making the delivery of services such as school bus transportation difficult. Since 1947, the state legislature has encouraged school districts to consolidate or align themselves into larger districts so that education services can be provided in a more cost-effective manner. The Dickinson Public School District is located in a more populous area. Therefore, the district chose not to reorganize. Prior to 1973, bus transportation in the district was free, although there was often a considerable distance from the bus stop to students' homes. Since 1973, the district has been charging a fee for door-to-door bus service for its students. In 1979, the state enacted a statute allowing the collection of fees for bus service, although most districts in the state provide bus service at no cost to students or their families.

In 1985, Mrs. Kadrmas lived with her husband, her daughter Sarita, and two preschool children, about 16 miles from Sarita's school. There was no dispute that the Kadrmas family was indigent at the time of the trial. The family's annual income was at or near the poverty line, and the family was heavily in debt, owing a total of $13,000. The fee for bus service for Sarita was $97 annually, approximately

11% of the actual cost of transportation. The Kadrmas family had agreed to pay the fee until 1985, when they fell behind in paying their bills. They refused to agree to the busing fee in 1985. Consequently, the bus no longer stopped at the Kadrmas home and they arranged instead to have Sarita transported to school privately. The cost for this private transportation was in excess of $1,000 a year.

In September of 1985, Mrs. Kadrmas filed a complaint with the state court to try to have the school district prevented from charging the bus fee. She was unsuccessful. In the spring of 1987, Mrs. Kadrmas signed a bus service contract for the remainder of that school year and paid part of the fee. Later she signed another contract for the 1987 school year, and paid about half of the fee. Sarita began taking the bus again in the spring of 1987.

Mrs. Kadrmas brought suit in state court, claiming that North Dakota's school bus fee statute violated her rights and that of her child's under the Equal Protection Clause of the Fourteenth Amendment. Both a North Dakota state court and the North Dakota Supreme Court dismissed Mrs. Kadrmas' claim. Mrs. Kadrmas appealed to the U.S. Supreme Court. Rendering its decision in favor of the school district, Justice O'Connor, speaking for the majority, reasoned:

> The Kadrmas family could and did find a private alternative to the public school bus service for which Dickinson charged a fee. That alternative was more expensive, to be sure, and we have no reason to doubt that genuine hardships were endured by the Kadrmas family when Sarita was denied access to the bus. Such facts, however, do not imply that the Equal Protection Clause has been violated....

> Applying the appropriate test—under which a statute is upheld if it bears a rational relation to a legitimate government objective—we think it is quite clear that a State's decision to allow local school boards the option of charging patrons a user fee for bus service is constitutionally permissible. The Constitution does not require that such service be provided at all, and it is difficult to imagine why choosing to offer the service should entail a constitutional obligation to offer it for free. No one denies that encouraging local school districts to provide school bus service is a legitimate state purpose or that such encouragement would be undermined by a rule requiring that general revenues be used to subsidize an optional service that will benefit a minority of the district's families. It is manifestly rational for the State to refrain from undermining its legitimate objective with such a rule....

> In sum, the statute challenged in this case discriminates against no suspect class and interferes with no fundamental right. Appellants have failed to carry the heavy burden of demonstrating that the statute is arbitrary and irrational. The Supreme Court of North Dakota correctly concluded that the statute does not violate the Equal Protection Clause of the Fourteenth Amendment.... (*Kadrmas v. Dickinson Public Schools,* 1988, pp. 461–465)

Justice Marshall, joined by Justice Brennan, wrote a strong dissenting opinion, noting that the majority has misconstrued the spirit of the Equal Protection Clause of the Fourteenth Amendment.

Today, the Court continues the retreat from the promise of equal educational opportunity by holding that a school district's refusal to allow an indigent child who lives 16 miles from the nearest school to use a school-bus service without paying a fee does not violate the Fourteenth Amendment's Equal Protection Clause.... I do not believe that this Court should sanction discrimination against the poor with respect to "perhaps the most important function of state and local governments...." [Citing *Brown v. Board of Education,* 1954, p. 491]. This case involves state action that places a special burden on poor families in their pursuit of education. Children living far from school can receive a public education only if they have access to transportation; as the state court noted in this case, "a child must reach the schoolhouse door as a prerequisite to receiving the educational opportunity offered therein" [Citing *Lane v. Wilson,* 1939, p. 275].

Indeed, for children in Sarita's position, imposing a fee for transportation is no different in practical effect from imposing a fee directly for education. Moreover, the fee involved in this case discriminated against Sarita's family because it necessarily fell more heavily upon the poor than upon wealthier members of the community.... (*Kadrmas v. Dickinson Public Schools,* 1988, pp. 466–469)

Citing *Plyler v. Doe* (1982), Justice Marshall maintained that the Fourteenth Amendment was intended "to abolish caste legislation" and that this intent is frustrated when the state takes action that tends to "entrap the poor and create a permanent underclass" (*Kadrmas v. Dickinson Public Schools,* 1988, p. 469). Thus, such actions should be subjected to exacting scrutiny.

A statute that erects special obstacles to education in the path of the poor naturally tends to consign such persons to their current disadvantaged status. By denying equal opportunity to exactly those who need it most, the law not only militates against the ability of each poor child to advance herself or himself, but also increases the likelihood of the creation of a discrete and permanent underclass. Such a statute is difficult to reconcile with the framework of equality embodied in the Equal Protection Clause....

The Court fails in its constitutional duties when it refuses, as it does today, to make even the effort to see. For the poor, education is often the only route by which to become full participants in our society. In allowing a State to burden the access of poor persons to an education, the Court denies equal opportunity and discourages hope. I do not believe the Equal Protection Clause countenances such a result. (*Kadrmas v. Dickinson Public Schools,* 1988, pp. 466–471)

Questions for Discussion

1. How might one view this case and the court's decision from a justice perspective?
2. Was Sarita treated in a caring manner? Why or why not?
3. How might this case be viewed through the lens of critique?

4. What would the profession expect of the Dickinson school officials?

5. Through a best interests perspective, was Sarita afforded her rights? In this respect, how might this situation have been handled differently? Better? Was Sarita afforded respect? Dignity? Why or why not?

6. What would you have done in this situation if you were officials at the Dickinson Public Schools?

GARRETT v. BOARD OF EDUCATION OF THE SCHOOL DISTRICT OF DETROIT
775 F. Supp. 1004 (E.D. Mich. 1991)[1]

On August 26, 1991, the School District of the City of Detroit, Michigan, planned to open three male-only academies, housing approximately 250 boys. The schools were to serve students from kindergarten to fifth grade, with Grade 6 though Grade 8 to open in the following few years. At the time of the suit, the district had spent $454,000 on the project. The students selected to attend the schools would come from a mix of achievement levels with high-needs "at-risk" students making up approximately one third of the population. In general, students were not assigned to any particular school within the district's 251 schools. Participation in the academy program was also to be voluntary.

The curriculum and structure of the school day would differ from that of traditional schools. The curriculum was described as pluralistic, with an Afro-centric focus and an emphasis on male responsibility. One class, called "Rites of Passage," would teach that males need to have a vision and a plan for life, as well as learn how to manage their emotions. Males, it said, need to "acquire skills and knowledge to overcome life's obstacles." Mentors and counselors would be available to assist students in acquiring these objectives. The program called for Saturday classes, an extended instructional day, and school uniforms.

The school district's rationale for such schools was to address high rates of unemployment, student dropout, and homicide among urban males. School officials felt that the traditional coeducational school setting had failed to improve educational performance in males, thereby contributing to these social problems. Females' achievement levels, on the other hand, did not seem to be adversely affected under the existing curriculum. The school district had observed some increased levels of achievement and fewer behavior issues in two experimental, but smaller scale, programs running within larger schools. Their plan with this larger experiment was to learn what type of curriculum and teacher training was most helpful for these male students and then use this information for the benefit of all students.

The parents of girls enrolled in the Detroit Public Schools challenged these academies on behalf of themselves and their daughters, contending that the goals of

---

[1] It should be noted that Shawn Garret and her 4-year-old daughter voluntarily withdrew from the suit, citing harassment from the community as the reason.

the school do not require a male-only atmosphere to succeed, that the problems facing the target male population are ones that face all children and adolescents, both male and female, and that there was also no equivalent school for females. Finally, although the schools' stated goal was to address social problems facing urban male youth, this "at-risk" population made up only one third of the school.

The federal district court for the Eastern District of Michigan granted the girls and their parents a preliminary injunction to stop the program. In rendering its decision, the court first looked at the likelihood of success that the girls might have in winning such a case. Here, claims included violation of (a) equal protection as guaranteed under federal and state constitutions; (b) Title IX (Education Act Amendments, 1972), which prohibits gender discrimination; (c) the Equal Educational Opportunities Act (EEOA), which prohibits assignment of students outside of neighborhood schools if the reassignment results in a greater degree of segregation on the basis of a number of factors including sex; and (d) Michigan's state code, which prohibits same-sex schools. The court found likely violations on all these counts and determined that no substantial harm would result if it prevented the operation of an unconstitutional school. Concluding with this statement as to its decision and the public interest, the court determined:

> Plaintiffs [the girls and their parents] argue that the public interest is better served by preventing the opening of an unconstitutional educational facility. Defendant [school district] argues the Academies seek a bona fide public good to the detriment of no one. Defendant further contends that the creation of the Academies is substantially related to the important governmental interest of the Detroit Public Schools in obtaining information directed toward meeting the special educational needs of inner-city males. This "pilot setting" affords the public schools the opportunity to evaluate the effectiveness of various curricula and other programs in meeting the educational needs of males ... This Court views the purpose for which the Academies came into being as an important one. It acknowledges the status of urban males as an "endangered species." The purpose, however, is insufficient to override the rights of females to equal opportunities. (*Garrett v. Board of Education of the School District of Detroit*, 1991, p. 1014)

Questions for Discussion

1. How might one view this case and the court's decision from a justice perspective?
2. How would one with an ethic of care approach this issue?
3. How might this case be viewed through the lens of critique?
4. What would the profession expect of Detroit school officials? Teachers working in the academy?
5. Through a best interests perspective, what does this case say about rights and responsibilities? About respect? About dignity?

6. What would you have done in this situation if you were the Detroit school officials?

TAXMAN v. BOARD OF EDUCATION OF THE TOWNSHIP OF PISCATAWAY
91 F. 3d 1547 (3rd Cir. 1996)

In 1980, Sharon Taxman was hired as a teacher in the Business Department at Piscataway (New Jersey) High School. In 1989, the Piscataway School Board acted on a recommendation by the Superintendent of Schools to reduce the teaching staff in the Business Department by one teacher. Based on New Jersey statutes regarding the dismissal of teachers, the school board's decision essentially came down to two choices, Taxman or Debra Williams. Ms. Williams, who is Black, was hired the same day in 1980 as Ms. Taxman, who is White. In addition, Ms. Williams was the only minority faculty member in the Business Department at the high school. The state statutes were so stringent that they essentially took away discretion from local school boards to choose between employees for layoffs, except where there was an exact tie in seniority between two employees.

The Superintendent of Schools, Burton Edelchick, recommended that the District's affirmative action plan be invoked in order to settle the dispute. While he believed that Taxman and Williams were equally qualified and tied in seniority, the school board should invoke the affirmative action plan to keep Williams because Williams was the only Black teacher in the Department. The board's affirmative action policy, however, did not provide a remedy in regard to the district's problem. Black teachers were neither underrepresented nor underutilized in the district. Further, statistics showed that the percentage of Black teachers employed by the district was at a higher rate than the percentage of Blacks in the available work force.

Theodore Kruse, the School Board President, stated that while debating the decision, the board considered the affirmative action policy to be applicable here because the community is "quite diverse" and there was value in the students seeing "in the various employment roles a wide range of background and that it was also valuable to the work force and in particular teaching staff that ... they see that in each other" (*Taxman v. Board of Education of the Township of Piscataway,* 1996, pp. 1551–1552). In a disposition, Kruse also stated that the students would have a clear message from the school board that the teachers and staff remain culturally diverse so that when the students come into contact with the faculty, "they are more aware, more tolerant, more accepting and more understanding of people of all backgrounds."

In the end, the school board unanimously voted to retain Williams in accordance with the affirmative action policy. Ultimately, Taxman filed legal claims under both Title VII (Civil Rights Act, 1964) and the New Jersey Law Against Discrimination (NJLAD, 1945). The New Jersey district court held the school board liable under both statutes for discrimination on the basis of race. Prior to the trial court assessing damages, Taxman was rehired at the high school due to the retirement of another teacher. The court awarded Taxman $134,014.62 for back pay, fringe benefits, and prejudgment interest under Title VII. An additional $10,000 was awarded to Taxman for emotional suffering under the NJLAD. She was also given full seniority in order to reflect continuous employment from her original date of hire. The school board appealed the district court's ruling.

In an 8–4 ruling, the Third Circuit Court of Appeals affirmed the district court's grant of summary judgment to Taxman. In writing for the majority, Judge Mansmann maintained that the court had to decide whether or not an employer with a racially balanced work force could show preference in order to promote "racial diversity." The court stated that there is a clear Title VII violation when an employer makes an employment decision based upon an employee's race. Judge Mansmann cited a U.S. Supreme Court decision in *United Steelworkers v. Weber* (1979), where the court determined that affirmative action plans do not violate Title VII's racial discrimination prohibition if they pass two prongs: "first 'have purposes that mirror those of the statute' and second, do not 'unnecessarily trammel the interests of the [non-minority] employees'" (*Taxman*, 1996, p. 1550. Citing *Weber*, 1979, p. 208).

The court affirmed the district court's decision to grant summary judgment to Taxman. Judge Mansmann concluded on behalf of the court: "We hold that Piscataway's affirmative action policy is unlawful because it fails to satisfy either prong of *Weber*. Given the clear anti-discrimination mandate of Title VII, a non-remedial affirmative action plan, even one with a laudable purpose, cannot pass muster" (*Taxman v. Board of Education of the Township of Piscataway,* 1996, p. 1550).

The Piscataway school board filed an appeal to the United States Supreme Court. Prior to court proceedings, Taxman and the school board agreed to a settlement. In a 5–3 vote, the board voted to settle with Taxman. The NAACP Legal Defense and Education Fund, who may have felt that another ruling against the school board in this matter would further restrict affirmative action in employment, supported the board in its decision to settle. The settlement amount was reported at $433,500, which included the amount of back pay mentioned in the original judgment, plus interest and legal costs.

Taxman remains employed as a teacher in the high school, and her classroom is adjacent to Ms. Williams' room. An Associated Press release reported that Ms. Williams wept after the school board voted for the settlement and was pained by the entire situation because she felt slighted that she was originally retained only because of her race. The case had gone on for 9 years before the settlement was reached (Westfeldt, 1997).

Questions for Discussion

1. How might one view this case and the court's decision from a justice perspective? Was the action taken against Ms. Taxman fair to Ms. Taxman? To Ms. Williams? Was the court's decision fair?

2. Were Ms. Taxman and Ms. Williams treated in a caring manner? Why or why not? How might school officials have treated them in a more caring way?

3. How might this case be viewed through the lens of critique?

4. What would the profession expect of Ms. Taxman? Ms. William? Superintendent Edelchick? Board President Kruse?

5. Through a best interests perspective, were Ms. Taxman and Ms. Williams afforded respect? Dignity? Why or why not? What message does the treatment of these teachers send to students? To other teachers? What message, if any, does the court's decision send?

6. What would you have done in this situation if you were Ms. Taxman? Ms. William? Superintendent Edelchick? Board President Kruse?

Part IV

CONCLUSIONS

Part IV of this book offers a chapter on conclusions that ties together the various concepts presented in this book, including legal issues, ethical paradigms, the best interests of the student model, and how the legal cases provided in Part II and Part III reflect these concepts. The chapter ends with a charge to school officials to view the discretion granted to them by the courts as a form of empowerment—one which enables them to make wise ethical decisions in the best interests of students.

15

Conclusions

The discussion in Part I articulated a threefold aim for this book. First, educators need to understand the inherent limitations of the law, especially as these limitations apply to everyday problem solving in schools. Sometime the law is wrong, as evidenced by the Jim Crow statutes, the *Bowers v. Hardwick* (1986) decision upholding Georgia's sodomy laws, and arguably a number of decisions presented in this book.

Regarding education and the law, for over half a century, we strongly believed the Court's assertion in *Brown v. Board of Education* (1954) that separate is inherently unequal was sacred. Yet, today we are presented with cases that support the possibility that separate schools based on race and gender might actually be in the best interests of some students of color and some males and females of all races and ethnicities.

In an effort to keep schools safe, we institute zero tolerance laws that appear to be evenhanded but have resulted in absurd scenarios, such as punishing a student for having a knife in his car when he did not even know it was there or expelling a student who took a weapon away from another student who was contemplating suicide. Trying to keep schools drug free, school authorities are often given the discretion to bring canines into the schools, call in the police, strip search students, and drug test many students who never use drugs. And, even when these actions prove illegal, the courts generally grant qualified immunity to these educators.

Regardless of whether the law is a good one, it may simply not be clear. As we have learned, laws are narrowly drawn, and frequently, courts in different circuits may disagree as to legal interpretations. Certainly, the Supreme Court could decide for everyone, but doing so in all cases where there is disagreement is virtually impossible. Moreover, it has long been held that states are free to pass laws that provide greater protection of rights for individuals. When there is no clear law in one's state or circuit, school officials are once again left to their own devices to solve these problems.

The cases presented in this book illustrate how this dissension among the courts plays out, especially as related to students' freedom of religion and free speech rights. What one administrator may view as free expression, another may see as disruption. What one educator may view as creativity and diversity in the curriculum, another may see as indoctrination or endorsement of certain political or religious beliefs. What some educators think of as reasonable restraint, others may condemn as censorship. Thus, many times, the answer lies not in the legal system, but in good professional practice and sound ethical decision making.

A second aim of this book is to understand the broad discretion courts have provided to school authorities. In short, courts do not want to tell educators how to run their schools. Nor do they want to tie school officials' hands. The Supreme Court in *Board of Education, Island Trees Union Free School District No. 26 v. Pico* (1982) pointed out that courts have long recognized "local school board discretion in the management of school affairs" (p. 863). As evidenced in a number of the cases in this book, even when courts do not agree with administrative decisions or think they are bad decisions, they are reluctant to overrule them because of the discretion issue.

Understanding the courts' views on discretion is a powerful insight. It can be freeing to competent administrators who prefer to rely on their own good judgment rather than on some top–down governmental directive. On the other hand, this knowledge and the empowerment that comes with it behoove school officials to use their discretion wisely and in an ethical manner that serves the best interests of the student.

Accordingly, the third aim of this book is to recognize the importance of self-reflection and inquiry in making ethical decisions that may, and often do, have a profound influence on students. We arrive at this aim by realizing that the legal system will not provide the answers that we as educators seek and that much of what we are searching for is within our discretion and lies in the realm of ethics. Ethics is grounded in culture, and it is contextually based. Moreover, many ethical decisions must be made quickly with little advance notice.

Thus, the time for self-reflection and inquiry is now, not when a crisis occurs. Being aware of the various ethical paradigms (i.e., justice, care, critique, the profession) and applying these concepts to real-life cases such as those prewsented in this book provide a basis for inquiry. Reflecting on one's own values and reactions to these situations sets the stage for what Starratt (2004) characterizes as authentic leadership. A vital part of this leadership is found in what Shapiro and Stefkovich (2005) describe as the ethic of the profession with the best interests of the student as its keystone. As articulated in chapter 3 of this book:

> Not all those who write about the importance of the study of ethics in educational administration discuss the needs of children; however, this focus on students is clearly consistent with the backbone of our profession. Other professions often have

one basic principle driving the profession. In medicine, it is "First, do not harm." In law, it is the assertion that all clients deserve "zealous representation." In educational administration, we believe that if there is a moral imperative for the profession, it is to serve the "best interests of the student." Consequently, this ideal must lie at the heart of any professional paradigm for educational leaders. (Shapiro & Stefkovich, this volume, p. 17)

To make ethical decisions in the best interests of the student necessitates that this term be understood, if not defined. This text presents a model for determining best interests in a manner that takes advantage of school officials' inquiry by asking that educators reflect on what truly is in the best interests of students, and by injecting student voices in the mix, not just their adult-centric views.

This best interests model focuses on the three Rs of rights, responsibility, and respect. Reciprocity is embedded in this model. Rights carry with them responsibilities. Responsibility necessitates that the student is responsible to him- or herself, to others, and to society and that the educator is responsible for taking advantage of teachable moments to help the student act in a responsible manner. Respect is based on mutuality. Thus, the student respects her- or himself and others, including school officials, and these educators in turn show respect toward the student.

Educators teach these three Rs by modeling such behavior. Thus, the school official who taped a misbehaving student to a tree was hardly demonstrating respect. Indeed, if there was a teachable moment here, it was when a fifth grader questioned the appropriateness of the administrators' actions. The educator who allowed other students to repeatedly bully and harass a student because he was gay, assuming that "boys will be boys," modeled neither responsibility nor respect and ignored the gay students' rights.

Finally, the cases in this book reflect a number of cross-cutting themes related to access, equality versus equity, inculcation of values, cultural differences in an everchanging society; and the rights of parents in relation to the school's responsibility to act *in loco parentis* (in the place of the parent). All of these themes carry with them ethical implications that bear directly on a student's best interests.

In conclusion, it is my hope that those reading this book may learn from any wisdom that it has to offer, will be encouraged to reflect on their own ethical concepts of *good* and *bad, right* and *wrong,* and will feel empowered with the understanding that courts allow considerable discretion to educators as they pursue what is truly in the best interests of the student.

Appendix

Law and Education Textbooks

Alexander, K., & Alexander, M. D. (2005). *American public school law* (6th ed.). Belmont, CA: Wadsworth Thomson Learning.

Essex, N. L. (2005). *School law and the public schools: A practical guide for educational leaders* (3rd ed.). Boston: Allyn & Bacon.

Fischer, L., Schimmel, D., & Stellman, L. R. (2003). *Teachers and the law* (6th ed.). Boston: Allyn & Bacon.

Goldstein, S. R., Silver, E. S., Gee, E. G., & Daniel, P. T. K. (1995). *Law and public education: Cases and materials* (3rd ed.). New York: Bender.

Imber, M., & Van Geel, T. (2005). *Education law* (3rd ed.). Mahwah, NJ: Lawrence Erlbaum Associates.

LaMorte, M. W. (2005). *School law: Cases and concepts* (8th ed.). Boston: Allyn & Bacon.

McCarthy, M. M., Cambron-McCabe, N. H., & Thomas, S. B. (2003). *Public school law: Teachers' and students' rights* (5th ed.). Boston: Allyn & Bacon.

Rossow, L. F., & Stefkovich, J. A. (2005). *Education law: Cases and materials*. Durham: Carolina Academic Press.

Russo, C. J. (2004). *Reutter's the law of public education* (5th ed.). Westbury, NY: Foundation Press.

Valente, W. D., & Valente, C. M. (2001). *Law in the schools* (5th ed.). Upper Saddle River, NJ: Prentice-Hall.

Yudof, M. G., Kirp, D., Levin, B., & Moran, R. (2002). *Education policy and the law* (4th ed.). Belmont, CA: Wadsworth.

References

Ambach v. Norwick, 441 U.S. 68, 80 (1979).

American Civil Liberties Union v. Black Horse Pike Regional Board of Education, 84 F.3d 1471 (3rd 1996).

Apple, M. W. (2001). *Educating the "right" way: Markets, standards, God, and inequality.* New York: Routledge Falmer.

Apple, M. W. (2003). *The state and the politics of knowledge.* New York: Routledge Falmer.

Aristotle. (2002). *Nicomachean ethics.* (C. Rowe, Trans.). Oxford: Oxford University Press.

Arons, S., & Lawrence, C. (1980). The manipulation of consciousness: A first amendment critique of schooling. *Harvard Civil Rights—Civil Liberties Law Review, 15,* 309–361.

Ashbaugh, C. R., & Kasten, K. L. (1995). *Educational leadership: Case studies for reflective practice* (2nd ed.). White Plains, NY: Longman Publishers.

Associated Press. (1983, November 17). Nine students suspended in textbook flap. *Miami Herald,* p. B5.

Audi, R. (Ed.). (1995). *The Cambridge dictionary of philosophy.* New York: Cambridge University Press.

Beck, L. G. (1994). *Reclaiming educational administration as a caring profession.* New York: Teachers College Press.

Beck, L. G. (1999). Metaphors of educational community: An analysis of the images that reflect and influence scholarship and practice. *Educational Administration Quarterly, 35*(1), 13–45.

Beck, L. G., & Murphy, J. (1994, April). *A deeper analysis: Examining courses devoted to ethics.* Paper presented at the American Educational Research Association, New Orleans.

Beck, L. G., Murphy, J., Mertz, N. T., Starratt, R. J., Shapiro, J. P., Stefkovich, J., et al. (1997). *Ethics in educational leadership programs: Emerging models.* Columbia, MO: The University Council for Educational Administration.

Begley, P. T. (2004). Understanding valuation processes: Exploring the linkage between motivation and action. *International Studies in Educational Administration, 32*(2), 4–17.

Begley, P. T., & Johansson, O. (1998). The values of school administration: Preferences, ethics, and conflicts. *Journal of School Leadership, 9*(4), 399–422.

Begley, P. T., & Johansson, O. (Eds.). (2003). *The ethical dimensions of school leadership.* Boston: Kluwer.

Bentham, J. (1948). *An introduction to the principles of morals and legislation.* New York: Hafner Publishing Company.

Bethel School District No. 403 v. Fraser, 478 U.S. 675 (1986).

Beussink v. Woodland R–IV School District, 30 F. Supp.2d 1175 (E. D. Mo. 1998).

Billings v. Madison Metropolitan School District, 259 F.3d 807 (7th Cir. 2001).

Bitensky, S. (1992). Theoretical foundations for a right to education under the U.S. Constitution: A beginning to the end of the national education crisis. *Northwestern University Law Review, 86*(3), 550–642.

Blase, J., & Blase, J. (2003). *Breaking the silence: Overcoming the problem of principal mistreatment of teachers.* Thousand Oaks, CA: Corwin Press.

Blase, J., & Blase, J. (2004). *Handbook of instructional leadership: How successful principals promote teaching and learning* (2nd ed.). Thousand Oaks, CA: Corwin Press.

Board of Education of Independent School District No. 92 of Pottawatomie County v. Earls, 536 U.S. 822 (2002).

Board of Education, Island Trees Union Free School District No. 26 v. Pico, 457 U.S. 853 (1982).

Boring v. Buncombe County Board of Education, 136 F.3d 364 (4th Cir. 1998).

Boroff v. Van Wert City Board of Education, 220 F.3d 465 (6th Cir. 2000), *cert. den'd,* 532 U.S. 921 (2001).

Bowers v. Hardwick, 478 U.S. 186 (1986).

Brooks, J. L. (2004). Suspicionless drug testing of students participating in non-athletic competitive school activities: Are all students next? *Wyoming Law Review, 4,* 365–396.

Brown v. Allen, 344 U.S. 443 (1953).

Brown v. Board of Education, 347 U.S. 483 (1954).

Buber, M. (1958). *I and thou.* (R. G. Smith, Trans.). New York: Scribner.

Callahan, R. E. (1962). *Education and the cult of efficiency: A study of the social forces that have shaped the administration of public schools.* Chicago: The University of Chicago Press.

Campbell, E. (1999). Ethical school leadership: Problems of an elusive role. In P. T. Begley & O. Johansson (Eds.), *Values and educational leadership* (pp. 151–163). Albany: SUNY Press.

Capper, C. A. (Ed.). (1993). *Educational administration in a pluralistic society.* Albany: SUNY Press.

C.H. v. Oliva, 226 F.3d 198 (3rd Cir. 2000).

Civil Rights Act of 1871, 42 U.S.C. §1983.

Civil Rights Act of 1964, Title VII, 42 U.S.C.A. §2000e *et seq.*

Connick v. Myers, 461 U.S. 138 (1983).

Convention on the Rights of the Child, Nov. 20, 1989, G.A. Res. 44/25, 44 U.N. GAOR. Supp. No. 49, at 165, U. N. Doc. A/44/736.

Cooper, J. M. (1995). *Teachers' problem solving: A casebook of award-winning teaching cases.* Boston: Allyn & Bacon.

Cornfield by Lewis v. Consolidated School District No. 230, 991 F.2d 1316 (7th Cir. 1993).

Czaja, M., & Lowe, J. (2000). Preparing leaders for ethical decisions. *The AASA Professor* (American Association of School Administrators), *24*(1) 7–12.

Davenport v. YMCA, 1999 U.S. App. LEXIS 29864, 1999 WL 1059829 (8th Cir. 1999), *cert den'd,* 530 U.S. 243 (2000).

Davis, N. (1993). Contemporary deontology. In P. Singer (Ed.), *A companion to ethics* (pp. 205–218). Malden, MA: Blackwell.

Diamond, D. A. (1978). Education law. *Syracuse Law Review, 29*(1), 103–152.

Diamond, S. (1981). The first amendment and the public schools: The case against judicial intervention. *Texas Law Review, 59*(3), 477–528.

Dillon, R. (1992). Respect and care: Toward moral integration. *Canadian Journal of Philosophy, 22*(1), 105–131.

Doe v. Pulaski County Special School District, 306 F.3d 616 (8th Cir. 2002).

Doe v. State of Hawaii Department of Education, 334 F. 3d 906 (9th Cir. 2003).

Ducote, R. (2002). Guardians *ad litem* in private custody litigation: The case for abolition. *Loyola Journal of Public Interest Law, 3,* 106–151.

Duke, D., & Grogan, M. (1997). The moral and ethical dimensions of educational leadership. In L. G. Beck, J. Murphy, N. T. Mertz, R. J. Starratt, J. P. Shapiro, J. A. Stefkovich, et al. (Eds.), *Ethics in educational leadership programs: Emerging models* (pp.141–160). Columbia, MO: University Council for Educational Administration.

Dupre, A. (1996). Should students have constitutional rights? Keeping order in the public schools. *George Washington Law Review, 65*(1), 49–105.

The Dustin Seal Story. (2003). Retrieved March 3, 2005, from Zero Tolerance Nightmares Web site: http://www.ztnightmares.com/html/dennis_story.htm

Eckes, S. E. (2005). Diversity in higher education: The consideration of race in hiring university faculty. *Brigham Young University Education and Law Journal, 2005,* 33–51.

Education Amendments of 1972, Title IX, 20 U.S.C. §§1681–1688.

Education for All Handicapped Children Act, 20 U.S.C. §1400 *et seq.* (1975).

Ehrensal, P. A. L. (2002, October). *Are we doing what is best for the children? Towards a radical ethical critique* (profiling new scholarship keynote address). Paper presented at the 7th Annual Values and Leadership Conference, Toronto, Canada.

Ehrensal, P. A. L. (2003). Constructing children in schools: Policies and the lessons they teach. *Journal of Curriculum Theorizing, 19*(2), 119–134.

Elementary and Secondary Education Act of 1965, 20 U.S.C.S. §6301 *et seq.*

Emmaus High School Web site. (2005). Retrieved March 3, 2005, from http://www.eastpenn.k12.pa.us/ehs/about.html#facts

Eshelman, A. (2004). *Moral responsibility.* Retrieved December 7, 2004, from Stanford Encyclopedia of Philosophy website: http://plato.stanford.edu/entries/moral-responsibility/

Estlund, C. L. (2005). Putting *Grutter* to work: Diversity, integration, and affirmative action in the workplace. *Berkeley Journal of Employment and Labor Law, 26,* 1–39.

Fleming v. Jefferson County School District, 298 F.3d 918 (10th Cir. 2002).

Fossey, R., & Zirkel, P. A. (2004). Liability for student suicide in the wake of *Eisel. Texas Wesleyan Law Review, 10*(2), 403–439.

Foster, W. (1986). *Paradigms and promises: New approaches to educational administration.* Buffalo, NY: Prometheus Books.

Freire, P. (1970). *Pedagogy of the oppressed.* (M. B. Ramos, Trans.). New York: Continuum.

Freire, P. (1985). *The politics of education: Culture, power, and liberation.* (D. Macedo, Trans.). Westport, CT: Greenwood.

Freire, P. (1993). *Pedagogy of the city.* (D. Macedo, Trans.). New York: Continuum.

Freire, P. (1998). *Pedagogy of freedom: Ethics, democracy, and civic courage.* New York: Rowman & Littlefield.

Friedelbaum, S. H. (2002). The quest for privacy: State courts and an elusive right. *Albany Law Review, 65,* 945–989.

Furman, G. C. (2003). The 2002 UCEA presidential address. Toward a new scholarship of educational leadership. *UCEA Review, 45*(1), 1–6.

Furman, G. C. (2004). The ethic of community. *Journal of Educational Administration, 42*(2), 215–235.

Garcia v. Miera, 817 F.2d 650 (10th Cir. 1987).

Garner, B. A. (Ed.). (2004). *Black's law dictionary* (8th ed.). St. Paul, MN: West's Publishing.

Garrett v. Board of Education of the School District of Detroit, 775 F. Supp. 1004 (E. D. Mich. 1991).

Gartner, S. A. (1997). Strip searches of students: What Johnny really learned at school and how local school boards can solve the problem. *Southern California Law Review, 70,* 921–978.

Gay Straight Alliance v. Boyd, 258 F. Supp. 2d 667 (E. D. Ky. 2003).

Gilligan, C. (1982). *In a different voice*. Cambridge, MA: Harvard University Press.

Giroux, H. A. (1994). Educational leadership and school administrators: Rethinking the changing meaning of democratic public culture. In T. Mulkeen, N. H. Cambron-McCabe, & B. Anderson (Eds.), *Democratic leadership: The changing context of administrative preparation* (pp. 31–47). Norwood, NJ: Ablex.

Giroux, H. A. (2000). *Stealing innocence: Youth, corporate power, and the politics of culture*. New York: St. Martin's Press.

Giroux, H. A. (2001). *Theory and resistance in education: Towards a pedagogy for the opposition*. Westport, CT: Bergin & Garvey.

Giroux, H. A. (2003a). *The abandoned generation: Democracy beyond the culture of fear.* New York: Palgrave Macmillan.

Giroux, H. A. (2003b, October). *Higher education, youth, and the crisis of public time: Educated hope and democracy's promise*. Keynote presentation at the 8th annual Values and Leadership Conference, State College, PA.

Giroux, H. A. (2004). *The terror of neoliberalism: Authoritarianism and the eclipse of democracy*. London: Paradigm Publishers.

Goldstein, J., Freud, A., & Solnit, A. (1973). *Beyond the best interests of the child*. New York: Free Press.

Goldstein, J., Freud, A., & Solnit, A. (1979). *Before the best interests of the child*. New York: Free Press.

Goldstein, J., Solnit, A., Goldstein, S., & Freud, A. (1996). *The best interests of the child: The least detrimental alternative*. New York: The Free Press.

Goodlad, J. I., Soder, R., & Sirotnik, K. A. (Eds.). (1990). *The moral dimension of teaching*. San Francisco: Jossey-Bass.

Green, P. C., & Mead, J. F. (2004). *Charter schools and the law: Establishing new legal relationships*. Norwood, MA: Christopher-Gordon Publishers.

Greenwood, G. E., & Fillmer, H. T. (1997). *Professional core cases for teacher decision-making*. Upper Saddle River, NJ: Prentice Hall.

Grenz, S. J., & Smith, J. T. (2003). *Pocket dictionary of ethics*. Downers Grove, IL: InterVarsity Press.

Gruenke v. Seip, 225 F.3d 290 (3rd Cir. 2000).

Grutter v. Bollinger, 539 U.S. 306 (2003).

Guardini, R. G. (1965). *The world and the person*. (S. Lange, Trans.). Chicago: Henry Regency Company.

Guinier, L., & Torres, G. (2002). *The miner's canary: Enlisting race, resisting power, transforming democracy*. Cambridge, MA: Harvard University Press.

Hanson, A. L. (2005). Have zero tolerance school discipline policies turned into a nightmare? The American dream's promise of equal educational opportunity grounded in Brown v. Board of Education. *UC Davis Journal of Juvenile Law and Policy, 9*, 289–379.

Harlow v. Fitzgerald, 457 U.S. 800 (1982).

Hasenfus v. LaJeunesse, 175 F.3d 68 (1st Cir. 1999).

Hazelwood School District v. Kuhlmeier, 484 U.S. 260 (1988).

Hearn v. Board of Public Education, 191 F.3d 1329 (11th Cir. 1999).

Heise, M. (1995). State constitutions, school finance litigation, and the "third wave": From equity to adequacy. *Temple Law Review, 68*(3), 1151–1176.

Heubert, J. P., & Hauser, R. M. (Eds.). (1999). *High stakes: Testing for tracking, promotion, and graduation.* Washington, DC: National Academy Press.

Hobson v. Hansen, 327 F. Supp. 844 (D. D. C. 1971).

Hoffman v. Board of Education, 64 A.D. 2d 369 (N.Y. App. Div. 1978).

Hyman, I. A., & Snook, P. A. (1999). *Dangerous schools: What we can do about the physical and emotional abuse of our children.* San Francisco: Jossey-Bass.

Immediato v. Rye Neck School District, 73 F.3d 454 (2nd Cir. 1996).

Ingraham v. Wright, 430 U.S. 651 (1977).

Ingrassia, D. (2004). *Thomas ex. rel Thomas v. Roberts*: Another photo finish where school officials win the race for qualified immunity. *Whittier Law Review, 26*, 621–651.

Interstate School Leaders Licensure Consortium. (1996). *Standards for school leaders.* Washington, DC: Author.

James, B., & Larson, J. E. (2004). The doctrine of deference: Shifting constitutional presumptions and the Supreme Court's restatement of student rights after Board of Education v. Earls. *South Carolina Law Review, 56*, 1–92.

Jergeson v. Board of Trustees, 476 P.2d. 481 (WY 1970).

Jones v. Clear Creek, 977 F.2d 963 (5th Cir. 1992).

Joye v. Hunterdon Central Regional High School Board of Education, 826 A.2d 624 (NJ 2003).

Kadrmas v. Dickinson Public Schools, 487 U.S. 450 (1988).

Kant, I. (1966). *The fundamental principles of the metaphysics of ethics.* (O. Manthey-Zorn, Trans.). New York: Appleton-Century-Crofts.

Kirshmann, R. E. (1996). *Educational administration: A collection of case studies.* Englewood Cliffs, NJ: Prentice Hall.

Kohlberg, L. (1980). Educating for a just society. In B. Munsey (Ed.), *Moral development, moral education, and Kohlberg* (pp. 455–471). Birmingham, AL: Religious Education Press.

Kohlberg, L. (1981). *The philosophy of moral development: Moral stages and the idea of justice* (Vol. 1). San Francisco: Harper & Row.

Krislov, M. (2004). Affirmative action in higher education: The value, the method, and the future. *University of Cincinnati Law Review, 72*, 899–907.

Lane v. Wilson, 307 U.S. 268, 275 (1939).

Larry P. v. Riles, 793 F.2d 969 (9th Cir. 1984).

Lassonde v. Pleasanton Unified School District, 320 F.3d 979 (9th Cir. 2003).

LaVine v. Blaine School District, 257 F.3d 981 (9th Cir. 2001), *reh'd en banc den'd*, 279 F.3d 719 (9th Cir. 2002).

Lawrence-Lightfoot, S. (1999). *Respect: An exploration.* Reading, MA: Perseus Books.

Lawrence v. Texas, 539 U.S. 558 (2003).

Lawson, J. (2003, July 6). With the fairness and legality of its policy in question, the Knox County School Board zeroes in on zero tolerance. *Knoxville News-Sentinel*, p. A1.

Lemon v. Kurtzman, 403 U.S. 602 (1971).

Levesque, R. (1996). International children's rights: Can they make a difference in American family policy? *American Psychologist, 51,* 1251–1254.

Levesque, R. (1997). The right to education in the United States: Beyond the limits of the lore and lure of law. *Annual Survey of International and Comparative Law, 4,* 205–252.

Lewis, M. A. (2001). Testing students for pregnancy: How far will the courts allow schools to go? *McGeorge Law Review, 33,* 155–186.

Lickona, T. (1991). *Educating for character: How our schools can teach respect and responsibility.* New York: Bantam Books.

Lippmann, W. (1928). *American inquisitors.* New York: Macmillan.

Lynch, T. (1998). Note, education as a fundamental right: Challenging the Supreme Court's jurisprudence. *Hofstra Law Review, 26*(4), 953–973.

Marshall, C. (2004). Social justice challenges to educational administration: Introduction to a special issue. *Educational Administration Quarterly, 40*(1), 5–15.

Mawdsley, R. D. (2003). Random drug testing for extracurricular activities: Has the Supreme Court opened Pandora's box for public schools? *Brigham Young University Education and Law Journal,* 587–621.

Mayshark, J. F. (1996, December 5). School board expels student after knife was found in his car. *Knoxville News-Sentinel,* p. A1.

McCarthy, M. M. (2004). Religious influences in public schools: The winding path toward accommodation. *Saint Louis University Public Law Review, 23*(3), 565–596.

Mead, J. F. (2002, winter). Conscious use of race as a voluntary means to educational ends in elementary and secondary education: A legal argument derived from recent judicial decisions. *Michigan Journal of Race & Law, 8,* 63–149.

Merseth, K. K. (1997). *Case studies in educational administration.* New York: Addison Wesley Longman.

Mill, J. S. (1978). *On liberty.* Indianapolis, IN: Hackett.

Mitra, D. L. (2001). Opening the flood gates: Giving students a voice in school reform. *Forum, 43*(2), 91–94.

Mitra, D. L. (2003). Student voice in school reform: Reframing student–teacher relationships. *McGill Journal of Education, 38*(2), 289–304.

Mitra, D. L. (2005). Adults advising youth: Leading while getting out of the way. *Educational Administration Quarterly, 41*(3), 520–553.

Moran, R. F. (2000). Sorting and reforming: High stakes testing in the public schools. *Akron Law Review, 34,* 107–135.

Mozert v. Hawkins County Board of Education, 827 F.2d 1058 (6th Cir. 1987).

Mulvey, E. P. & Cauffman, E. (2001). The inherent limits of predicting school violence. *American Psychologist, 56*(10), 797–802.

Murphy, J. (2005). Unpacking the foundations of ISLLC standards and addressing concerns in the academic community. *Educational Administration Quarterly, 41*(1), 154–191.

Nabozny v. Podlesny, 92 F.3d 446 (7th Cir. 1996).

Nettleton School District v. Owens, 329 Ark. 367 (Ark. 1997).

New Jersey Law Against Discrimination. (1945). N.J.S.A. 10:5–1 *et seq.*

New Jersey v. T.L.O., 469 U.S. 325 (1985).

Noddings, N. (1984). *Caring: A feminine approach to ethics and moral education.* Berkeley: University of California Press.

Noddings, N. (1992). *The challenge to care in schools: An alternative approach to education.* New York: Teachers College Press.

Noddings, N. (2002). *Educating moral people: A caring alternative to character education.* New York: Teachers College Press.

Noddings, N. (2003). *Caring: A feminine approach to ethics and moral education* (2nd ed.). Berkeley: University of California Press.

Olmstead v. United States, 277 U.S. 438 (1928).

O'Neill, P. T. (2003). High stakes testing law and litigation. *Brigham Young University Education and Law Journal, 2003,* 623–659.

Ozar, T. (1986). Rights: What they are and where they come from. In P. Werhane (Ed.), *Philosophical issues in human rights: Theories and applications* (pp. 9–10). New York: McGraw-Hill College.

P.B. v. Koch, 96 F.3d 1298 (9th Cir. 1996).

Pennsylvania Garb Statute. (1895). 24 PA. Cons. St. Ann. §11–1112.

People Who Care v. Rockford, 111 F.3d 528 (7th Cir. 1997).

Pierce v. Society of Sisters, 268 U.S. 510 (1925).

Plyler v. Doe, 457 U.S. 202 (1982).

Professional Standards Commission v. Smith, 571 S.E.2d 443 (Ga. Ct. App. 2002).

Purpel, D. E. (1989). *The moral and spiritual crisis in education: A curriculum for justice and compassion in education.* New York: Bergin & Garvey.

Purpel, D. E. (2003). Review essay: The decontextualization of moral education. *American Journal of Education, 110*(1), 89–95.

Ratner v. Loudoun County Public Schools, No. 00-2157, 1-6 (4th Cir. 2001), *cert. den'd* 534 U.S. 114 (2002).

Ravitch, D. (2003). *The language police: How pressure groups restrict what students learn.* New York: Alfred A. Knopf.

Rawls, J. (1999). *A theory of justice.* (Rev. ed.). Cambridge, MA: Belknap Press of Harvard University Press.

Reyes, A. H. (2001). Alternative education: The criminalization of student behavior. *Fordham Urban Law Journal, 29*(2), 539–559.

Rochin v. California, 342 U.S. 165, 172–74 (1952).

Rossow, L. F., & Barnes, S. (1992). Dress for success, not religion: Commentary. *Religion and Public Education, 19*(1), 47–51.

Rossow, L. F., & Stefkovich, J. A. (2005). *Education law: Cases and materials.* Durham: Carolina Academic Press.

Rossow, L. F., & Stefkovich, J. A. (2006). *Search and seizure in the public schools* (3rd ed.). Dayton, OH: Education Law Association.

Rousseau, J. J. (1967). *The social contract and discourse on the origin of inequality.* New York: Simon & Schuster.

Russo, C. J., & Gregory, D. L. (1999). Legal and ethical issues surrounding drug testing in schools. *Law Review of Michigan State University—Detroit College of Law, 1999,* 611–644.

Salomone, R. C. (1996). Common schools, uncommon values: Listening to the voices of dissent. *Yale Law and Policy Review, 14,* 169–235.

Salomone, R. C. (2000). *Visions of schooling: Conscience, community, and common education.* New Haven: Yale University Press.

Salomone, R. C. (2003). *Same, different, equal: Rethinking single-sex schooling.* New Haven: Yale University Press.

Satterfield, J. (2003, March 7). Judge weighs future of suit against schools; Father requests a jury in case involving expelled son's suicide. *Knoxville News-Sentinel,* p. B3.

Schaill v. Tippecanoe, 864 F.2d. 1309 (7th Cir. 1989).

Seal v. Morgan, 229 F.3d 567 (6th Cir. 2000).

Selman v. Cobb County School District, 390 F.2d 1286 (2005).

Sergiovanni, T. J. (1994). *Building community in schools.* San Francisco: Jossey-Bass.

Sernak, K. (1998). *School leadership: Balancing power with caring.* New York: Teachers College Press.

Settlegoode v. Portland Public Schools, 371 F.3d 503 (9th Cir. 2004).

S.G. v. Sayreville Board of Education, 333 F.3d 417 (3rd Cir. 2003).

Shapiro, J. P., & Stefkovich, J. A. (2001). *Ethical leadership and decision making in education.* Mahwah, NJ: Lawrence Erlbaum Associates.

Shapiro, J. P., & Stefkovich, J. A. (2005). *Ethical leadership and decision making in education* (2nd ed.). Mahwah, NJ: Lawrence Erlbaum Associates.

Sharif by Salahuddin v. New York State Education Department, 709 F. Supp. 345 (S.D.N.Y. 1989).

Shields, C. M. (2004). Dialogic leadership for social justice: Overcoming pathologies of silence. *Educational Administration Quarterly, 40*(1), 111–134.

Shouse, R. C. (2005). Some current threats to humanistic pupil control. In W. K. Hoy & C. G. Miskel (Eds.), *Educational leadership and reform* (pp. 301–318). Greenwich, CT: Information Age.

Skrla, L., Scheurich, J. J., Garcia, J., & Nolly, G. (2004). Equity audits: A practical leadership tool for developing equitable and excellent schools. *Educational Administration Quarterly, 40*(1), 135–163.

Smith, P. S. (1997). Addressing the plight of inner-city schools: The federal right to education after *Kadrmas v. Dickinson Public Schools. Whittier Law Review, 18,* 825–862.

Stanley v. Georgia, 394 U.S. 557 (1969).

Starratt, R. J. (1991). Building an ethical school. *Educational Administration Quarterly, 27*(2), 185–202.

Starratt, R. J. (1994). *Building an ethical school.* London: Falmer Press.

Starratt, R. J. (2004). *Ethical leadership.* San Francisco: Jossey-Bass.

Starratt, R. J. (2005, October). *Cultivating authenticity in both cognitive and human development: A new perspective on moral educational leadership.* Paper presented at the 10th annual Values and Leadership Conference, State College, PA.

Stefkovich, J. A. (1992). Religious garb in the schools: A different time, a different place. Commentary. *Religion and Public Education, 19*(1), 43–46.

Stefkovich, J. A., & O'Brien, G. M. (2004). Best interests of the student: An ethical model. *Journal of Educational Administration, 42*(2), 197–214.

Stefkovich, J. A., O'Brien, G. M., & Moore, J. (2002, October). *School leaders' ethical decision making and the "best interests of students."* Paper presented at the 7th annual Values and Leadership Conference, Toronto, Canada.

Stefkovich, J. A., & Torres, M. S. (2003). The demographics of justice: Student searches, student rights, and administrator practices. *Educational Administration Quarterly, 39*(2), 259–282.

Stefkovich, J. A., & Torres, M. S. (2006). Comprehensive database of student search court decisions in public schools since *New Jersey v. T.L.O.* Unpublished database on file with Stefkovich, the Pennsylvania State University, 1–200.

Stiffler, L. (2000, February 26). Violent poem not a threat, judge says; Student at Blaine High gets his record cleared. *Seattle Post-Intelligencer,* p. B1.

Strike, K. A., Haller, E. J., & Soltis, J. F. (1998). *The ethics of school administration* (2nd ed.). New York: Teachers College Press.

Strike, K. A., & Soltis, J. F. (1992). *The ethics of teaching* (2nd ed.). New York: Teachers College Press.

Taxman v. Board of Education of the Township of Piscataway, 91 F.3d 1547 (3rd Cir. 1996).

Thimmig, P. (1998). Not your average school day—Reading, writing, and strip searching: The eleventh circuit's decision in *Jenkins v. Talladega City Board of Education. Saint Louis University Law Journal, 42,* 1389–1416.

Thomas v. Roberts, 323 F.3d 950 (11th Cir. 2003).

Thro, W. (1989). Note, To render them safe: The analysis of state constitutional provisions in public school finance reform litigation. *Virginia Law Review, 75,* 1639–1679.

Thro, W. (1998). A new approach to state constitutional analysis in school finance litigation. *Journal of Law and Policy, 48,* 525–540.

Timothy W. v. Rochester School District, 875 F.2d 954 (1st Cir. 1989).

Tinker v. Des Moines Independent Community School District, 393 U.S. 503 (1969).

U.S. Department of Education, No Child Left Behind Act of 2001, 20 U.S.C. 6301 et. seq. (2002).

U.S. Department of Education (2003). Guidance on constitutionally protected prayer in public elementary and secondary schools, 68 Fed. Reg. 9645–9646.

United States v. Board of Education for the School District of Philadelphia, 911 F.2d 882 (3rd Cir. 1990).

United States Constitution, Amendment I. (1791).

United States Constitution, Amendment IV. (1791).

United States Constitution, Amendment V. (1791).

United States Constitution, Amendment XIV. (1868).

United States v. Summers, 268 F.3d 683 (9th Cir. 2001).

United Steelworkers v. Weber, 443 U.S. 193 (1979).

Universal Declaration of Human Rights, G.A. Res. 217 A, (31) U.N. GAOR Res. 71, U.N. Doc A/810 (1948).

Universal Declaration of Human Rights. (1948). In *United Nations, human rights: A compilation of international instruments,* Vol. I (First Part), 1–7.

Vernonia School District 47J v. Acton, 515 U.S. 646 (1995).

Walker, K. (1995). The kids' best interests. *The Canadian School Executive, 15*(5), 2–8.

Walker, K. (1998). Jurisprudential and ethical perspectives on "the best interests of children." *Interchange, 29*(3), 283–304.

Walsh, T. J. (1993). Education as a fundamental right under the United States Constitution. *Willamette Law Review. 26,* 279–296.

Washington Administrative Code §180–40–295.

West, R. (2001). The constitution and the obligations of government to secure the material preconditions for a good society: Rights, capabilities and the good society. *Fordham Law Review, 69,* 1901–1932.

West Virginia State Board of Education v. Barnette, 319 U.S. 624, 642 (1943).

Westfeldt, A. (1997). Associated Press. Retrieved from http://www.washingtonpost.com/wp-srv/national/longterm/supcourt/stories/ap112197.htm

Wikipedia Online Encyclopedia. Retrieved December 7, 2004, from http://en.wikipedia.org/wiki/Best_Interests

Willower, D., & Lacata, J. (1997). *Values and valuation in the practice of educational administration.* Thousand Oaks, CA: Corwin Press.

Wisconsin v. Yoder, 406 U.S. 205 (1972).

Wood v. Strickland, 420 U.S. 308 (1975).

Yudof, M. (1995). Tinker tailored: Good faith, civility, and student expression. *St. John's Law Review, 69,* 365–377.

Yudof, M. (1998). Personal speech and government expression. *Case Western Reserve Law Review, 38,* 671.

Yudof, M., Kirp, D., Levin, B., & Moran, R. (2002). *Educational policy and the law* (4th ed.). Belmont, CA: Wadsworth Thomson Learning.

Zirkel, P. A. (2003). Courtside: Testing behavior. *Phi Delta Kappan, 84*(9), 647–712.

Zubay, B., & Soltis, J. F. (2005). *Creating the ethical school: A book of case studies.* New York: Teachers College Press.

Author Index

Foster, W., xi, 34
Freire, P., 12, 13, 111, 112
Freud, A., 19
Friedelbaum, S. H., 83
Furman, G. C., 14

G

Garcia, J., 113
Garner, B. A., 3
Gartner, S. A., 83
Gee, E. G., 161
Gilligan, C., 11, 24
Giroux, H. A., 12, 13, 96
Goldstein, J., 19, 21
Goldstein, S., 19, 21
Goldstein, S. R., 161
Goodlad, J. I., xii
Green, P. C., 144
Greenwood, G. E., xii
Gregory, D. L., 84
Grenz, S. J., 3
Grogan, M., 14
Guardini, R. G., 25
Guinier, L., 112

H

Haller, E. J., 9
Hanson, A. L., 96
Hauser, R. M., 111
Heise, M., 22
Heubert, J. P., 111
Hyman, I. A., 97

I

Imber, M., 161
Ingrassia, D., 136
Interstate School Leaders Licensure
          Consortium, 5

J

James, B., 83
Johansson, O., 14

K

Kasten, K. L., xii
Kirp, D., 56, 121, 161
Kirshmann, R. E., xii
Kohlberg, L., 10, 24
Krislov, M., 32

L

Lacata, J., 14
LaMorte, M. W., 161
Larson, J. E., 83
Lawrence, C., 120, 121
Lawrence-Lightfoot, S., 25, 26
Lawson, J., 100
Levesque, R., 21, 22
Levin, B., 56, 121, 161
Lewis, M. A., 83
Lickona, T., 24, 25
Lippmann, W., 56
Lowe, J., 14
Lynch, T., 22

M

Marshall, C., 13
Mawdsley, R. D., 83
Mayshark, J. F., 100
McCarthy, M. M., 58, 161
Mead, J. F., 121, 144
Merseth, K. K., xii
Mertz, N. T., 4
Mill, J. S., 9, 23
Mitra, D. L., 21
Moore, J., 19, 20
Moran, R. F., 56, 121, 161
Moran, R., 111
Mulvey, E. P., 51
Murphy, J., xii, 4, 5

N

Noddings, N., xii, 4, 11, 15, 24
Nolly, G., 113

Subject Index

D